LONDON RECORD SOCIETY
PUBLICATIONS

VOLUME LIX

THE PERIODICALS OF FERDINAND PELZER (1833–1857)

A German Musician in London

EDITED BY

SARAH CLARKE

LONDON RECORD SOCIETY
THE BOYDELL PRESS
2024

© London Record Society 2024

All Rights Reserved. Except as permitted under current legislation
no part of this work may be photocopied, stored in a retrieval system,
published, performed in public, adapted, broadcast,
transmitted, recorded or reproduced in any form or by any means,
without the prior permission of the copyright owner

Editorial material © Sarah Clarke

First published 2024

A London Record Society publication
Published by The Boydell Press
an imprint of Boydell & Brewer Ltd
PO Box 9, Woodbridge, Suffolk IP12 3DF, UK
and of Boydell & Brewer Inc.
668 Mt Hope Avenue, Rochester, NY 14620–2731, USA
website: www.boydellandbrewer.com

ISBN 978-0-900952-09-8

A CIP catalogue record for this book is available
from the British Library

The publisher has no responsibility for the continued existence or accuracy of
URLs for external or third-party internet websites referred to in this book, and
does not guarantee that any content on such websites is, or will remain, accurate or
appropriate

MIX
Paper | Supporting
responsible forestry
FSC
www.fsc.org FSC® C013056

Printed and bound in Great Britain by
TJ Books Limited, Padstow, Cornwall

CONTENTS

ILLUSTRATIONS

All are from private collections unless otherwise noted

The editor and publisher are grateful to all the institutions and persons
listed for permission to reproduce the materials in which they hold
copyright. Every effort has been made to trace the copyright holders;
apologies are offered for any omission, and the publisher will be pleased
to add any necessary acknowledgement in subsequent editions.

ACKNOWLEDGEMENTS

I am very grateful to Kate Eaton of the Guildhall School of Music and Drama Library for permission to use the Appleby volume and for helping in many ways, and to Ainara Urrutikoetxea and other library staff who have welcomed and assisted me. I am indebted to Christopher Page and James Westbrook who have so promptly answered numerous questions and given me invaluable advice. Others to whom I am grateful for help include Teresa Breathnach of the Dublin City Library and Archive, Robert Coldwell, Sandys Dawes, Anne Edgar, Declan Hickey, Martin Holmes of the Bodleian Libraries, Gerhard Penn, Erik Stenstadvold, and Jeff Wells of the Austin-Marie Collection. I am also grateful to staff at the British Library, Cambridge University Library, Camden Local Studies and Archive Centre, City of Westminster Archive Centre, the Institute of Historical Research, London Metropolitan Archives, the National Archives, the Royal Academy of Music Library, and Tring Library. Lastly, great thanks are due Jerry White, Honorary General Editor of the London Record Society, who has overseen the project; he has given me constant encouragement and many insightful suggestions.

ABBREVIATIONS

GMO   *Grove Music Online*
ODNB   *Oxford Dictionary of National Biography*
TG   *The Giulianiad*

NOTE ON THE TEXT

The text has been transcribed from the volume of Pelzer's periodicals in the Appleby Collection of Guitar Music held by the library of the Guildhall School of Music and Drama in London. However, in that volume six pages are missing from the *Guitarist's Companion*, four of the text (pages 1, 2, 7 and 8) and two of the music (pages 1 and 2). The text for these pages has been transcribed from the copy held by the Bodleian Libraries, with permission.

The original spelling and punctuation has been retained throughout; places where there could be doubt have been confirmed with [*sic*]. American spelling is used on many occasions, although not consistently.

In the Appleby volume *The Giulianiad* (1833–c.1835) is first, the *Guitarist's Companion* (1857) is second, and the *Musical Herald* (c.1841/43) is last. In this edition the order has been rearranged so that the periodicals are in chronological order. Thus, *The Giulianiad* remains as the first, the *Musical Herald* is second, and the *Guitarist's Companion* is last.

Both *The Giulianiad* and the *Guitarist's Companion* have separate 'text' and 'music' sections with separate pagination. Footnote references to these are all to the 'text' sections unless 'music' is specified.

The quotations from newspapers in the leaflets about Pelzer's choral teaching that follow the *Musical Herald* have been checked against the original articles and differences noted with the exception of two. Copies of the *Drogheda Argus* for 24 September 1842 and 1 October 1842 could not be located.

INTRODUCTION

The Periodicals of Ferdinand Pelzer (1833–1857): A German Musician in London comprises the text of three periodicals, and a few leaflets, that are bound together in one volume. It is part of the Appleby Collection which is currently housed in the library of the Guildhall School of Music and Drama in London. This volume is one of the most significant items in the collection, which comprises music, periodicals, and other documents relating to the guitar in the last 200 years. Wilfrid Appleby (1892–1987) was an astute and uncompromising advocate of the classical guitar best remembered as editor of *Guitar News*, a bimonthly periodical published in Cheltenham from 1951 until 1973. Its readership was wide, and Appleby corresponded with guitarists from many parts of the globe. Everything in this volume is almost certainly connected to the work of a German musician from Trier, Ferdinand Pelzer (1801–64), who arrived and settled in London in about 1829. Three periods of Pelzer's career in this country are evidenced here. From the 1830s is a rare complete volume of the guitar periodical *The Giulianiad*. From the 1840s is another periodical, the *Musical Herald*, accompanied by some leaflets concerning his choral teaching. From the 1850s is his *Guitarist's Companion*. Together these documents give a unique overview of the career of a nineteenth-century musician in England.

Some of the provenance of the volume is known. The name 'Ernest Shand' is written inside. Ernest Shand (1868–1924) was an outstanding English guitarist of the very late Victorian era who had, in addition, a more lucrative career as a comic actor. Appleby was given it by Shand's widow, Louisa Nellie Shand, née Smith (1872–1948), an actress who used the stage name Louie Stafford. Appleby suggests that the volume would have belonged to Pelzer, whose daughter, Catharina, probably gave it to Shand. Nothing, however, has been found to confirm this theory.[1] In addition to Shand's name there is another inscribed on the inside cover. Although

[1] For a biography of Shand see Stanley Yates, 'Introduction', in Ernest Shand, *Guitar Music from Late Victorian England*, ed. Stanley Yates (Tennessee, 2022), 11–28. For Appleby's account of how he acquired the volume see Wilfrid Appleby, 'The Story of a Guitar, Chapter 1 – Autobiographical', *Guitar News* 64 (1962), 6–11, at 11. Catharina Pratten, née Pelzer (1824–95), was the most well-known guitarist in London in the Victorian era. She styled herself Madame Sidney Pratten after her marriage in 1854 to the flautist Robert Sidney Pratten.

Figure 1. Ferdinand Pelzer [1840], engraved by C. E. Wagstaff, after Brown, Courtesy of the Austin-Marie Collection. The guitar he is holding is likely to have been made by Joseph Gerard in London. James Westbrook, *Guitar Making in Nineteenth-Century London: Louis Panormo and his Contemporaries* (Halesowen, 2023), 387.

partially scratched out, this is probably that of 'Lady Lucy Dawes' and the address given is 'Heathfield Lodge, Grove Road, Surbiton'. Lucy Dawes (1835–1921) was the wife of Edwyn Sandys Dawes (1838–1903), a successful shipowner who was knighted in 1894.[2] They lived in Heathfield Lodge from around 1869, after a time in India, until roughly 1875 when they went to live on the family estate at Mount Ephraim in Kent. Edwyn's

[2]   John Orbell, 'Dawes, Sir Edwyn Sandys', *ODNB*. If the book had belonged to Lucy it is unclear why the word 'Lady' precedes her name. She would not have had this title until after her husband was knighted in 1894.

Figure 2. Guitar attributed to Joseph Gerard, 1831. Courtesy of the Austin-Marie Collection. On the label of the guitar Pelzer's daughter, Catharina (Madame Sidney Pratten), states that the instrument had belonged to her father.

Figure 3. Label of guitar attributed to Joseph Gerard, 1831. Courtesy of the Austin-Marie Collection.

surviving diaries record how Lucy sang and enjoyed musical evenings at home, as one would expect of a woman of her class at that time. No specific mention of a guitar has been found, so why she had this volume, if it was hers, must remain a mystery for now.[3]

According to Pelzer's marriage record of 1823 from Trier, he was the son of the musician Anton Peltzer of Jülig (possibly Jülich, near Cologne).[4] In about 1829 he came to London with his wife, Maria, and daughter, Catharina.[5] He was one of many foreign musicians who made the journey during the first half of the nineteenth century; London was then the largest and richest city in the world and provided ample opportunities for concert giving and teaching. Some came to escape troubled times in their own countries. Spaniards fled the oppressive regime in their country after 1813.[6] Many guitarists left Italy for a variety of reasons that included the difficult economic situation in the north of the country at the end of the Napoleonic wars. Moreover, although there were opportunities for guitarists as accompanists, their instrument did not suit large Italian theatres. European cities elsewhere provided not only more suitable performance environments in smaller salons but also better publishing houses and a greater chance of winning patronage.[7] Guitarists from the continent usually found work easily in London

---

[3]   The Dawes's were looking at houses in Grove Road in December 1868. Their house in Surbiton (Heathfield Lodge) was sold in July 1875. Anne Edgar, *Sir Edwyn Dawes – Merchant through the Suez* (Private printing, 2014), I, 85, 207. This book includes transcripts of Edwyn Sandys Dawes's diaries for 1868, 1870, and 1875.

[4]   Trier, Stadtarchiv Trier, Heiratseintrages Nr 49/1823 vom 22 April 1823. In this record 'Pelzer' is spelt 'Peltzer'. A twenty-two-page document 'Memoirs of Giulia Pelzer' in the Appleby Collection gives a different account and states that Pelzer's father was a mathematician named Jacob Pelzer. The provenance of these 'Memoirs', probably dating from 1938, is unknown and they must therefore be treated with caution. Giulia Pelzer (1838–1938) was one of Pelzer's younger daughters who taught guitar and mandolin at the Guildhall School of Music in London in the 1880s and 1890s.

[5]   In London Pelzer and his wife Maria (1804–63) had five more children in addition to Catharina and Giulia: Jane (1831–46) who was a pianist, Annie (1833–97) who played and published music for the concertina until her marriage in 1859, Ferdinand (1837–?), Cunigunda (1840–78) who taught concertina and guitar, and Christian (1842–45).

[6]   Brian Jeffery, *Fernando Sor, Composer and Guitarist*, 3rd edn (London, 2020) [e-book], 121–22.

[7]   Thomas Heck, *Mauro Giuliani: A Life for the Guitar*, GFA Refereed Monographs, 2 (Palos Verdes Peninsula, 2013) [e-book], Chapter 2, Section 2.3. Immigrant Italian guitarists were particularly influential in bringing the guitar to London in the early nineteenth century. Robert Spencer, '19th-Century Guitar Music: The Type of Edition We Should Play From', *EGTA Guitar Journal* 6 (1995), 15–18, at 18.

STEAM EXCURSION.

PLATE I.

Figure 4. George Cruikshank, 'The Steam Excursion', in Charles Dickens, *Sketches by Boz* (London, 1837), 371.

and were often welcomed by the upper-class English who had some preference for seemingly exotic foreign musicians.[8]

In the 1830s Pelzer was known principally as a guitarist. By then the guitar, often referred to at that time in England as the 'Spanish guitar', was established in this country with six single strings, having evolved from earlier instruments of varying numbers of strings and courses. The three treble strings were made of gut while the three basses were of silk floss overwound with silver wire. The usual tuning, but not the pitch, was the same as that of a modern guitar although the instrument was a little smaller.[9] It was being played in this country by 1800; the earliest known method book was by Bonaventura Sperati, published in London in 1802.[10] Within a few years it seems that interest was fuelled by officers returning from the Peninsula war.[11]

By 1830 enthusiasm for the guitar was great and what has been labelled as the 'Great Vogue' for this romantic instrument was well under way in London.[12] The guitar was relatively cheap, could be easy to play, and was portable.[13] Writers later in the century looked back with some nostalgia. One commentator of 1888 talked of 'the guitar craze [...]

---

[8]   Nicholas Temperley, 'Xenophilia in British Musical History', in *Nineteenth-Century British Music Studies*, ed. Bennett Zon, 3 vols (Aldershot, 1999–2003), i (1999), 3–19, at 12–13. One inevitable consequence of this was that some English musicians made attempts to appear foreign; one journal, referring to an English guitar teacher who was struggling, noted that he became very successful after 'Italianising' his name. Anon, 'I remember once', *Literary Garland* 1:5 (1839), 232. The writer of the 'Introduction' in *The Giulianiad* suggests that guitarists from the continent were largely responsible for making the instrument popular in London. 'Introduction', *TG* 1:1 (1833), 1–2, at 2.

[9]   The usual tuning of the guitar today, using the Helmholtz scale in which middle c is c', is E-A-d-g-b-e'. Victorian pitch was higher than today's. However, there is evidence from tutor books of the time that guitars were tuned a tone lower in order to lessen the chances of strings breaking.

[10]   Bonaventura Sperati, *New and Complete Instructions for the Spanish Guitar* (London, [1802]). For an account of who was playing the Spanish guitar prior to 1814 in England see Christopher Page, *The Guitar in Georgian England* (New Haven, 2020), 89–110.

[11]   This was a commonly held belief at the time. For an account of the Peninsula war and the officers with guitars see Page, *Guitar*, 111–31.

[12]   This 'Great Vogue' for the instrument in Western Europe began around 1800 and was dwindling by about 1840. Christopher Page, 'The Great Vogue for the Guitar: an Overview', in *The Great Vogue for the Guitar in Western Europe 1800–1840*, ed. Christopher Page, Paul Sparks, and James Westbrook (Woodbridge, 2023), 29–40.

[13]   For the better off it could easily be taken on excursions where a cumbersome pianoforte would have been impractical. Thus Dickens describes the performance of the three Misses Briggs on their guitars on a steam ship in his *Sketches by Boz*. Charles Dickens, *Sketches by Boz* (London, 1836), 370. In addition, in *David Copperfield* (London, 1850–51) Dora Spenlow is rarely without a guitar, one of the endearing qualities that persuades David to propose marriage.

fostered in this country about seventy years ago. At that period – but only for a time – the guitar drove the pianoforte out of the field. Every young lady played it, and young men made it accompany the expression of much romantic sentiment.'[14] The choice of instruments for amateurs was then a gendered affair; men generally played certain orchestral instruments, often the flute and violin. Women, on the other hand, were expected to play keyboard or plucked string instruments and for many girls learning to play them was an essential accomplishment needed to enhance their chances in the marriage market. Among men there had been negative attitudes towards music in the eighteenth century, which persisted to some extent into the nineteenth.[15] Nevertheless, amateur music making was enjoyed by men such as Lord Saltoun who had fought in the Peninsula war. An account by William Gardiner of his playing the guitar at home with other instrumentalists gives an indication of his enthusiasm: 'At Lord Saltoun's I heard parts of the new operas cleverly arranged for his lordship's parties […] Lord Saltoun [played] the guitar.'[16]

Pelzer won praise soon after his arrival in London; a writer in the *Sunday Times* of 1829 noted that Felix Horetzky and Pelzer were 'the best masters of the instrument in London'.[17] In spite of suffering from nerves when performing Pelzer was nevertheless included later in the 'Collard Jubilee Festival' after having spent just over ten years in the capital.[18] This festival was held in honour of F. W. Collard (1772–1860) of the piano manufacturer Collard and Collard. Some 120 people attended the dinner in the Albion Tavern, Cheapside, and it is an indication of how Pelzer was regarded that he was named with a few other prominent

---

[14]   'Dramatic and Musical', *Daily Telegraph*, 29 June 1888.

[15]   These negative attitudes were illustrated by the often-quoted view of the earl of Chesterfield, who, in 1749, urged his son to avoid music making as it would lead him to keep bad company and waste time. Arthur Loesser, *Men, Women and Pianos* (New York, 1954), 213, 268. A commentator of 1874 summed up the attitude well: 'Music hardly comes within the scope of a boy's education […] while it is almost compulsory on girls whether they have talent for it or not.' Anon, 'The Education of Women', *Nature* 10:255 (1874), 395–96, at 395.

[16]   William Gardiner, *Music and Friends; or Pleasant Recollections of a Dilettante*, 3 vols (London, 1838, 1853), ii (1838), 692. William Gardiner (1769–1853) was a stocking manufacturer from Leicester who was also a keen musician and writer. Jonathan Wilshere, 'Gardiner, William', *GMO*. Alexander Fraser, 16th Lord Saltoun, served in the Peninsula war and was an accomplished amateur guitarist. Page, *Guitar*, 128–31.

[17]   'Varieties', *Sunday Times*, 23 August 1829. The Polish guitarist Felix Horetzky (1796–1870) may have studied with Giuliani in Vienna. Robert Coldwell, 'Introduction', in 'Felix Horetzky Quatre Variations Op 22', *Soundboard* 37:4 (2011), 60–61.

[18]   His nervousness was commented on in one review: 'He has a fine tone, and a just idea of expression […] but his nervousness in a large room, renders these qualities ineffective.' 'Messrs Dressler and Pelzer's Concert', *TG* 1:5 (1833), 49.

My child-wife's old companion

Figure 5. Hablot Knight Browne,'My Child Wife's Old Companion', in Charles Dickens, *David Copperfield* (London, 1850), 544.

orchestral musicians in the review.[19] It was to be expected that someone of his standing would be associated with the most significant London publication for the guitar in the 1830s, *The Giulianiad*.

THE GIULIANIAD (1833–c.1835)

The Giulianiad has long been regarded as important by historians of the guitar because it was the first periodical dedicated to the guitar that included both text and music sections, or so it did in its first six numbers, with the two sections having separate pagination. It is the text from these six numbers that is transcribed here. As such it offered a change in direction from the guitar periodicals, consisting only of music, that had preceded it.[20] This format, however, was not new for a musical periodical and it would seem likely that the editor(s) drew inspiration from earlier publications. As early as 1774 *The New Musical and Universal Magazine* had included literary pages in addition to music. In the nineteenth century *The Harmonicon* was the best-known example; it spanned the years 1823 to 1833 and the quality of the text, which included musical essays, reviews, and news, made it an influential publication.[21] It is possible that the editor(s) of *The Giulianiad* were also influenced by the *Flutist's Magazine* of 1827 which may have been the first English journal with text and music dedicated to a single instrument.

The Giulianiad bears witness to the great esteem with which the Italian guitarist Mauro Giuliani (1781–1829) was held in this country. This was all the more interesting since, as far as we know, he never visited England, whereas another great guitarist of the time, the Catalan Fernando Sor (1781–1839), had lived in London from 1815 until 1822.[22] Fervour for Giuliani's playing may be partly attributed to the enthusiasm of the few guitarists living in London in the 1830s who had, or had probably, known him in Vienna.[23] Listeners were particularly impressed

---

[19] 'The Collard Jubilee Festival', *Musical World* 16:294 (1841), 312–14. Collard and Collard was one of the largest piano manufacturers in nineteenth-century London. Ehrlich shows that later in the century it was second only to Broadwood. Cyril Ehrlich, *The Piano, a History* (London, 1976), 144.

[20] There were many guitar periodicals consisting of music published on the continent and in England prior to 1833. A few included short instructions on how to play, such as those by Bartolomeo Bortolazzi. His 'Periodical Amusements' for guitar reached thirty in number by 1829, the first, c.1807, was his *Compleat Instructions, for the Spanish Guitar. Made Perfectly Simple and Easy.*

[21] *The Harmonicon* had literary and music sections each with separate pagination. It is possible that the editor(s) of *The Giulianiad* took inspiration from its layout.

[22] For Sor's biography see Jeffery, *Sor*, 3rd edn, and Erik Stenstadvold, 'Fernando Sor (1778–1839)', in *Great Vogue*, eds Page, Sparks, and Westbrook, 203–20.

[23] The guitarists in London who would have heard Giuliani play before he left Vienna in 1819 were Andreas Schulz (born c.1787) and his son Leonard Schulz (1813–60). Schulz senior accompanied Giuliani in a concert in August 1817. Erik Stenstadvold,

by the way that he could make the guitar sing, not an easy thing to do on a plucked string instrument that by its nature can offer much less 'sustain' than a bowed string instrument. So it was that *The Giulianiad* commemorated him with the suffix *-iad*, possibly an allusion to Greek and Roman epics. Perhaps there is an element of humorous satire in making a guitarist, the exponent of an instrument often belittled, into an epic hero.[24] A reviewer in *The Harmonicon* went so far as to say that in 'the concert-room it [...] becomes as ineffective as a piping bullfinch perched on a trombone in the midst of a great military band'.[25] Its position with amateurs was not helped by the common perception that it was often the chosen instrument of young women for whom high standards of performance were not generally encouraged.[26] The guitar was therefore, as Andrew Britton puts it, 'inseparable from the devaluation and trivialisation of women's musical activities by European society in general'.[27]

It has been possible to piece together some of *The Giulianiad*'s publication history from the few surviving copies that have their original thin green wrappers and from newspaper advertisements. The first was dated January 1833 as we can see from the wrapper on the copy held in the Spencer Collection at the Royal Academy of Music in London.[28] The second was published in February and the fourth in April; the third would have been in March.[29] Production slowed in that summer; the fifth was published in July and the sixth in October, completing the first

'"The Worst Drunkard in London": The Life and Career of the Guitar Virtuoso Leonard Schulz', *Soundboard* 38:4 (2012), 9–16, at 9. In addition, Felix Horetzky (1796–1870) claimed to have studied with Giuliani. Coldwell, 'Introduction', 60–61.

[24] Many works took the suffix *-iad* after the publication of Pope's mock-heroic satire *The Dunciad* of 1728. Richmond Bond, '*-IAD*: A Progeny of the Dunciad', *Publications of the Modern Language Association* 44:4 (1929), 1099–1105.

[25] 'Three Rondos for Two Guitars', *The Harmonicon* 7:14 (1829), 48.

[26] David Golby, *Instrumental Teaching in Nineteenth-Century Britain* (Aldershot, 2004), 47.

[27] Andrew Britton, 'The Guitar in the Romantic Period: Its Musical and Social Development, with Special Reference to Bristol and Bath' (unpublished doctoral dissertation, University of London, 2010), 99. To some extent the instrument was seen as a new consumer item. This is illustrated by the way that it was sometimes included as a prop in fashion plates in women's periodicals. For example, see 'Evening Dress', *Lady's Magazine* 4 (1823), after 486. For an outline of this consumer place for the guitar see Page, 'Overview', 32–33.

[28] This first issue was possibly produced in December 1832. An advertisement in the *Morning Herald* on 14 December 1832 announced that the first number was to be published that day. It was reviewed in *The Express* (Dublin) on 31 December 1832. Robert Spencer (1932–97) was a singer, lutenist, guitarist, and musicologist who was an important figure in the early music field. His extensive collection of music and instruments is now held by the Royal Academy of Music, London.

[29] For the second issue see 'Advertisements', *The Examiner*, 3 February 1833. The copy of the fourth held by the British Library is dated April 1833.

Figure 6.
'Evening Dress', *Lady's Magazine*, 4 (1823), after 486.

Evening Costume

Printed by Mrs Bryant & engraved for the Lady's Magazine N.º 122

volume.[30] The beginning of the second volume with number seven was published in January 1834.[31] Number ten was available by November 1834[32] which suggests that number eight was published in April and number nine in July of that year. The publication dates of the remaining three issues are not clear.

Some were reissued later. It is not known how many were printed initially, but there probably were not many as the high price of two shillings and sixpence for each number would have limited purchasers to the well-off.[33] It seems, however, that the publisher underestimated demand and that some were reprinted in later editions. An advertisement announcing the publication of the second number added that the second edition of the first from January was also ready.[34] In number four there is a footnote to say that the previous number (three) would be reprinted with the addition of English words for a German song, 'The Minstrel's Lay'.[35] The individual copy of this number in the Spencer Collection is a first and shows that this was done. Only German words are given for the song 'Frölich und wohlgemuth'. In later copies English words are added.[36]

In addition to the bound complete volume, the Appleby Collection also contains five copies of individual numbers with their wrappers. Four of these indicate that Pelzer was issuing them much later in the 1840s. Numbers two, three, six, and nine all state on the covers that they are available from Mr Pelzer at 55 Great Marlborough Street. This appears to have been a business address that he used in that decade; no reference to any family events there have been found. This raises an interesting question of how the periodical was printed. The music sections were printed from engraved plates which could have been kept indefinitely and used for later reprints. The text sections were printed from letterpress. This would have cost less because a skilled engraver would not have been required and instead a jobbing printer could have done the work. The problem was, though, that the letterpress forme would not have been kept after its first use; the printer would have dismantled it and used the type for something else. For the copies reissued in the 1840s either extra copies of the text section had been printed initially and

---

30   For the fifth see 'Advertisements', *The Age*, 16 June 1833. For the sixth see 'Advertisements', *The Age*, 22 September 1833.

31   'Advertisements', *Figaro in London* 3:112 (1834), 16.

32   'Advertisements', *True Sun*, 26 November 1834.

33   Of the nine copies seen with their original green wrappers, eight give the price of two shillings and sixpence. The copy of number four in the British Library gives a price of two shillings. Using the Bank of England inflation calculator, two shillings and sixpence in 1833 would be worth approximately twelve pounds and twenty-five pence in 2024.

34   'Advertisements', *The Examiner*, 3 February 1833.

35   'The Minstrel's Lay', *TG* 1:4 (1833), 41.

36   'Frölich und wohlgemuth', *TG* 1:3 (1833), Music 29.

stored somewhere, or new letterpress formes were made, or permanent stereotype plates were made from the original letterpress formes at extra expense.[37] It is not clear what was done, although one minor mistake in the early printing of issue six remained uncorrected in the reissue of the 1840s, so it is likely that extra copies were printed initially.[38]

As was the convention of the time, the editor(s) of *The Giulianiad* remained anonymous.[39] It is, however, now widely accepted that Pelzer was involved, either as sole editor or with others. The earliest reference to suggest that Pelzer had an editorial role came in 1954 in the second edition of Philip Bone's book about the guitar and mandolin.[40] Later writers have taken a similar stance and its inclusion in this Appleby volume with other of Pelzer's works points to this being so. There are other indications of his involvement. The individual copy of number ten in the Appleby Collection, which appears to be a first edition, states that both the 'Proprietor' and 'F Pelzer' live at 39 Great Portland Street and therefore seem to be one and the same.[41] This is a very plausible theory, but there were probably other households at that address as well so, although unlikely, one of the other residents could have been the 'Proprietor'. In the 1841 census, by which time the Pelzers had moved on, the building contained five households and it seems likely that it was equally as crowded in the mid 1830s.[42]

Another way to assess whether Pelzer may have been the editor is to compare the contents of *The Giulianiad* with other of his works and in particular the *Guitarist's Companion* of 1857 in which Pelzer is named as editor. There are similarities between the two. The words of all the songs in the later periodical were written by William Ball, who also

---

37   To make stereotype plates a plaster of Paris mould was taken from the forme and then used to make an iron plate. For a full description of the process see 'The Commercial History of a Penny Magazine, No. iii, Compositors work and Stereotyping', *Penny Magazine*, Monthly Supplement, 31 October 1833.

38   The mistake in number six, page 56: 'ins trument' goes uncorrected. The Spanish guitarist Dionisio Aguado (1784–1849) published his *Nuevo método* in 1843; it is interesting to note what he did. Like *The Giulianiad* the text of his book was printed from letterpress and the music from engraved plates. At his death in 1849 he left 560 copies of the letterpress section plus the plates for the remaining section as well as sixty complete copies of the book. Erik Stenstadvold, 'Printing and Publishing Music for the Guitar', in *Great Vogue*, eds Page, Sparks, and Westbrook, 57–75, at 62.

39   Leanne Langley, 'The English Musical Journal in the Early Nineteenth Century' (unpublished doctoral dissertation, University of North Carolina at Chapel Hill, 1983), 117.

40   Philip Bone, *The Guitar and Mandolin*, 2nd edn (London, 1954), 140–41. Pelzer's possible connection to the periodical is not mentioned in the first edition of this book published in 1914.

41   Stewart Button, *The Guitar in England 1800–1924* (New York, 1989), 119.

42   In the 1831 census for Great Portland Street there is no entry for number 39. This would have indicated how many families lived in the house.

provided words for some thirty-two of the songs and two poems in *The Giulianiad*. Two of the songs in the publications are the same but with new English words by Ball in the *Guitarist's Companion* replacing Italian ones of *The Giulianiad*.[43] The text section of the later publication also owed much to the earlier periodical. Both the introduction and the first article, 'The Guitar as an Accompaniment to the Voice', are largely taken from the introduction to 'On the Comparative Merits of the Pianoforte and Guitar as an Accompaniment to the Voice' in *The Giulianiad*. Some of the text is quoted exactly without acknowledgement. This blatant plagiarism does not in itself mean that the two had the same editor as articles were often recycled in different journals at that time.[44] In spite of these common components the two periodicals have differences. *The Giulianiad* was wide-ranging and its readership was intended to range from beginner amateurs to advanced players and professors.[45] In contrast, the *Guitarist's Companion* was just for amateurs. They could both have been the work of Pelzer who, after a gap of some twenty years, aimed his later work at a slightly narrower market.

A less obvious comparison but nevertheless an illuminating one can be made by looking at Pelzer's *Instructions for the Spanish Guitar*. In particular, the differences between the first edition of 1830 and the second of 1833 are important. All the pieces by Horetzky and John Nüske in the first edition are removed and replaced with pieces by other composers, changes which would have involved some expense with the engraving of eight new plates. The removal of the pieces by Nüske is surprising because Pelzer gives him particular praise in a lengthy paragraph at the end of the first edition.[46] A similar hostility to these two guitarists developed in *The Giulianiad*. Horetzky's playing was praised in the first issue but then his compositions were ridiculed

---

43 The melody of 'Povera Signora', *TG* 1:2 (1833), Music 20–21, is used for 'Child of the Mountain', *Guitarist's Companion* 1 (1857), Music 2–3. The melody of 'Al Tempo Felice', *TG* 2:9 (1834), Music 115, is used for 'The Aspirant's Dream', *Guitarist's Companion* 1 (1857), Music 3. William Ball (c.1784–1869) wrote lyrics for many songs. 'Death of Mr. William Ball', *The Era*, 23 May 1869.

44 Langley, 'Musical Journal', 128–29.

45 The introduction specifies that the journal should 'instil in those who are almost commencing, and keep alive in those who are already advanced, an interest in their instrument,—and finally to provide food for a little chit-chat amongst the best professors themselves'. 'Introduction', *TG* 1:1 (1833), 1–2, at 2.

46 John Abraham Nüske (1796–1865), originally from Russia, was a prominent guitarist in London at this time. Pelzer says in the first edition of his method book, 'I beg to assure all who are real lovers of the Art, and of this romantic and scientific instrument; that from the period when I began to play the Compositions of Mr. Nüske, I have experienced a higher degree of pleasure in teaching it.' Ferdinand Pelzer, *Instructions for the Spanish Guitar* (London, [1830]), 59.

in the third.[47] Likewise with Nüske, he was praised in the second but then none of his compositions appeared after the fifth issue. Perhaps some rivalry developed and as this can be seen in both Pelzer's work and in *The Giulianiad* this adds to the likelihood that he was involved with the latter.[48]

In reality, there may have been a team of editors for part or all of the periodical's life. If there had been changes in the composition of this team this would help account for the inconsistent content. Thus, the text section offered promises of future articles that were not fulfilled and finally ceased altogether after the sixth issue. The wrapper of the fourth issue, held in the British Library, refers to the proprietors in the plural.[49] Further evidence to support this theory comes with the publication details on the front cover. There we are told that it is 'published for the Proprietor by Sherwood & Co'. This wording suggests that the 'Proprietor(s)' took the financial risk and paid for the production of the periodical and the publisher named sold it for some commission.[50] In order to spread the cost it is likely that there was more than one 'Proprietor',[51] although it would be impossible now to know who others might have been without some further evidence.[52]

---

[47] The first issue states that Horetzky's performance 'approaches perfection'. 'Giuliani', *TG* 1:1 (1833), 7–8, at 8. In the third issue a review of his compositions says that they have 'little originality or invention' and 'The higher attributes of writing, this composer does not appear to possess.' 'Review of Music', *TG* 1:3 (1833), 33.

[48] Thomas Heck has observed this possible rivalry that developed between Horetzky and the editor(s). Thomas Heck, 'Horetzky e la Giulianiad', *Il Fronimo* 3:12 (1975), 23–26.

[49] However, four other wrappers on copies that are almost certainly first editions refer to the 'proprietor', singular. They are numbers one and three in the Spencer Collection, number three in New York Public Library, and number ten in the Appleby Collection.

[50] For details of the possible ways that publications were financed see David Rowland, 'Composers, Publishers, and the Market in Late Georgian Britain', in *Music Publishing and Composers (1750–1850)*, ed. Massimiliano Sala (Turnhout, 2020), 85–112, at 94–104.

[51] Leanne Langley in her work suggests that the capital needed to start a journal was beyond the means of a single individual and ownership would have been syndicated. She also notes that having more than one editor could lead to inconsistencies in the publication. Langley, 'Musical Journal', 128–29. Such problems are evident in *The Giulianiad*.

[52] Whoever was involved, a phrase in *The Giulianiad* suggests that at least one writer's first language may not have been English and could have been German. It says, 'It is not to be denied.' 'The Westminster Review and the Guitar', *TG* 1:2 (1833), 18–19, at 18. This is a characteristically German way to begin a sentence. There is a similarly awkward phrase in the *Guitarist's Companion*, 'they should be always repeated.' 'Exercises', *Guitarist's Companion* 1 (1857), Music 10.

As already described, the aim of the periodical was very far-reaching and the first number succeeded in having something for everyone. In the music section there are four short easy guitar solos, a solo from Giuliani's third guitar concerto, and a song with guitar accompaniment that would have been presentable at any drawing-room occasion. In the text section there are articles about the guitar, including one in praise of Giuliani. There is a poem, a review of some music, and 'chit-chat' with comments on musical life in London and Vienna that is largely gleaned from other periodicals. However, not all the issues were so well balanced and some articles promised in the text section never saw the light of day after the demise of the text at the end of 1833. The ninth, by which time text had ceased to be a part, comprised five songs with moderate accompaniments and an extended 'German Air with Variations' by Pelzer. There was nothing for the elementary player. This inconsistency may have contributed to its ultimate end, although the usual life of a journal in this period was two years and four months, which would make *The Giulianiad*'s production span about average.[53]

By the mid 1830s the vogue for the guitar was in decline, and as was usual for musicians at that time, Pelzer diversified his activities. This was a sensible business strategy since life could be uncertain. Musicians nearly always taught more than one instrument; guitarists usually offered singing, piano, or flute lessons, in addition to the guitar. Some were also involved in activities that had nothing to do with music, many branching out into language teaching, which must have been an obvious choice for those from abroad.[54] Pelzer himself published method books for both the piano and concertina.[55] It was, however, with singing teaching that his career moved forward in the 1840s.

---

[53] Langley, 'Musical Journal', 54.

[54] Sarah Clarke, 'An Instrument in Comparative Oblivion? Women and the Guitar in Victorian London' (unpublished doctoral dissertation, the Open University, 2020), 64–69. One such was the German Karl Eulenstein (1802–90), who played the jew's harp and guitar. He spent much of his career in England and moved to the West Country in the mid 1830s where he started teaching German as well as the guitar. Victor de Pontigny, revised by Paul Sparks, 'Eulenstein, Charles', *GMO*. By 1842 he was better known for language teaching than for music; he was listed in a trade directory as a teacher of German only in Bath. *Pigot and Co's Directory of Somersetshire* (London, 1842), 18. He published a German grammar that ran to at least five editions.

[55] Ferdinand Pelzer, *A Practical Guide to Modern Piano Forte Playing* (London, 1842). No extant copy of his *Practical Guide* for the concertina has been located; it is listed in *Catalogue of the Universal Circulating Library, Novello, Ewer & Co.* (London, [1860]), 237.

THE *MUSICAL HERALD* (c.1841/43)

Another musician from Trier who was the same age as Pelzer was also a teacher of singing. This was Joseph Mainzer (1801–51). He had spent a brief time as an apprentice mining engineer before becoming a priest and as a singing master at the seminary in Trier he wrote his didactic work, *Singschule*, which was subsequently used in schools in Prussia. His involvement in political activity became regarded as subversive by the authorities, so he fled first to Brussels and then Paris in 1834. Mindful of the conditions of the miners that he had experienced, he organised singing classes for workmen in the French capital in an effort to alleviate their lot. The classes were offered gratis; for his income he depended upon the sale of his books, and the spectacle of large numbers of working people singing attracted visitors including Henry Chorley of *The Athenaeum* in London, who published an account of the events.[56] However, as enthusiasm for Mainzer's classes fell and the Parisian authorities became concerned about the possibility of political intent, he moved to London in 1841 and conducted classes there.[57] He published his *Singing for the Million* in 1841.[58]

Meanwhile in England in the late 1830s Parliament was seeking to improve the provision of education in the country and a Committee of Council on Education was established. The secretary was James Kay (later Kay-Shuttleworth) and it was his personal philosophy and resulting proposals that largely held sway. He sought to promote singing in schools because of its civilising effect and because it might improve public worship. In addition, something that could provide contentment for working people, and distract them from drink and political agitation, was welcomed by those in authority who were becoming nervous of the activities of the Chartists.[59] Here the philanthropic aim of promoting something that was enjoyable was mixed with a desire to influence the lower orders.[60]

Prior to Mainzer's arrival textbooks aimed at improving congregational singing included those by John Turner in 1833 and Sarah Glover in 1835, and in 1836 W. E. Hickson (1803–70) published *The Singing Master*, a book for teachers providing secular songs for children. Hickson was also instrumental in founding the Society for the Encouragement of Vocal Music in 1838, which sought to cater for all classes 'As a Means

---

[56]   Henry F. Chorley, 'Foreign Correspondence', *The Athenaeum* 527 (1837), 881.
[57]   Details about Mainzer are taken from Bernarr Rainbow, *The Land Without Music* (London, 1967; repr. Aberystwyth, 1991), 104–7.
[58]   Joseph Mainzer, *Singing for the Million* (London, 1841).
[59]   Rainbow, *Land*, 111–20.
[60]   Rosemary Golding, 'Music and Mass Education: Cultivation or Control?', in *Music and Victorian Liberalism: Composing the Liberal Subject*, ed. Sarah Collins (Cambridge, 2019), 60–80, at 60.

of softening the Manners, refining the Taste, and raising the Character of the great Body of the People'.[61] Kay, though, looked abroad for inspiration. He employed a young musician, John Hullah (1812–84), to visit Paris to witness Mainzer's classes. However, Hullah arrived after the classes had ceased and instead found those of the French teacher G. L. Bocquillon Wilhem (1781–1842). Back in London Hullah taught in a new training school established by Kay for teachers in Battersea and also established a singing school for teachers in Exeter Hall in February 1841. For these he adapted Wilhem's method, publishing it as *Wilhem's Method of Teaching Singing* with the blessing of the Committee of Council on Education.[62]

The work of these and other teachers led to what can only be described as a craze for choral teaching and singing that swept the country in the early 1840s. Large classes were being taught: a report in March 1842 of Mainzer teaching a class of some 500 was representative, the writer noting that singing 'was the certain precursor of increased morality and good conduct'. It was said that plans were afoot to build a music hall that could accommodate 10,000 pupils since no existing hall in London was sufficiently large.[63] There was also enthusiasm in the provinces, a correspondent in Hampshire writing of the 'irrational mania [...] upon these new modes of spontaneously generating any given number of vocalists'.[64]

This was the movement that Pelzer joined. With different teachers working with differing methods discussions and rivalries were inevitable. So it was that Pelzer made a plea for unity of purpose in his *Musical Herald* in place of 'selfishness and pride of heart'.[65] Pelzer himself had much in common with Mainzer. It is probable that they had known each other in Trier and Mainzer is likely to have contacted his old friend when he first arrived in London after hastily leaving Paris. He was not known to have played the guitar but was nevertheless listed as one of the late subscribers to Pelzer's *One Hundred and Fifty Exercises* for the instrument in 1840.[66]

---

[61] 'Prospectus for the Society for the Encouragement of Vocal Music', British Library, 1879.cc.13.(11.). Hickson was the son of a wealthy industrialist who, in 1840, purchased the *Westminster Review*. Bernarr Rainbow, *Four Centuries of Music Teaching Manuals 1518–1932* (Woodbridge, 1992), 183.

[62] Rainbow, *Land*, 122–25. Hullah published Wilhem's method in 1842. John Hullah, *Wilhem's Method of Teaching Singing, adapted to English use* (London, 1842).

[63] 'Singing for the Million', *Morning Post*, 24 March 1842. The proposed new hall was never built.

[64] 'Class Singing', *Hampshire Telegraph and Sussex Chronicle*, 21 November 1842.

[65] Ferdinand Pelzer, *Musical Herald* (London [1842]), 8–9.

[66] Ferdinand Pelzer, *One Hundred and Fifty Exercises for Acquiring a Facility of Performance on the Spanish Guitar* (London, 1840). Two copies of this have been found, one in the Spencer Collection in the Royal Academy of Music, London, and a later edition in the Nakano Collection, Japan. A few extra subscribers are

The singing methods of the two men were, in the early stages, strikingly similar. Pelzer presented his system in his *Music for the People* of 1842,[67] published a year after Mainzer's book. Their similarity is well illustrated by a comparison of two newspaper accounts of their lessons. In these reports the simplicity of both methods was stressed, noting that no new theories as such were being offered. Both used a blackboard and started with the group singing exercises on one note, G, or *sol* in the *solfa* system. Both teachers added subsequent notes in the same order, first ascending as far as C and then adding lower notes. The satisfaction of achieving much in just one session was noted.[68] It is not completely clear which of the two men devised this procedure. However, since Mainzer published his book a year before Pelzer published his, and nothing has yet been found to suggest that Pelzer was involved with choral teaching before the early 1840s, it is probable that Mainzer developed his system first and that Pelzer then adapted some of his methods. It is even possible that Pelzer visited Paris in the 1830s to witness Mainzer's work there, although no evidence to confirm this has been found.

Pelzer's *Musical Herald*, given here, outlines his philosophy and aims. His ambitious plan aimed to establish a Society for the Diffusion of Musical Knowledge whose members would promote vocal work for the 'regeneration of the people from debasing habits'.[69] This would not

added in the latter, among whom was Mainzer. Mainzer's younger brother, Jacob Mainzer (1804–76), also taught choral singing and played the guitar. 'Singing for the Million', *The Sun*, 14 December 1843.

[67] Ferdinand Pelzer, *Music for the People on Universal Principles, Practically Arranged by Ferdinand Pelzer, and Theoretically Explained by H. Doherty, esq.* (London, 1842). The date of first publication, 20 July 1842, is confirmed by its registration at Stationers' Hall. National Archives, Records of the Copyright Office, Stationers' Company, COPY 3/1. In order to secure copyright at this time publications had to be registered at Stationers' Hall; in practice many were not because of the cost involved. A second edition, with an added introduction, was published in 1858. The only known copies of both editions are held by the British Library. Its copy of the first stops at page 80, the first page of the fifth part; it is possible that some subsequent pages are missing. The first eighty pages are the same in both, so it is not clear what, other than the introduction, was added for the second edition. H. Doherty was probably Hugh Doherty, who published the newspaper the *London Phalanx* (1841–43) which promoted the ideas of the French socialist thinker Charles Fourier (1772–1837). Reference to Fourier's book *Universal Unity* is made on page 142 in Pelzer's *Music for the People*.

[68] For the description of Mainzer's lesson see 'Provincial', *Manchester Times*, 19 February 1842. Pelzer's lesson is in a newspaper quotation in Pelzer's first leaflet about his choral work that is transcribed here. The reference given is: 'Music for the People', *Drogheda Argus*, 24 September 1842. No copy of the original newspaper has been located and the quotation has therefore not been checked.

[69] 'Proposals', *Musical Herald*, 1. The philanthropic aim of the society echoed that of the Society for the Diffusion of Useful Knowledge (1826–46), established by

have been the first organisation established to promote choral singing; there was Hickson's Society for the Encouragement of Vocal Music and Mainzer also had plans for an association.[70] Pelzer added an interesting proposal that others had not made: he wanted to include a benefit fund 'for professional members of the society when disabled by illness or other misfortune from following their profession'.[71] This enlightened scheme would have recognised how difficult things could be for those unable to work, for many musicians fell on hard times, through illness or want of employment, at some point in their careers.[72] It seems, however, that this plan was not realised, nor were any of the promised future issues of the *Musical Herald*.[73]

Although Pelzer was in London when he developed his method, he also put it into practice in the provinces, as revealed by the three leaflets of newspaper reports that follow the *Musical Herald* and track his progress. After the publication of his method *Music for the People*, he went to Ireland in the autumn of 1842 and then to Hampshire. In the early part of 1843 he was in Surrey, and by the end of the year in Devon. At this time the whole family moved to Exeter and lived at 6, Longbrook Terrace.[74] While in the West Country Pelzer taught singing in Devon, Cornwall, and Bristol in 1845. The newspaper reports attest to

Henry Brougham, which sought to provide cheap periodical literature. Rosemary Ashton, 'Society for the Diffusion of Useful Knowledge', *ODNB*.

[70] Mainzer's initial plans were outlined in a leaflet that is bound into the British Library copy of his *Singing for the Million* of 1841, shelf mark 785.g.21. Hickson's prospectus for his Society for the Encouragement of Vocal Music among all Classes of 1838 gave detailed plans, but the society did little after Kay and the Committee of Council on Education backed Hullah in 1841.

[71] 'Benefit Fund', *Musical Herald*, 2.

[72] Deborah Rohr, *The Careers of British Musicians 1750–1850* (Cambridge, 2001), 157–60. Some were helped by institutions or charities; the most well-known of these was the Royal Society of Musicians founded in 1738 to help 'Decayed musicians or their families' if in need. Pippa Drummond, 'The Royal Society of Musicians in the Eighteenth Century', *Music and Letters* 59:3 (1978), 268–89, at 268. The society continues today to give help to musicians. Those who had exhausted all other options could turn to the workhouse.

[73] Mainzer had more success with his journal. He first published his *National Singing Circular*, which was produced irregularly, in August 1841. This was replaced by *Mainzer's Musical Times* in July 1842, published twice monthly. In 1844 it was taken over by Joseph Novello, who continued it as *The Musical Times and Singing Class Circular*. No copies of the *National Singing Circular* have been located.

[74] Their departure from 47, Poland Street, their last known address in London before they moved out of the city, is confirmed in the rate books. A note in the 'remarks' column of the record for 1843 crosses out Pelzer, noting that he left at Michaelmas (late September). London, City of Westminster Archives, Rate book for Poland Street in the Parish of Saint James, 1843, D182, page 39. The Pelzer family moved home on an almost annual basis while in London in the 1830s. This was not unusual. Jerry White, *London in the 19th Century* (London, 2007), 115.

the great success he had on many occasions in teaching large groups of pupils. However, no references to his choral work after 1846 have been found. Several causes may have contributed to the decline in interest, not least the very harsh economic climate that developed in the winter of 1846 that hit Devon and Cornwall hard. The price of food rose and in Exeter about one quarter of the population sought assistance from the Famine Relief Fund.[75]

There was, in addition, an intrinsic problem with the system that Pelzer was almost certainly using that could present seemingly insurmountable difficulties to amateurs after the initial stages, regardless of their social class. Hullah and Mainzer used Italian *solfa* syllables in the French way with a fixed *doh* that always represented C. Pupils were able to make good progress while everything remained in the key of C major. Problems arose when accidentals, and other keys, were introduced. The music critic Joseph Bennett recalled the effect these had on a class he attended in 1842 that used Mainzer's system: 'Ah miserable sharp! It knocked the class off its bearings [...] while the names of the notes remained unchanged each might represent three different sounds [...] The old enthusiasm began to wane, attendance became irregular.'[76] It can be seen that there was a pattern in the way that Mainzer worked; he tended to keep moving from place to place, which suggests that it was difficult to make progress beyond a certain level. It is almost certain that Pelzer also used this fixed *doh* system and that he was encountering the same difficulties in his work.[77] The accounts of the singing lessons that he gave leave no doubt that he was a very committed teacher, and it was often noted how simple his method was and how clear were his instructions. Nevertheless, as with Mainzer, he was constantly moving to new places and various series of lessons that he started did not seem to last. For example, in Ireland in 1842 he taught the children from St Peter's Orphan Society for just three weeks. With the help of a Mr Searle, he gave a demonstration

---

75 R Swift, 'Food Riots in Mid-Victorian Exeter, 1847–67', *Southern History* 2 (1980), 101–27, at 104.

76 Joseph Bennett, 'Some Recollections', *Musical Times and Singing Class Circular* 39:665 (1898), 451–53, at 453. The alternative to the fixed *doh* system is relative *solfa* in which *doh* is applied to the tonic of all major keys. This was advocated by John Curwen (1816–80), who adopted the method of Sarah Glover with minor changes. This system flourished in the late nineteenth century and was used in the twentieth by the Hungarian Zoltan Kodaly.

77 In his book *Music for the People* Pelzer is not completely clear with this matter. He uses fixed *solfa* syllables throughout with *doh* as C. Confusion comes with a footnote at the bottom of page 69 in which minor scales are given. He says that 'these scales may be sung to the *sol, fa*, instead of the numerals bearing in mind that the tonic or first note of each must be *do*, the second *re*, etc.' However, this instruction makes no sense when applied to minor scales since for them the tonic would not be *doh*.

of his work at a dinner of the musical professors of Dublin and Pelzer received a toast for his magnificent work. In spite of such a splendid send-off it appears that Pelzer did not return.[78] In January 1843 Searle was still giving lessons in schools using the method but no evidence has been found of him continuing with it after that.[79]

Personal tragedy may have contributed to Pelzer's final decision to leave Devon. His infant son Christie died in January 1845 and his daughter Jane, aged fifteen, died in November 1846.[80] An announcement was made in April 1847 that he had returned to London 'with a view of organizing Classes in the Metropolis'.[81] It is not certain if most of the family moved back as well at that point; his eldest daughter, Catharina, continued to teach guitar and concertina in Devon until late 1848 when she returned to London.[82] It is likely that she stayed on in Exeter after the rest of the family had gone.

THE *GUITARIST'S COMPANION* (1857)

Back in London Pelzer appears to have returned to the guitar, for no reports of the intended singing classes have been found. To this end, he published the *Guitarist's Companion* in 1857 which, as already outlined, had much in common with *The Giulianiad*. However, it was aimed at a narrower amateur market. It acknowledges the portability of the instrument and that it was generally used to provide accompaniment to songs.[83] In twelve issues, it sought to provide the amateur guitarist and singer with a 'travelling library' of music.[84] The first issue only is included here; the contents of the proposed second number are outlined

---

78 'Public Dinner to Mr. Pelzer', *Freeman's Journal*, 3 October 1842. This review is quoted in Pelzer's first leaflet transcribed here.

79 'Advertisements', *Freeman's Journal*, 25 January 1843.

80 An announcement of Jane's death noted that she had been 'an extraordinary pianist' and that 'Her death falls as a heavy calamity on a worthy family, who have been tried with many sorrows.' 'Deaths', *Western Times*, 21 November 1846.

81 'Brief Chronicle of the Last Month', *Musical Times and Singing Class Circular* 2:35 (1 April 1847), 87. The classes referred to would have been singing classes. Pelzer had left Exeter before the food riots of May 1847 in which 'emaciated' women and children took part. 'Food Riots', *Exeter and Plymouth Gazette*, 22 May 1847.

82 For an announcement of Catharina's return to London see 'Advertisements', *The Times*, 8 December 1848. She advertised guitar and concertina lessons extensively in the Exeter newspapers between 1846 and 1848 and is listed in White's directory of Devon of 1850. William White, *History, Gazetteer, and Directory of Devonshire* (Sheffield, 1850), 170. It is probable that information for this directory was gathered some time before publication. Ferdinand Pelzer is not included.

83 The guitar accompaniments in the later periodical are all easier than those for the same songs in *The Giulianiad*.

84 'Introduction', *Guitarist's Companion*, 3–4, at 4.

but as no extant copy has been found it is probable that no more were published. There is in this issue some text, a selection of six songs with easy guitar accompaniments with English words, a few left hand exercises, and two extended solo guitar pieces.[85]

The page that gives most insight into Pelzer and his work is the second. The wording derives from an advertising flyer, a copy of which is leafed into the depositions taken at the inquest following his death in 1864.[86] Perhaps it was placed there as a tribute to his work. It says that he offers guitar and singing lessons to individuals and large groups; of particular interest is the emphasis placed upon the art of performance which should go hand in hand with an understanding of the 'science', or theory, of music and composition. Pelzer further observes that many beginners are taught by governesses who themselves have had scant education and here he offers to teach 'intelligent ladies how to instruct in the elementary principles'. He notes that this knowledge is needed for the enjoyment of classical music and the emphasis he places on this aspect of study would confirm its usual neglect.[87] The statement would have reflected how Pelzer had first taught his own five daughters, four of whom had careers as professional musicians in adult life. Catharina in particular developed into a composer in addition to being a teacher and performer; her considerable number of pieces for the guitar have had some years of neglect but are once more gaining in popularity.[88]

---

[85] It is curious that, if this volume was intended for an elementary amateur, no easy solos are included as they are in the first issue of *The Giulianiad*. The list of contents of the proposed second issue indicates that they would not have been included there either.

[86] London, London Metropolitan Archives, Middlesex Central Coroner's District Depositions, Ferdinand Pelzer, 14 July 1864, COR/B/016. Depositions were witness statements. At the time of his death Pelzer, aged sixty-three, was living in a lodging house in Ernest Street, just east of Regent's Park. The coroner concluded that nothing untoward had taken place and the cause of death was recorded as heart disease.

[87] Nearly all the older pupils of governesses would have been girls. The notion that harmony and composition should be taught to girls was stressed by a piano teacher, Eleanor Geary, in the early 1840s. Like Pelzer she noted that this study was important for the understanding of music and would not necessarily lead a pupil to become a composer. Eleanor Geary, *Musical Education* (London, 1841), 10–11. The poor teaching of theory to girls was noted by a contemporary musician, Henry Banister. He recalled that when he was a student at the Royal Academy of Music in the late 1840s the study of counterpoint was introduced only for boys studying composition, it was not taught to the girls. Henry Banister, *George Alexander Macfarren* (London, 1891), 25. For the importance of governesses in the teaching of music see Christopher Page, 'Being a Guitarist in Late Georgian Britain', *Early Music* 46:1 (2018), 3–16, at 12–15. By 'Classical Music' Pelzer would almost certainly have been referring to the works of the Viennese classical composers Haydn, Mozart, and Beethoven.

[88] There can be little doubt that he taught all his daughters. In his piano tutor he says that the book was written from experience of teaching his own children. It is

MR PELZER, THE CELEBRATED GERMAN PROFESSOR OF MUSIC

Pelzer is best remembered today as the patriarch of the Pelzer family that was to dominate the Victorian guitar world. His skill as a teacher is reflected in the successes of his daughters and Catharina in particular. Her pupils included one member of the royal family and those who became teachers in their turn often mentioned her name in advertisements as a guarantee of competence.[89] Pelzer, however, was ambitious and had an interesting and varied career in his own right that reflected the times in which he lived.

The periodicals transcribed here give some indication of just how ambitious he was. *The Giulianiad* was intended for everyone who was interested in the guitar, both amateurs and professionals. It has illuminating content, and more articles were planned about Sor and English guitar makers. In the *Musical Herald* he laid out plans to establish a Society for the Diffusion of Musical Knowledge. In the *Guitarist's Companion* he set out to produce a complete little travelling library for the amateur. Not everything that he hoped for materialised, but achievements there were. *The Giulianiad*, the first periodical for the instrument to include both text and music, and to which he made a large contribution, established a pattern that was to be used by many guitar journals that followed. His singing method may have been flawed in some respects but nevertheless his work was part of a choral movement that embedded singing in the school curriculum.[90] We do not know how much vocal teaching he continued with in the last years of his life, but it is significant that his death certificate recorded his occupation as 'teacher of singing'.

---

not clear if he also taught his sons. 'Introductory Remarks', in Pelzer, *Practical Guide*.

[89] Catharina gave guitar lessons to Princess Louise, daughter of Queen Victoria.

[90] Rainbow, *Land*, 138.

THE GIULIANIAD

The
GIULIANIAD
OR
Guitarist's Magazine,

[Image of a Guitar]

VOL.

———

LONDON,

Published for the Proprietor by Sherwood & Co. 23 Paternoster Row,
Chappell, Music Seller to the King 30, New Bond Street
and Duff; 65, Oxford Street.
*Price Bound 1st Vol. . / in Numbers each 2/6
and to be had of the Proprietor 39 Great Portland Street.*

[First unnumbered page][1]

TUITION ON THE GUITAR.

———

F. PELZER

Respectfully informs the Nobility and Gentry, that he has removed his residence to No. 39, GREAT PORTLAND STREET, where he receives Pupils for Instruction on the SPANISH GUITAR, on the usual Terms.

———

NOTICE.

The present Number (XII.) of THE GIULIANIAD closes the Second Volume of the Work, for which a Title-Page and Table of Contents are herewith given.[2]

The Numbers of the GIULIANIAD will continue to be issued, as usual, one every three months, containing, at least, three or four Songs or Duets of the most approved character, with original English words,

---

[1]   In this volume six unnumbered pages comprising advertisements and lists of contents are placed after the title page and before the start of the first number. Some of these were first published with various issues of the journal. The first and second unnumbered pages would have accompanied the twelfth issue c.1835.

[2]   One further and final number, the thirteenth, was subsequently published. It was the first number of what would have been the third volume.

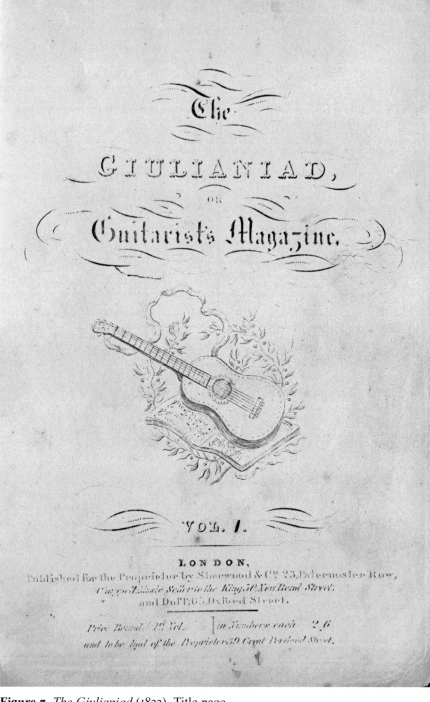

Figure 7. *The Giulianiad* (1833), Title page.

and easy accompaniments for the Guitar, together with a proportionate selection of subjects as Instrumental Pieces, by the most celebrated masters, with compositions and arrangements by the Editor of the Work.

THE GIULIANIAD is published at 2s. 6d. each Number.

[Second unnumbered page]

CONTENTS OF VOL. II. OF THE GIULIANIAD.[3]

No. VII.

Song – "My home in the Forest!"	*German.*
Air – La Sentinelle, with Variations for the Guitar	*Giuliani.*
Song – "Strew with me those tribute roses"	*German.*
Song – "If you are cashless"	*Weber.*
Song – The Linden Tree	*German.*
Song – May Morn	*Mozart.*
Song – "Time is spending"	*J. C. T. Muncki.*
Minuetto, with Variations for the Guitar	*W. Matiegka.*

No. VIII.

Galopade	
Con quell occhietto	*Blangini.*
Song – Sereny	*Spanish.*
Waltz	*Spanish.*
Song – Hope told a flattering tale	*Italian.*
Al tempo felice	*Italian.*
Du! Du!	*German.*
Andante, with Variations	*F. Calegari.*
Song – "Let my lot rest unknown"	*German.*
Air – The Swiss Boy	*Swiss.*
Air – Non Piu Mesta	*Italian.*

No. IX.

Song – Memory	*French.*
Duett – "Dost thou remember him?"	*German.*
Song – "Al tempo felice"	*Italian.*

---

3   The third volume is not included here. The music from number thirteen, the only known issue from that volume, contains: Song – "Why Should I Seek Another Land", words W. Ball; The Favorite Reichstadt Waltz; Marcia; Galoppade; German Air; Song – "Oh! Lady; ask me not, I Pray", Lanza; Song – "Le Retour de Pierre"; Song – "My Sister Jane!" by J. Valentine; Song – "The Ruined Home", words by W. Ball; Rondo by Giuliani.

Duett – "Midnight is here"	*French.*
The Song of Joseph	*Mehul.*
German Air, with Variations for the Guitar	*F. Pelzer.*

No. X.

Song – The Absent One	*German.*
Song – Faintly as dies the Vesper sound	*Italian.*
Song – The Water Party	*Hurka.*
Duett – Les Adieu à la Suisse	*Bruguiere.*
Duett – with Variations for the Guitar	*F. Horetzky.*
Rondino for the Guitar	*M. Giuliani.*
Air, with Variations for Guitar	*F. Carulli.*
Song – The Castle	*Pacini.*
Theme and Variations	*F. Carulli.*

No. XI.

Serenade – "Sweet, Good Night!"	*German.*
Arietta – "Oh! cease, love, to grieve thee"	*German.*
Song – The Minstrel's Home	*Styrian.*
Extract from	*Legnani.*
Song – "Ich sap und spaun"	*German.*
Song – "Ye happy ones!"	* * * *
Song – "Minnesold"	*German.*
Solfegge for the Voice and Guitar	

No. XII.

Song – "Softly fall the dews of night"	*Swiss.*
Extract from Op. 16.	*Horetzski.*
Song – "The Soldier's Flask"	*German.*
Song – "Yes, there are meadows"	*Parry.*
Song – "The Deceived"	*German.*
Song – "Angel of Peace"	*Hungarian.*
Song – "O listen, listen, Lovers"	*French.*
Air	*Venetian.*

[Third unnumbered page][4]

The 1st. Volume of **THE GIULIANIAD** is just Completed

Containing 6 Nos. The following are the Contents.

CONTENTS OF NO. 1.

Musical Literature.

Introduction.
On the capabilities of the Guitar.
Stanzas to my Guitar by E. M.
Giuliani – His performance & compositions.
On the comparative Merits of the Piano Forte
and Guitar as an Accompaniment to the Voice.
Review of Music. Chit Chat &c.

Music.

1st Four Pages (Popular Music) Six popular Airs (Easy)
2nd Four Pages (Classical Music) four Pieces by Giuliani.
3rd Four pages (Vocal Music) Song "Fair Evening Star," by Miss E.
    Mounsey.

CONTENTS OF NO. 2.

Musical Literature.

"I do not like the Guitar!" being an examination of the objections
raised against that instrument.
Guitar Song by Mrs. L. Miles.
Westminster Review and Guitar:
The Farewell Gift by W. Ball.
Reviews, Chit chat &c &c.

Music.

Four Pages of Popular Airs, Music by Sor.
Song with French Words.
Song by Weber, with English and
German Words.
Waltz, by Sor.

---

[4]   The third unnumbered page would have been first published with the sixth issue
        of the journal (October 1833). It is present in the copy of that individual issue held
        in the Appleby Collection. In addition, this individual issue also contains copies of
        the fourth and fifth unnumbered pages that follow here. However, as the Appleby
        copy is a later reissue from the 1840s these contents may not have been present
        in the first issue of 1833.

CONTENTS OF NO. 3.

Musical Literature.
Horace's Cithara or Guitar.
Sing to thy Sweet Guitar.
The Fancy Ball, a fragment.
Extracts from Gardiner's Music of Nature.
Foreign News, Chit Chat &c.
Sor, His compositions & performance.
Music.
Four Pages of Popular Airs.
German Song (German and English words.)
Theme Varied by Giuliani.
Theme by Sor.
Song, "The Captive to his Guitar."
Italian Song, "La Smorfia."
German Song, "Der Frühlings. abend."

CONTENTS OF NO. 4.

Musical Literature
Observations on Music in preceding numbers.
On Public performances on the Guitar.
The Minstrel's Lay.
Review of Music.
Musical Intelligence.
Music.
Andantino & Larghetto by Sor.
Swiss Waltz, Galopade, & German Air.
Waltz, & Monferrino by Giuliani.
God Save the King & Variations.
Song "I hail thee in thy beauty."
Minuet & Alpine Sanger.
Allemand & Waltz.
2 French Songs.
English Song, "My heart is with thee."

CONTENTS OF NO. 5.

Musical Literature
The Cithara of the Ancients, the Modern Guitar.
Guitar Professors, Guitar Makers & Sellers.
Notices of Concerts. Miss Mounsey's, Messrs.
Dressler & Pelzer's, Miss Bruce's, Mr. Schultz's,
Mr. Sagrini's, Miss Fanny Woodham's, and
Miss F. Healey's.
Music.
Song. "El inocente Pastor", De Busto.
Grand Variations on the French Air

"Portant pour la Syrie." by Giuliani.
Theme by Mozart, varied by Nüske
Gebet während der Schlacht
Prayer during battle by Himmel.
German song.

CONTENTS OF NO. 6.

Musical Literature.
Instructions to My Daughter for playing on the
Enharmonic Guitar.
Pelzer's Instructions.
Foreign Guitar Makers & English
Music Sellers.
Reviews. Chit Chat &c.
Music.
Fantasia. by M. Giuliani.
Divertimento. by M. Nüske.
Canzonet, by Donald Walker.
Spring Song of the Poles in 1831.
Song. "The Wish," by W. Newland.
Song. "The Warrior to his Son."
Song. "The Hermit's Evening Song."

[Fourth unnumbered page]

TO THE
ADMIRERS OF CLASSICAL GUITAR MUSIC.

GIULIANI'S THIRD CONCERTO,
TO BE PUBLISHED BY SUBSCRIPTION.

MESSRS. JOHANNING & CO. respectfully beg to acquaint Amateurs of the Guitar, that at the solicitation of many eminent Professors of that Instrument (all of whom have become Subscribers), they have been induced to publish

GIULIANI'S GRAND THIRD CONCERTO.

This piece is acknowledged by every class of Musicians to be the masterpieces of that great genius; and the publishers flatter themselves that its publication in England will be hailed with enthusiasm by all the real admirers of this magnificent little instrument.[5]

---

5   The concerto probably originally dates from 1816. Brian Jeffery, 'Introduction', in
      Mauro Giuliani, *Concerto for Guitar and Orchestra, Opus 70*, xxx: *The Complete*

The price of the CONCERTO (with Piano-forte Accompaniment,) will be 10s. 6d. It will be ready for sale on the 1st of November, and Subscribers' Names will be attached to it.

It is not necessary, perhaps, to state the high opinion which the Musical world has attached to this composition; but to those who are quite unacquainted with its merit, it should be mentioned that the celebrated HUMMEL wrote full Orchestral Accompaniments for it; an honour which he has not conferred on any similar production.[6] CZERNY has also adapted it, as a Piano-forte Concerto, on which instrument it is likewise held in such high estimation that MADAME DULCKEN has performed it with great applause in public.[7]

That such a production therefore – with such manifold attestations of its genius – should remain without a Publisher in England, would argue that good players on the instrument were very limited. It is therefore now proposed to engrave it in the best style; and the publishers rely with confidence that such a work will not remain unpatronised by Amateurs.

6, JOHN STREET, OXFORD STREET.

[Fifth unnumbered page]

OPINIONS OF THE PRESS ON "THE GIULIANIAD."

———

From "THE WESTMINSTER REVIEW" *for April,* 1833, *No.* 36.

ARTICLE, MUSICAL PERIODICALS. – HARMONICON – GIULIANIAD.

"If the Harmonicon is a chief of a staff, the other is the leader of a small *manipulus* or company, which he is anxious to make the most effective

---

Works in Facsimiles of the Original Editions, ed. Brian Jeffery (Vienna, [1822]; facs. edn, with introduction by Brian Jeffery, London, 1987). The edition advertised here was published in London c.1833 and is included in a later list of guitar music in *The Giulianiad*. 'Foreign Guitar Makers and English Music Sellers', *TG* 1:6 (1833), 56–57, at 57. A solo from the concerto is included in the music section of the first issue of *The Giulianiad. TG* 1:1 (1833), Music 5. See Appendix 1.

[6]   It is not completely certain if the pianist Hummel was responsible for the orchestration of the concerto. Marco Riboni, 'Il Concerto op. 70 di Giuliani e il Concerto op. 28 di Czerny', *Il Fronimo* 187 (2019), 24–37. Letters by Erik Stenstadvold, Gerhard Penn, and Marco Riboni in 'Idee a confronto', *Il Fronimo* 188 (2019), 50–53. Johann Nepomuk Hummel (1778–1837) was a Hungarian pianist and composer. James Brown, *Biographical Dictionary of Musicians* (London, 1886), 337.

[7]   Carl Czerny, *Piano Concerto, Op. 28* (Vienna, [1822]). Czerny (1791–1857) was an Austrian composer and pianist. Louise Dulcken (1811–50) was a German pianist who settled in London. Brown, *Dictionary*, 195, 220.

its magnitude will admit of. And he manifestly has the root of the matter in him. The guitar is an instrument even now not comprehended in this country. People cannot find out that it is an orchestra in little, a miniature painting of *le donne, i cavalier, l'arme, e gli amori.*[8] Its forte is the picturesque; meaning thereby the presenting of pictures – *des tableaux.* It wants force, as a miniature wants acres of canvass, but is not less a painting for that. A young lady with her guitar is neither Mr. Harpur with his trumpet, nor the Petrides with their horns; but it does not therefore follow she is nothing.[9] She may be compared to an artist, who, for some reason, has no great depth of shadow at command; the keeping may be more difficult, but it is not impossible. The great countervailing power is in the intimate connexion between the performer and the instrument, giving a command over the strength and quality of tone, which can scarcely be equalled but on the violin, and then there must be at least a trinity of performers to approach to the same effects. The authors of 'The Giulianiad' have proved that they understand the thing. They are the first, or nearly so, that have shown they comprehend the bounty of Providence in the guitar. On many points they go so close to what has been impressed in the present utilitarian organ, that it may not be misplaced to state, there is no community of source. They are altogether a second voice in the desert, returning a responsive halloo to the other.

"The music, in their two first Numbers, throws more light on what the guitar is meant for, than could be got by the pillage of a music-shop."[10]

———

From "THE SUN," *Feb.* 11, 1833.

"The Giulianiad contains, in addition to some very sweet music for the guitar, many able essays, especially that on the capabilities of this delightful instrument."[11]

---

8   Women, cavaliers, weapons, and loves.

9   Thomas Harper (1787–1853) was a prominent trumpet player. Brown, *Dictionary*, 303. The Petrides brothers were French horn players from Prague who settled in London in 1802. John Sainsbury, *A Dictionary of Musicians*, 2nd edn, 2 vols (London, 1827), ii, 283–85.

10   [T. P. Thompson], 'Musical Periodicals: Harmonicon-Giulianiad', *Westminster Review* 18 (1833), 471–74. T. Perronet Thompson (1783–1869), who had a military and political career, had a great interest in the science of musical instruments. For a biography see L. G. Johnson, *General T. Perronet Thompson* (London, 1957). He was one of the editors and co-owner of the *Westminster Review* from 1829 until 1836. This glowing review of *The Giulianiad* in the *Westminster Review* was followed by a favourable review of Thompson's *Instructions* in *The Giulianiad*. 'Instructions to my Daughter for playing on the Enharmonic Guitar, by a Member of the University of Cambridge', *TG* 1:6 (1833), 51–53. The latter review may not have been unbiased and was perhaps published in some gratitude.

11   'Literature', *The Sun*, 11 February 1833. The review says: 'This "Guileaniad" [*sic*] contains, in addition to some very sweet music, some clever written "Stanzas to

―――――

From "THE DUBLIN EXPRESS," *Jan.* 1833.

"We have long been accustomed to see music pursuing her way in scientific loneliness, wooed only by her own disciples – those favourite few who have had the happiness of being ranked amongst the initiated. Times are now changed. Music, like her sister arts, goes hand in hand with literature; and the reproach, that 'musicians were ignorant of everything but music,' will no longer be cast upon the professors of this delightful science. We have been led into these remarks by the examination of the first Number of a new Guitarists' Magazine, to which the appropriate title of "THE GIULIANIAD" has been given, as it professedly takes for its 'patron saint' that prince of guitar players and composers, 'Giuliani,' of whom a brief but interesting memoir will be found in the pages of the present Number. The music is divided under three heads – Popular – Classical – and original Vocal Music – together with some pretty 'Stanzas to My Guitar,' and a cleverly-written article on the capabilities of the instrument. There are also candid Reviews of Music, Musical Chit Chat, &c. &c.; altogether forming a cheap, elegant, and desirable acquisition to the portfolio of every lover of that justly admired instrument.[12]

―――――

From "THE LITERARY GAZETTE," *January,* 1833.

"Some very pretty guitar music, with able, instructive, and pleasant information for the guitarist."[13]

---

my Guitar," together with an able essay on the capabilities of that delightful little instrument. Among musical men, the work, we think, is likely to be popular. At any rate it deserves to be so.'

[12] 'Music', *The Express*, 31 December 1832. The newspaper review, which uses the incorrect spelling '*Guilianiad*' throughout, adds: 'The publishers announce in their preface that the objects of "*The Guilianiad*" are to bring the compositions of Guiliani [*sic*], Carulli, Lor [*sic*], and other distinguished Masters, more under the notice of the amateur and professor of the Guitar; to discuss the relative merits of their writings, to instil in beginners, and to keep alive in proficients, an interest in this romantic instrument; and, finally, to provide food for a little chit–chat amongst its professors and admirers of every class.' Ferdinand Carulli (1770–1841) was an Italian who was best remembered for his many didactic works for the guitar. 'Lor' was a misspelling of 'Sor'.

[13] 'Varieties', *Literary Gazette* 833 (1833), 13. The review says: 'we have No. 1 of the *Giulianiad* [...] with some very pretty guitar music, and pleasant musical infor-mation'. The musical information then listed is all taken from the 'chit-chat' in *The Giulianiad* on page twelve. Reviews in the weekly *Gazette*, founded in 1817, were highly regarded and for novels a good one could ensure good sales. There was some lessening of its success in the early 1830s. Robert Duncan, 'Literary Gazette', in *British Literary Magazines: The Romantic Age 1789–1836*, ed. Alvin Sullivan (Westport, 1983), 242–46. The *Literary Gazette* and the *Westminster Review* were

[p. 1 – Issue 1, January 1833]

INTRODUCTION.

———

OF all kinds of music the Guitar is the instrument of romance and sentiment; its name is handed down to us associated with deeds of chivalry and love, and awakening in the memory a thousand traditions of its enchanting power. From the time of its first rude construction, composed of the shell of the tortoise,* to its present modern shape, – from the period that Apollo first drew forth its notes, to the time that a Giuliani touched with masterly perfection its strings, – the guitar has, in varied forms, in most civilized countries been studied with delight, and heard with approbation and rapture.

The Egyptians, with the guitar, as with all kinds of musical instruments, were skilful adepts: and scarcely can we read a tale of the Moors, their history, or that of Spain since their introduction into that country; whether we read the renowned Don Quixote, or its rival in fame Gil Blas, we find the guitar is brought forth to aid and heighten the charm of romantic truth or fiction.[14]

Perhaps in no other civilized country has the instrument been so superficially studied, till of late years, as in England. In Spain, France, and Germany, and indeed in most countries on the Continent, it has been appreciated, and has attained a high degree of celebrity. Giuliani's performance on the guitar in Vienna, in the very seat and centre of musical learning, was the wonder and delight of the most distinguished dilettante. The announcement

*A well known historical fact. A brief history of the guitar will be given in the forthcoming pages of this work.[15]

[p. 2]

of his performance at a concert was the sure source of a numerous audience. In short, Giuliani was the Paganini on his instrument.[16] We bring this forward merely as a proof that the most ambitious musician

both foremost journals and the good reviews in them show how well regarded *The Giulianiad* was at first.

[14] These two fictional travellers in Spain encounter the guitar played by ordinary Spanish people. Miguel de Cervantes, *El ingenioso hidalgo don Quixote de la Mancha* (Madrid, 1604–05, 1616). Alain-René Lesage, *L'Histoire de Gil Blas de Santillane* (Paris, 1715–35). Popular English translations quickly followed these publications.

[15] This proposed article was not later published.

[16] Nicolò Paganini (1782–1840), best known as a violin player, was also a virtuoso on the guitar. Frederic Grunfeld, *The Art and Times of the Guitar* (New York, 1969), 200. He very rarely played the latter in public.

may study it to advantage, and that, as an instrument, it possesses good and substantial qualities for the approbation of the most fastidious.

The successful introduction of the guitar into England has been comparatively of recent date. Till the peace of 1815, it may be assumed that few persons in this country were acquainted with its full and varied powers. From that time, however, to the present moment, no instrument can be brought in comparison with its rapid advancement in public estimation. No instrument in fifteen years has attained such decided success and extensive circulation. This may in a very great degree be ascribed to the many excellent masters with which the Continent has furnished us: to them must we concede the merit of having given the guitar a character which antecedently was unknown in England, and of having brought it to its present high state of fashionable popularity. But although these masters have effected much, a great deal more remains to be done. Giuliani, Carulli, Sor, and other distinguished masters are yet, at best, but imperfectly understood.

To bring their compositions more under the notice of the amateur and English professor, – to discuss the relative merits of their writings, – to instil in those who are about commencing, and keep alive in those who are already advanced, an interest in their instrument, – and finally to provide food for a little chit-chat amongst the best professors themselves, – these are briefly the objects of THE GIULIANIAD, a name, by the bye, which we hope our readers will have no objection to see thus apotheosized. Whether our efforts will be crowned with success remains to be seen: all that we can promise is, to use our best exertions to deserve it. In the mean time, as the guitar is here still in its infancy, we naturally call upon its professors and admirers to aid our labors for the advancement of this particular instrument.

[p. 3]

ON THE CAPABILITIES OF THE GUITAR.

————

THE powers of the guitar are much more extensive, far more varied, and its execution infinitely more perfect, than the English amateur has hitherto given it credit for. We propose, in the following brief attempt in a summary of its merits, to view it in the three following lights:-

1st, As an instrument of harmony;

2d, As an instrument of melody; and

3d, As an instrument of execution, in which is combined its power of developing its resources in both harmony and melody.

The strongest position which an advocate for the guitar will insist upon, and on which he will never fail of convincing, is most undoubtedly that on the point of harmony. In this respect, in its facilities of developing the most intricate combinations of harmony, it excels all other instruments, the piano-forte alone excepted; for, the harp, although admirable to a certain extent in harmony, yet as its difficulties in expressing it increase, in proportion to the accidental half tones introduced, (these being on that instrument produced by the foot), it cannot, as to facility, for a moment, be compared to the guitar. We are not about to broach an apparent paradox in asserting that the guitar rivals, in the wide ocean of harmony, the piano-forte; but we confidently affirm that within the three octaves and a half, to which the guitar may be strictly said to be limited, its powers are as equally varied, as equally perfect, and as equally inexhaustible, as the piano-forte itself. Let us see whether in his point of view we are borne out by facts; for we would not bring a weak argument to sustain our views, or one that will not bear the test of the most severe examination.

And here we will bring no less a testimony than M. Czerny, the celebrated piano-forte player, who, in his great admiration of one of Giuliani's concertos (the third), has actually written the whole piece for the piano-forte. An extract from this concerto will be seen at page 5 of our music; and if this, or the remainder of the concerto be referred to, it will be found, that not only has M. Czerny, in his arrangement for the piano-forte, preserved the melody as Giuliani wrote it, but he has throughout used the same identical harmony, (making, of course, allowance for the superior compass of the instrument); thus

[p. 4]

showing, most confessedly, that the guitar was capable of producing the same harmony and melody in conjunction, as the piano-forte itself.[17] Were other instances wanted, we could cite Sor, who has given many examples of its capabilities in this respect.

We hope, then, to have proved that within the three octaves and a half, that is, from E below the line to A in alt,[18] that the guitar has equal resources in harmony to the piano-forte itself. But our little instrument has this great advantage over the cumbersome and unwieldy, though admirable piano-forte, viz, that of its extreme portability. How easily is it conveyed from one place to another! What a small addition does it make to the musician's travelling equipage! Even from the lap of beauty in her carriage may its softly swelling tones be drawn forth, to dissipate the ennui of travel! No advantages of this nature attend the

---

[17]   By the 1830s most piano makers were producing instruments with a six and a half octave compass. David Rowland, 'The Piano Since c.1825', in *The Cambridge Companion to the Piano*, ed. David Rowland (Cambridge, 1998), 40–56, at 46. However, older shorter pianos would still have been in use.

[18]   The guitar usually has a range of three and a half octaves from the open E on the sixth string to A on the seventeenth fret of the first string.

piano-forte. Here, it is true, we find a combination of excellencies; but where we find it, there must it remain until we return to it: no carriage companion, – no musician's solace in his pilgrimage, – no portability. It is for this great convenience – and we are not overrating this quality, for it is of essential importance – that our greatest musicians were always fond of this instrument. Bach, Mozart, Haydn, even the mighty Beethoven himself, played the guitar; not perhaps alone for effect, but because it was an instrument of easy conveyance, and because it was capable of expressing every variety of harmony.[19] Paganini is also a modern instance of a great musician being a guitar player. The violin, splendid and perfect as it is in sustained or rapid melody, is deficient in its power of expressing harmony. When Paganini was asked why he played the guitar, when he was so miraculous in his performance on the violin? "I love it," says he, "for its harmony; it is my constant companion in all my travels."[20]

It is as an instrument of harmony, then, that the chief beauty of the guitar exists.

To come to our second point, "as an instrument of melody" it is surpassed by all sustained instruments, by which we mean, all wind instruments, and all the class of violin, violoncello, &c. – but in comparison to the piano-forte or harp in this respect, the advantage must, most assuredly, be given to the guitar. Those who have ever heard Giuliani touch this instrument will not hesitate one moment in confirming this. That unrivalled performer brought tones as pure, as thrilling, and almost as sustained as the violin itself – but, of course, we do not insist, that because this wonderful man produced these sostenuto sounds, that it is a characteristic of the instrument itself – this only proves the triumph of true genius over a great difficulty. There are, how-

[p. 5]

ever, masters enough in this great metropolis, who, having had the good fortune to study under Giuliani, or had the advantage of hearing him, will easily convince the hearer, that, as a sostenuto instrument, the guitar surpasses both the harp and piano-forte – and those who are sceptical on this point, have only to hear the perfection of its glide, – so perfect as even to rival the violin – to become fully convinced of its superiority.

---

[19]   No evidence has been found to suggest that Bach, Mozart, Haydn, or Beethoven played the guitar.

[20]   It is not known where this quotation is from. Paganini's enthusiasm for the guitar may not have been as great as is suggested here. In 1829 he was quoted as saying: 'I do not like the guitar, but consider it a sort of guide to thoughts.' 'Biography, Paganini', *Literary Gazette* 653 (1829), 491–92, at 492.

To come to our third position, "that of its powers of execution," we will candidly confess, that in this respect we are not such enthusiastic advocates as many of its professors; not that we are insensible to its manifold beauties when in the hands of a skilful performer – but because we see in the instrument greater perfection in the higher qualities of tone, harmony, and expression. Did the guitar but possess these rare qualities, apart from the doubtful excellence of execution – it would be an instrument worthy of the regard of the true musician and every "lover of the concord of sweet sounds."[21] But although we are not enthusiastic enough to view it as an instrument perfect in its powers of execution – that is, in the velocity by which it can express certain passages – yet we confess it has powers sufficient to execute well any passage short of legerdemain: and from conjurers and mountebanks on the instrument, we eschew their influence even from this, our first commencement. The real guitar player will adhere to the music of Giuliani, Sor, and Carulli, and to some of our modern composers, who sufficiently value these great masters by making them their models; of these we shall often have occasion to speak, in the review department of our Magazine.

We could mention many minor details, but we leave that to a future opportunity – yet there remains one other beauty of the guitar, which we have reserved for our concluding observations on this head, because it is one in which our fair readers will, and ought pertinaciously to insist – we mean the delightful accompaniment of the guitar to the voice. In the performance of what other instrument can we so well blend the poetry, the romance of the subject? What instrument so completely drown in oblivion the cares of this "earth's weary pilgrimage," and live for a time as it were, in a world of our own imagination, as when the voice dwells and lingers in "fondest sympathy" with the elastic touch of our sweet instrument? So harmoniously – so twin-like are the song and instrument attuned to each other, that our own divine bard must surely have had these alone in view, when he sung,

"If music and sweet poetry agree,
As needs they must, the sister and the brother,
Then must the love be great 'twixt thee and me,
For thou lov'st one, and I the other." – *Shakspeare's Sonnet.*[22]

---

[21] 'Concord of sweet sounds', William Shakespeare, *The Merchant of Venice*, v. 1. 92.

[22] This poem, by Richard Barnfield, was wrongly ascribed to Shakespeare. Sidney Lee, 'Introduction', in William Shakespeare, *The Passionate Pilgrim* (London, 1599; repr. with introduction by Sidney Lee, Oxford, 1905), 29.

[p. 6]

STANZAS "TO MY GUITAR."

BY A LADY.

————

COMPANION of the exiled brave!
Beloved, alike in peace or war,
The peasant wakes thee, and the slave,
Weeps fondly o'er his mute Guitar.

Solace of Scotia's beautious Queen
In captive hours – when Chatelar
Divinely touch'd thy chords between
Despair and hope, – my lov'd Guitar![23]

Dream of the long-forgotten dead!
Whose tones remind of scenes afar –
The scattered leaves of roses fled
Thy numbers breathe, my lone Guitar!

When o'er the festive song I wake,
Forgetting that e'en mirth may mar
Its own enjoyment – should I break
One feeling string, my own Guitar –

I'll take the moral to my breast,
Nor ever strain a *chord* so far
As wound a heart, which rudely prest
Would break, like thine, my sweet Guitar.

E. M.[24]

[p. 7]

GIULIANI.

————

IT may be expected, that having done honor, so far as in us lay, to the name of Giuliani, by having made it the title of our monthly work, that we should attempt to give some general idea to the reader of his own inimitable performance on the guitar. The tone of Giuliani was brought to

---

[23] Engravings of *Chatelar playing the lute to Mary Queen of Scots* by the French artist Fradelle were made in this period. In the picture the poet, Chatelard, is depicted playing a lute to the queen.

[24] It is not known who the author was. Variations of the poem were subsequently published, one of which was attributed to a certain Mrs Miles. Mrs L. Miles. 'The Guitar', *Monthly Magazine* 24:142 (1837), 357.

the greatest possible perfection; in his hands the guitar became gifted with a power of expression at once pure, thrilling, and exquisite. He vocalized his adagios to a degree impossible to be imagined by those who never heard him – his melody in slow movements was no longer like the short unavoidable staccato of the piano-forte – requiring a profusion of harmony to cover the deficient sustension of the notes – but it was invested with a character, not only sustained and penetrating, yet of so earnest and pathetic a description, as to make it appear in reality the natural characteristic of the instrument. *In a word, he made the instrument sing.* It may be easily supposed that with this singular faculty of giving expression to melody, Giuliani, gave to the guitar a character, which, it was thought before was totally alien to its nature. It is necessary that we should dwell on this characteristic, or style of Giuliani's tone, and that the reader should remember it, because it is one which belongs exclusively to his school, and which, as we are persuaded, it is the most effective and best, we shall take every means of enforcing in our future numbers.

We need not tell the experienced reader, that, it is by the elastic touch of the fingers of the right hand (properly supported, of course, by the pressure of the left), that this, the *ne plus ultra* of tone in guitar playing, is to be attained. Without great attention to the disposition of the right hand, the slightest approach to this beauty cannot be effected. But in another number of this work we shall more minutely discuss its acquirements, although all attempts at description must fall infinitely short of the practical example and instructions of a good master.[25]

But Giuliani's tone however perfect in itself was secondary, as it ought to be, to the grand quality of expression. Tone is only the means to an end – that end being expression; without expression, tone is like the rough diamond in the mine – intrinsically valuable it is true – but as yet unpolished – uncut into brilliance and beauty. Tone, (so to speak), is the material whereof expression is composed – but expression is the "cunning workman," which gives it life and animation. The *Venus de Medicis* was but a block of marble until the sculptor fashioned it into surpassing beauty.[26]

Expression, then, being the grand aim, not only of the guitar player, but of every musician – and not only of every musician, but alike of the poet,

[p. 8]

the painter, and the sculptor, Giuliani left for awhile the minor qualities of tone and execution, in the shade, and guided by his own good natural taste, assiduously analysed and cultivated expression in all its lights and shadows, in all its depth and variety.*

---

[25] This proposed article was not later published.
[26] The 'Medici Venus' marble statue is housed in the Uffizi Gallery, Florence.

Proceeding on this, the only true principle of music – and having, as we have seen, brought his tone to a high degree of perfection, it is no longer a matter of surprise, that he surpassed in his performance every other player on the instrument. His execution, (although he made it entirely subservient to tone and expression), was not the less wonderful, taking into consideration the nature of the instrument. It was clear, dexterous, animated, and impressive – and being, like a beautiful racer, under the curb and control of a consummate master, it never ran riot out of its destined course.

We should say to the guitar player, then, imitate Giuliani – sacrifice execution to tone, and tone to expression. We shall close our remarks on this subject with an observation of Mr. Horetzky, on the style of this master; as far as it goes, it confirms our own views on the subject.

"Among the professors of the Spanish guitar, it is well known that the justly celebrated Mauro Giuliani, is not only the first and most distinguished performer thereon, *but he must be considered as the inventor of a new method of playing,* by which he has demonstrated the abundance of harmony, and the beauty and power of which this agreeable instrument is capable."

This well-deserved compliment of M. Horetzky is appended to some of his own ingenious studies published in London,† and as he, in his own performance, approaches very near perfection, his authority must be allowed to possess much weight.

About twelve months ago, Giuliani paid the debt of nature. In him the little world of guitar players have lost their idol: but the compositions he has left behind him are a rich legacy, to which the present and future generations will, we have no doubt, pay every homage of respect and admiration.

*Those guitar players (and there are not a few of them) who fancy that execution is the first of all qualities to be attained, – assuming that tone, and even expression, must give way to its influence, – should be reminded, that Pasta's superiority over every other vocalist must be attributed to her expression alone.[27] In tone and execution she is surpassed by many. Look again to Kean, whose many absurdities would never have been brooked, were not his readings given with, and his countenance susceptible of, the most exquisite expression.[28] Whatever the passion he has to depict – whether of love or jealousy, madness or revenge, his expression bears him throughout triumphantly successful,

[27]   The Italian soprano, Madame Pasta (1797–1865), was established as one of the greatest singers in Europe in the 1820s. Kenneth Stern, 'Pasta [née Negri], Giuditta', *GMO*.

[28]   Edmund Kean (1787–1833) was an actor famed for his Shakespearian performances. Peter Thomson, 'Kean, Edmund', *ODNB*.

in despite of a voice, which every one must admit might have been more musical.

ϒBoosey and Co.[29]

[p. 9]

ON THE COMPARATIVE MERITS

OF THE

PIANO-FORTE AND GUITAR, AS AN ACCOMPANIMENT

TO THE VOICE.

———

WHAT the piano-forte is to an entire orchestra, the guitar is to a quartett of instruments; what the former possesses in power, the latter has in sweetness; the force of the one is counterbalanced by the variety of the other. If that instrument which can be the representative of the greatest number of sounds is to be considered the best, the piano-forte has then the deciding advantage over every other. But, for the reasons we shall now state to our readers, there are many points in which the preference may be fairly given to an instrument of less compass, which, possessing within itself peculiar powers and advantages, retains many of the good qualities of the fine instrument we have mentioned. This is precisely the case with the guitar. Indeed, we will go farther, and say to the player of the one instrument, that he should cultivate the other. We are none of those who are exclusively prejudiced in favor of any one instrument, nor would we recommend our readers to be so; as it narrows the judgement, and cramps the means, which are easily available, of enlarging the field of the perceptive powers of their enjoyment. For these reasons we would recommend the pianists' attention to the guitar; for the nature of stringed instruments* is so little understood by them, and forming, as they do, the leading feature of all orchestral accompaniments, a knowledge of them would teach piano-forte players their specific properties, and enable them to appreciate their combination in relation to each other, as well as to the human voice.

But to come more immediately to the subject of our article. For our fair readers who, of course, are excluded from the performance and practice of the violin, there is no fitter instrument to attain the means we have above stated, than the study of the guitar. We have elsewhere shown how Paganini

---

[29] Felix Horetzky, *Instructive Exercises for the Guitar, Op. 15* (London, [1827]). For a review of this see 'Review of Music', *TG* I:1 (1833), 11.

*An Essay on the Rise and Progress of Stringed Instruments, but more particularly that of the Guitar, will be given in our next Number.[30]

[p. 10]

himself has appreciated this instrument, and could cite numerous other instances, were it necessary; but if the great violinist has availed himself of its powers, how much more advantageous will it prove to the piano-forte player and singer.

As an accompaniment to the voice, in contradistinction to the piano-forte, the guitar possesses many desirable qualifications. The piano-forte, however out of tune, and however discordant, from variations of temperature, or from any other cause, cannot, on the instant, be remedied, – a disadvantage which is likely to prove very detrimental to the ear of a tyro; whereas the guitar can be tuned, not alone to any instrument with which it is accompanied, but to the then state or compass of the voice of the singer; adapting itself admirably to those who possess weak voices (which we take to be the case in nine instances out of ten), and improve and practise the ear in the nicest shades of tone. The piano-forte, from its powers, is certainly calculated for exhibiting in the drawing-room the full and instrumental accompa-niments of modern composers and dramatic performances; but then it necessarily must overpower and drown the slender voices to which we have alluded, as the works of Rossini, Pacini, Bellini, and other noisy composers, will sufficiently testify.[31] But for the plaintive ballad, the heroic verse of romance, or for any simple melody pourtraying some of the finest feelings of poesy, the all-subduing tones of the guitar are unquestionably the fittest.

There is also another recommendation in favor of our instrument, which, with little practice, may readily be attained, namely, that of making extemporaneous accompaniments to songs written only for the piano. This opens a vast field for the player's ingenuity, and will exercise his genius for harmony and composition; and setting aside all other considerations, this alone will amply compensate him for the little pains necessary to be bestowed in learning this instrument. We feel no hesitation in saying, that the practice of these extemporaneous accompaniments will so fascinate and wed him to the guitar, that it will convert him to an enthusiastic admirer in its favor. We here stake our reputation of the fact, that no piano-forte player has ever studied the other instrument, but has been subjected to its powers of fascination.

---

[30]   This proposed article was not later published.

[31]   Pacini referred to here was almost certainly Giovanni Pacini (1796–1867), an Italian composer whose operas were much influenced by Rossini. Brown, *Dictionary*, 435.

Another important thing is, that it teaches the performer to play with feeling; which, in reference to the piano, it possesses in a superior degree. The keys of the latter are not susceptible of so nice a degree of passion as the strings of the former: the pressure of the left hand, and the motion of the right, whether struck at the bridge, or midway between the bridge and the twelfth fret, can produce such a variety of tone, and such amplifications of expression, as the piano-forte certainly cannot reach.

[p. 11]

To all this may be added, its lightness, which enables it to be a constant companion and attendant, whether at home or abroad. Its conveyance is not of so much difficulty as the piano, whose unwieldiness may prove rather a cumbersome escort in a short journey to the country. In conclusion, there is something so social, so friendly, in the instrument we are recommending, it can be taken up or laid aside with so much ease, – and with its means, in a circle of your friends, whether in town or country, you have the power of dispensing (without noise or bustle) such quiet and full enjoyment, as taken altogether, belongs to no other instrument whatever. Thus we see it improves the ear, exercises the mind with regard to composition, inculcates feeling, extends the knowledge of stringed instruments, improves the taste, and is alike adapted to the strength of an infant, or the powerful hand of man. It is equally agreeable in the hands of either sex; there is nothing exclusive in the use of it, being fitted for all. It lends a charm to the graceful appearance of the one sex, and realises the romantic ideas of the other.

REVIEW OF MUSIC.

Instructive Exercises for the Guitar; containing Twenty-four Progressive Lessons. In two books. Composed by F. HORETZKY. *Op.* 15. Boosey and Co.

IN noticing these *Exercises*, written by a pupil of Giuliani – in which he has caught the true spirit of that master – we do so under the full persuasion that they are well adapted for the improvement of the scholar, both as regards the fingering and the "touch." The intention of each *Exercise* is explained in the introductory remarks of the first twelve, to which we recommend the pupil strictly to adhere. Although the leading features of Mr. Horetzky's compositions are easily traceable to the school which he has evidently made his model, he has, with much taste, seized those ideas which were not his own, and in a pleasing form collated them for the progress of his pupils. His harmonies, however, are pleasing and effective. The melodies of Nos. 12 and 18 are original and extremely good; and the whole of them, without exception, are calculated to ensure a knowledge of the various positions, firmness of finger, and strength of tone.

[p. 12]

Musical Intelligence, Chit-Chat, &c.

THE Contessa Rossi, (late Madlle. Sontag), has formally and unequivocally contradicted the statement which appeared in many of the Foreign and British Journals, relative to her return to the lyric stage. She utterly disclaims any such intention.[32]

MR. MOSCHELLES, – This celebrated Pianist has just arrived in London, having completed a musical tour on the Continent. On the 17th of October, he gave his first Concert at the Opera House in Berlin, where he performed his last Concerto before a splendid audience with complete success. His other performances were his "Recollections of Denmark," and an extemporaneous Fantasia. On the 22nd of the same month, his second Concert took place at the great room in Leipsic: the Band, congregated and led by Mathei, is one of the finest in Germany. On the 25th, Mr. Moschelles performed at the Court of Saxe Weimar; Hummel conducted, and all the most distinguished Nobility were present. The success of the Artist was of the most gratifying description. The Grand Duchess made him a present of a splendid diamond ring, and the Grand Duke of a gold snuff box. On the 7th of November, he gave his fourth Concert at the Theatre at Franckfort; and his last took place at Cologne, on the 13th of November which met with the greatest success. He was to have proceeded to the Hague, but the warlike aspect of affairs in that quarter, hastened his arrival in London. Had he proceeded to Antwerp he might have given us a musical bombardment![33]

PHILHARMONIC SOCIETY. – This Society has engaged the Hanover Square Rooms for the next season.[34] The rooms are now

---

32 This is taken from: 'Diary of a Dilettante', *The Harmonicon* 10:58 (1832), 232–35, at 234. Henriette Sontag (1806–54) was a successful German soprano who renounced the stage for a few years after her marriage. John Warrack, 'Sontag [Sonntag], Henriette', *GMO*.

33 This is taken from: 'Mr. Moscheles' Recent tour', *The Harmonicon* 10:60 (1832), 281. The article notes that Mathei 'ranks as one of the finest in Germany'. Ignaz Moscheles (1794–1870) was a Bohemian pianist and composer who was living in London at that time. Brown, *Dictionary*, 435. In November 1832, in the war of Belgian independence, a French army laid siege to Antwerp, held by the Dutch, in support of the Belgians.

34 The Hanover Square Rooms were on the east side of Hanover Square with an assembly room on the first floor that could seat 600 people. They played an

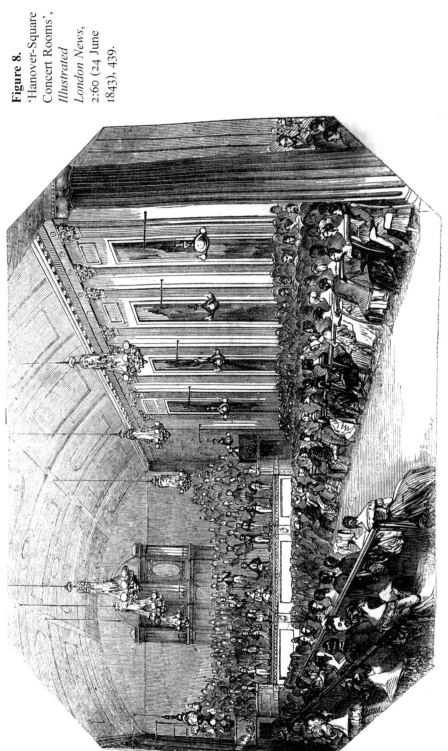

HANOVER-SQUARE CONCERT ROOMS.

Figure 8.
'Hanover-Square Concert Rooms', *Illustrated London News*, 2:60 (24 June 1843), 439.

undergoing extensive alterations; the orchestra is to be enlarged and brought lower in front, which it is thought will greatly facilitate and propel the sound into the body of the room. A large organ will also be added to the orchestra, the occasional use of which in the hands of a skilful performer, in grand orchestral pieces, will produce fine effects. A meeting was held on the 6th November, at which a resolution was passed to offer Messrs. Mendelsohn Bartholdy one hundred guineas for a new symphony, overture, and concerted vocal composition. We are happy to add, also, that our own countrymen are not quite neglected by the Society – on the 12th of the same month, they commissioned Mr. J. B. Cramer, and Mr. Cipriani Potter to write each an instrumental piece, and likewise Mr. Bishop, a concerted vocal piece, with full accompaniments. These compositions are to be finished in time to be performed in the ensuing season. This spirited conduct augurs well for the high reputation of the Society, and will unquestionably operate as a powerful stimulus to professors in this country.[35]

Madame Malibran (de Beriot's) engagement to sing at *La Scala* at Milan (the Grand theatre), is necessarily broken off, on account of her situation, which will confine her during great part of the season in which she had undertaken to perform. She has announced that she cannot appear in public, before the *primavera* (Spring).

Madame Pasta gave a grand Concert for the poor at Como, on the 20th of September; and intends, it is said, to retire to a beautiful villa she has been building on the banks of that lake.[36]

VIENNA, – At a concert recently given at this place for the benefit of the Institution for the Blind, the most remarkable features were, the *Battle of Vittoria*, and Mehul's overture *La Chasse*, with twenty-four French horns. There were sixteen piano-forte players, who performed

---

important part in London's musical life from 1775 until 1874; nearly all important vocalists and instrumentalists performed there. Robert Elkin, *The Old Concert Rooms of London* (London, 1955), 92–104. In December 1832 the orchestra area was enlarged. The building was demolished in the early twentieth century.

35   This is largely taken from: 'Diary of a Dilettante', *The Harmonicon* 10:60 (1832), 281–84, at 282, 283. The Philharmonic Society was founded by musicians in 1813; Cramer and Bishop were founding members and Potter was an associate. The works commissioned from Mendelssohn included his Italian symphony. Stanley Lucas, 'Philharmonic Society', in *A Dictionary of Music and Musicians*, ed. George Grove, 4 vols (London, 1879–89), ii (1880), 698–701. Johann Baptist Cramer (1771–1858) was a German pianist, composer, and publisher who founded the music publishing firm J. B. Cramer & Co. Cipriani Potter (1792–1871) was an English composer and pianist. Sir Henry Bishop (1786–1855) was an English composer. All three were leading composers in London at the time. Brown, *Dictionary*, 185, 481, 94–95.

36   References to Malibran and Pasta are taken from: 'Diary of a Dilettante', *The Harmonicon* 10:60 (1832), 281–84, at 283. Maria Malibran (1808–36) was a Spanish soprano who married her second husband, Charles de Bériot, in 1836. Brown, *Dictionary*, 411.

Carl Czerny's arrangements for eight and four piano-fortes, and at the end of the concert, by way of *bonne-bouche*, forty trumpeters played a stunning triumphal march! *The Harmonicon* asks whether the concert ought not to have been given for the benefit of the *deaf* instead of the *blind*?[37]

DRURY LANE THEATRE. – Captain Polhill is making the most amazing exertions – not, we hope, as the wag of the Globe says, to the road to ruin – but to secure a competent and admirable company of German performers. Already are not only Madame Shrœder Devrient, and M. Haitzinger engaged, but Madame Malibran performs at Drury Lane in May, at the enormous salary of £165. per night for twelve nights.[38]

[p. 13 – Issue 2, February 1833]

I DO NOT LIKE THE GUITAR!

Being an Examination of the Objections raised against that Instrument.

———

As we wish to meet fairly all objections that can be made against this instrument, and to dispassionately discuss its merits and demerits, *sui generis* (for where is the instrument that has not some defect), we will boldly meet them in fair argument; and, we trust, triumphantly put at rest all unjust prejudices.

To the prejudiced observation, "I do not like the guitar," we will consider, first, who are the persons that generally make it; secondly, what are their arguments against the instrument; and lastly, whether they, not playing it, are capable of judging.

Persons who generally object to the guitar are those who play on other, and fuller-toned, instruments, and who are accustomed to full orchestral accompaniments. These judge of the guitar by its power, compared with other instruments, and because, forsooth – it cannot drown a church-organ, a grand piano-forte, or double-actioned harp – straight condemn, and pronounce it to have no effect. Such persons are, perhaps, generally piano-forte players. Others there are who sit in judgement on every instrument by its effects taken singly, and its defects abstractedly. They have but

---

37   This is taken from: 'Foreign Musical Report, Vienna', *The Harmonicon* 10:60 (1832), 284–86, at 284.

38   Captain Polhill (1798–1848) was lessee of the theatre who used his personal resources to keep it afloat. 'The Theatre Royal: Management', in *Survey of London: Vol 35, the Theatre Royal, Drury Lane, and the Royal Opera House, Covent Garden*, ed. F. H. W. Sheppard (London, 1970), 9–29. *British History Online*, http://www.british-history.ac.uk/survey-london/vol35/pp9-29 [accessed 9 June 2022]. Devrient (1804–60) was a German soprano and Haizinger (1796–1869) was an Austrian tenor. John Warrack, 'Schröder-Devrient [née Schroder], Wilhelme', *GMO*. John Warrack, revised by Elizabeth Forbes, 'Haizinger [Haitzinger], Anton', *GMO*.

one universal standard by which they appreciate all of them, and that standard is, by concerto playing. The next and last class of persons who imbibe the strongest prejudices against the instrument, without the least consideration, are those who may be said to be bigots in everything; who will take up an opinion in an instant, and obstinately retain it for an age. Such persons (in their own opinion) can never be wrong: their dictum is so infallible, that the approach of the smallest difference to it hermetically seals their eyes and ears for ever, in mulish adherence to their hasty and first-pronounced judgment.

With some of them, we admit, it may be a matter of genuine feeling, but certainly not of judgment. These men have impulses, and nerves so finely strung – and so susceptible are they of the nicest variation of sound, that they would faint at a discord, and be pierced to death through the tympanum, by any accidental cause, whilst hearing any instrument for the first time.

The arguments which are brought by one and all of these personages are, that its powers are confined; that it is a tinkling, twanging toned instrument; that there is no effect in it; that it is difficult, and decidedly inferior to any other; and that its tones do not combine with those of any other instrument. With respect to the first objection of its confined powers, we admit the fact, but deny the inference. We would ask, whether a volume of tone, from a lesser instrument, is to be expected to preponderate over the greater – yet such is generally the test by which all instruments are judged, as the following anecdote will show:–

[p. 14]

"A manager of a provincial theatre was desirous of engaging an orchestra for the purpose of getting up an oratorio, and had made applications to various professors on different instruments for their services. The terms which they demanded being rather exorbitant, the manager objected to them; when the following arguments were urged by the different professors, as setting forth their various merits. Thus, the double bass, said, he could play his instrument as sweetly as the violin; the violin as loud as the bass; the flute could play as loud as a trumpet; the trumpet as soft as a flute; the clarionet as sweet as the oboe; the oboe as loud as the clarionet.[39] 'If these are your only merits, gentlemen,' said the manager, 'the best way will be, that you should play the instrument you strive to imitate itself, and that would save you a very great deal of trouble!'"

Just as well then may we expect a whole orchestra to play like the guitar, as a guitar like a whole orchestra. Loudness or smallness of

[39] Clarionet was the usual spelling for clarinet at this time.

tone has nothing to do with the merits of this instrument. We therefore dismiss this part of the objections as totally untenable.

With respect to the tinkling, twanging tone of the guitar: This, we are sorry to admit, is the weightiest objection of all that its enemies can bring against it, (though this we by no means admit to be valid); nor are we at all surprised that such impressions should be imbibed, when there are so many causes which contribute to show this apparent defect. At present we shall merely touch upon them; but in the course of our work we shall have much, very much, to say upon these causes. The first we shall allude to is the imperfect manner in which the generality of instruments are constructed. As well might we condemn the violin, hearing it played on a Dutch toy, instead of a Cremona, as the guitar, when heard on instruments that usurp its name, in ninety-nine cases out of one hundred. The multitudinous defects that are found in their construction will be treated of in our next, – such as the finger-board, the nice adjustment of the frets, the height of the bridge, the various woods of the sides and backs, the greenness of the materials, and the badness of strings – these all contribute to mar the proper effect of the instrument. The laws of acoustics are so imperfectly understood; the lowness of price at which they are manufactured; the time, expense, and incessant labour, which are required is consequently not bestowed on their formation; and in this country, in particular, it is least understood, or, if understood, not attended to. The attributes of the instrument, therefore, from these causes, cannot properly be elicited; nor can it be marvelled at any longer, that these defects are not easily surmounted by a good, much less an indifferent player. We now have an objection to urge against the generality of good performers, in their method of playing. We regret extremely that they should miscalculate wherein lies the power of their instrument. They say the true tone of the guitar is to be produced by playing near the bridge; but from which we decidedly and entirely dissent. By playing so near the bridge, they produce a *wiry tone* – the very tone which is objected to. This wiry tone is yclept *twanging*, or *tinkling*; and it is to us most unaccountable that the first professors should be insensible to it, and still continue to adopt the placing of the right hand where this objectionable tone is created. The defect (if defect it to be), then, is not in the instrument, but in the player: he has only to lower his hand nearer the aperture of the guitar, when he will have a fine, clear, harpy tone, to which the most fastidious ear cannot object.

[p. 15]

We know that it is almost heresy to state thus much to the professors, who may be startled at this innovation to their long-habituated and prescriptive rules; but we would ask them what manner of tone would the violin or violoncello produce, were they always played *ponticello* (at the point of the bow), and near the bridge?[40] Would it not, we would ask them, produce the same nasal, disagreeable tone, which is brought forth on the guitar in the same situation? It really would appear to us as if they actually wished to imitate the old English guitar, the strings of which were entirely composed of wire – and from which, indeed, the cognomen of tinkling has no doubt been derived – instead of emulating the tones of the harp, which are more agreeable and fascinating.[41] Thus much for these opprobrious epithets.

With regard to its producing no effect, much of the foregoing observations will apply; but there are others which we may enumerate, and which mar its effect.

These are also in the construction of the instrument. Should the fingers of the player be large and thick, and the strings set too close to allow free motion between them, the slightest collision in rapid passages must necessarily deaden the sound – acting like dampers on a pianoforte – destroying at once the vibrations of the open strings. Another, and yet important, feature is in using too great a force with the right hand; for, in endeavouring to produce the greatest *quantum* of tone by mere manual strength, they jar the strings, and weaken the real tone. All this might be obviated. Nor must we forget the precision with which the strings themselves should be evenly made in the whole of their length, without the smallest variation of thickness – any inequalities producing false notes, and a bad quality of tone. Damp hands is also prejudicial to tone. This, therefore, clearly proves that the "want of effect" is not in the instrument itself.

The last objection we have to notice is, that it is difficult, and decidedly inferior to every other; and that its tones do not combine with other instruments. Now, as to its difficulties, they are, as we have already anticipated in the course of this article, purely derivable from a want of proper knowledge in the construction of the instrument; and in the application of the ends to the means, all the difficulties consist. Practice, very little practice, by playing slowly at first, attending to tone, and eschewing execution – the bane not alone of this instrument, but of all others – are all that is requisite to surmount. Why the guitar, more than any other instrument, should be compared unfairly with them, when the uses and purposes of it are so diametrically opposite, we are at a loss to conjecture. Most other instruments are part and parcel of an orchestra; – this is to supply the place of one, and is chiefly applicable to the human voice. The comparison of one instrument to another is

[40]   A *ponticello*, or metallic, sound can be achieved on the guitar by plucking the strings close to the bridge.
[41]   The 'English Guittar', occasionally spelt 'Guitar', was a wire strung instrument usually tuned to a C major chord that had been popular from the middle of the eighteenth century. By 1825 it was largely forgotten.

no proof of the superiority or inferiority of either, unless their uses are for the same purpose.

That its tone does not amalgamate with other instruments, is so general and loose an observation, that it hardly requires one word of refutation from us. Every professor has merely to turn to his music portfolio, to give this assertion a direct contradiction, as he there finds music from time immemorial arranged for all instruments within the compass of the guitar, (except the double bass, organ, and trombone, unless, indeed, it is insisted on that the latter instruments form a proper criterion).

The best musicians in Germany have joined the powers of the guitar with

[p. 16]

those of the piano-forte. Hummel, who is the first composer on the latter instrument, perhaps in Europe, has often devoted his extraordinary talents to an union with them: so far even has he gone, that in his enthusiastic admiration for Giuliani's third concerto,* he has actually written full orchestral accompaniments for it; and again, in his Op. 79, Hummel has written conjointly with Giuliani, in a grand pot pourri. We might also mention Moschelles, who, with Giuliani, has written a grand duett: but the instances are so numerous, that, were it necessary, we could fill one of our Numbers with them.[42] The misfortune is, they are not known in England; the knowledge, however, is so much a desideratum, that we hope in time, through our pages, to make them pretty generally understood.

This then forms the *summum bonum* of all that has been, within our knowledge, brought against our favorite instrument, which we have shewn has been bred in prejudice, nurtured by accidental causes, and condemned by those only who never essayed its beauties, tried its effects, or applied its capabilities. The want of application in some, the lack of judgment in others, the misappropriation of its free powers, and abuse of its qualities, are the chief features that are apparent in its hostile detractors. We have endeavoured, in our humble power, to controvert these opinions; and if we have failed, it is not for want of argument, but entirely owing to our own incompetency to sustain it.

---

[42] Heck notes that Giuliani's few pieces for guitar and piano were mainly written in conjunction with Hummel or Moscheles. Heck, *Giuliani*, Chapter 6, Section 1.2. Mentioned here are: Mauro Giuliani and Johann Hummel, *Grand Pot-Pourri National, Opus 93* (Vienna, [1818]), (Opus 79 in Hummel's catalogue). Ignaz Moscheles and Mauro Giuliani, *Grand Duo Concertant* (Vienna, [1814]), (Opus 20 in Moscheles's catalogue).

The dominion which this little instrument has held over the feelings of mankind, from the earliest ages to the present time, is evidence sufficient that it is not to be banished from the world by a few dogmatical assertions or satirical epithets. Against the dissenting few, we have the millions many; the majority of the world is in our favour, and poetry and painting have equally vied in perpetuating and celebrating its praise.

*A specimen of this was given in the 1st Number of this Work.[43]

[Illustration of instruments including a harp, violin, lyre, and trumpet.]

[p. 17]

GUITAR SONG.*

BY MRS. L. MILES.

———

1.
A light breathing cadence is played.
SONG – List! – heard ye not a sigh
Amid the strings?
Some magic must be nigh –
A spirit sings.

11.
A low air, – in imitation of a voice.
SONG – Again, the chords are stirr'd,
While soft and low
The dulcet strain is heard,
In deeper flow.

111.
A bold and lofty measure.
SONG – Wild as the wave and deep,
Is borne away
In full and length'ned sweep,
The inspiring lay.

1V.
A pause.
SONG – Oh, cease! – my soul is gone
To yonder skies;
And like a wounded swan,
The music dies.

———

[43]   'Solo by Giuliani (from his 3rd Concerto)', *TG* 1:1 (1833), Music 5.

*We have hesitated in putting these beautiful lines to music in the first instance, choosing rather that the amateur should exercise her or his judgment, in giving them effect in music, unassisted. In the 4th or 5th Number, however, the words will be wedded to music by a distinguished composer.[44]

[p. 18]

THE WESTMINSTER REVIEW AND THE GUITAR.

ABOUT twenty years ago, the guitar in this country was looked upon as a sort of *rara avis;* our music shops were destitute of its exhibition – and a musician who played upon it, was looked upon not only as one who wished to appear singular in his pursuits, but with a feeling nearly akin to contempt, for making choice of, as was then supposed, so barbarous an instrument. Years have rolled away, and with them much of the ignorance and prejudice towards both foreigners and guitars. The Peninsula campaign, in which our brave soldiers took so prominent and important a part, effected that, which it is no fallacy to suppose would, without that event, have taken at least half a century to accomplish. Mixing, as did our warriors, with the people of Spain and Portugal; and domesticated as many of them were, and are to this day, with the families of those countries, it was only natural that they should have discovered the immense influence which the guitar there possessed, and have felt themselves, the witching powers of its fascination. It is not to be denied, that the introduction of this instrument in Britain, has taken place chiefly through the agency of British officers; and we are not risking too much in asserting, that by them and their families, and through their influence, the guitar in England is at the present moment chiefly supported. They have travelled in and over the land of romance; and in war, where a tinge of the romantic is always prevalent amongst the enterprising and enthusiastic, it would have been clearly impossible for them to behold the veneration in which our delightful instrument was held both by peer and peasant in the Peninsula, without the consciousness "that there must be some inward grace where there was much outward feeling."

How delightful must be the associations connected with this instrument to those who first heard its sound, and learnt its touch, amid the danger and terror of warfare, now that they can recall to their memories those days of chivalry and romance, by their own peaceful hearths in old England! Perhaps, while yet *bivouaching* in the soft twilight, conjuring in imagination the one dear form of her he left in his native land,

---

44   No accompaniment to these words was given in later issues.

touching in sympathy the strings of his guitar, might the mandate be given to arouse and prepare for the expected battle! And now that those days of strife and hostility have happily ended, how sweet to "fight his battles o'er again," and surrounded by those he holds most dear, again in vivid colours bring to his mind's eye the

[p. 19]

first moment when he felt the influence of an instrument, which no one better than he understands, is

"Beloved alike in peace or war."

Introduced then, as the instrument has been, into the bosom of our families, by the educated, and by the wise and the brave, we, in our humble capacity, have had by their means our path made smooth and pleasant, in putting forth its claims to praise.

It is with pride and gratification that we see the colossus of our present periodical literature, "The Westminster Review," lend its gigantic powers to bespeak a favourable reception for an instrument, which the reviewer says "brings an orchestra to every man's fire-side, for about the cost of an alderman's dinner."[45]

The reviewer in the course of noticing "Gardiner's Music of Nature,"[46] makes the following observations:–

"It is rather hard, that after commemorating every thing that squeaks, or squalls, or hums through the nose, no other mention should have been made of the descendant of the cithara of the ancients, the lute of our well-favoured ancestresses.[47] A murrain on the man who hath no leaning towards gentle antiquity! If instruments were estimated by their effect divided by their magnitude, the guitar, with its hundred tones, would hold considerable rank. But musicians love to come forth, and call upon their gods; and think scorn to commune with an instrument that brings an orchestra to every man's hearth for about the cost of an alderman's dinner. It is true its scale is not absolutely the purest; for it

45 The most well-known guitar maker, Louis Panormo (1784–1862), was advertising guitars from two to fifteen guineas. For further details of the Panormo family of instrument makers, see Westbrook, *Guitar Making*. As interest in the instrument declined in the mid 1830s some advertisements offered 'very cheap' guitars without specifying the price. Clarke 'Instrument', 44–45. Guitars could also be bought from pawnbrokers' shops and auctions. Page, *Guitar*, 222.

46 William Gardiner, *The Music of Nature* (London, 1832). Gardiner sought to show that music is derived from the sounds of the natural world. The lengthy article about it in the *Westminster Review* is an indication of the interest that the book generated.

47 The kithara (or cithara in Latin) was a large lyre first referred to in ancient Greece. Martha Maas, 'Kithara', *GMO*. Many writers in the early nineteenth century believed that this instrument was an antecedent of the guitar.

Figure 9. Label of a Guitar by Louis Panormo, 1843. The label reads:
LOUIS PANORMO. / The only Maker of / Guitars in the Spanish Style.
/ 46, High Street, Bloomsbury. / 2020 LONDON 1843 / Guitars of every
description from 2 to 15 Guineas. Panormo used this price description on his
labels from 1828 until around 1854. Westbrook, *Guitar Making*, 88.

is that division of the octave into twelve equal intervals, which was the
subject of great expectation with musicians while it was thought difficult
and rare. But this is of small import in an age which finds beauties in
untuneableness, and believes exact intonation would be an evil and a
loss. Its intonation is in some keys inferior to the pianoforte's; but the
pianoforte cannot warble, or articulate, or sigh, or wail, or tremble,
like the human voice under emotion, as the guitar; it cannot effect that
oblivion of worldly ills, which a philosopher said was produced on
him by a moonlight night, and Lord – by Vestris' ancle.[48] It may be
assumed that in every instrument the power of expression will be in
proportion to the immediateness of the contact between the sounding
materials and the performer. Hence, of all wind instruments, the bagpipe
is the least sentimental; and strings are fully conscious of the difference
between being touched by a maiden's fingers, and by the intervention of
a stick. None but the lute can have the *vox humana* tones – the distinct
soprano, mezzo, contr'alto, and tenor voices – which reside about the
middle of the thinner strings, and the miniature Dragonetti that lurks
within the thickest, interchangeable at will with the cumbrous alacrity

---

[48]   This would refer to the French Vestris family of dancers and musicians. Ivor Guest,
   'Vestris family', *GMO*.

of the bassoon.[49] The forte of the lute kind is imitation – not of beasts or birds, or things material, but of musical expressions; – the conjuring up of all recollections that hang by sounds, from a simple melody to the triumphant 'Orquesta'[50] of the Spanish cadet that forsook Ferdinand and a lieutenancy for love – of his guitar. Of all dulcet sounds, none can surpass a duet of Huerta's on the middle of the second and third strings, emerging from a wilderness of notes, deficient indeed in noise, but giving the

[p. 20]

liveliest idea in miniature of an overture by a full band.*[51] It is Lord Byron's image for sweet things – 'the voice of girls.'[52] Or the same frail machine can produce a *retraite,* that would draw two souls out of one adjutant – an old soldier may positively see the little drum-boy straddle, or stir his barrack-fire, and think upon the dew-drop pendant at the bugler's nose; – varied on the harmonics with a *ran plan plan* worthy of him who at midnight musters the spectre Guard, with the palpable flavour of parchment, as it would come from his marrowless knuckles across the ghastly heath. And then can come pipes, and reeds, and oaten stops, and distant choirs – priests chanting merrily, or mass, or requiem, and poor lost Italy – curse on all traitors and *justes milieus* of the earth – and fair romantic Spain, and floating forms, and dark mantillas, and castanets that turn the air to rhythm. All these cannot be had from a spinet. But they require some husbandry – a parlour twilight, or a turret lone, when gabbling boys are fast abed; and there is one peculiar tone, whatever be the cause, is never brought out but in the small hours of the morning. Above all, these things are hid from simpletons, who seek them in a crowded theatre, and then declare they nothing heard. They might as well line the stage with miniatures, and view them from the upper boxes. But he has missed the strangest effect of music, who has not heard the 'Carnival of Venice' in the long gallery that leads down to the tombs of the Pharaohs.[53] Organs would have been pompous mockeries; but the small voice of the guitar said 'All flesh is grass,'[54] in a way there was no resisting. It was as if the *domus exilis*

---

49   Domenico Dragonetti (1755–1846) was a double-bass virtuoso.
50   Orchestra or group of musicians who play together.
51   Trinidad Huerta (1800–74) was a Spanish guitarist who played in a flamboyant and improvisatory style and inspired romantic poetry such as that here by Madame de Girardin. Britton, 'Guitar', 193–95.
52   George Gordon Byron, *Don Juan,* 2 vols (London, 1849), i, 98.
53   The *Carnaval de Venise* was a popular air to which many composers wrote sets of variations. Gustave Chouquet, 'Carnaval de Venise', in *Dictionary,* ed. Grove, i (1879), 316.
54   The Bible, Isaiah 40:6.

Plutonia[55] was piping the joys and cares, that four thousand years have swept into eternity. Nothing ever gave a man such a vehement desire to cry; – not even the little duck-tails of Signore Passalacqua's nankin jacket could break the charm.[56] It is hard the author could tell no story of the guitar. Did he never hear of the Portuguese army – would it were Miguel's – that fled and left eleven thousand guitars upon the field? Or of the surprise of quarters in the Succession war in Spain, where the foremost cavalier found the enemy's vedette[57] tuning his guitar as he sat on horseback, and perceiving he did it ill, took it from his hands, and returned it, saying, 'Ahora es templada,' – 'Now it is in tune,' and passed on? There must be some inward grace, where there are so many outward signs. Men have not so forgotten themselves in peace and war, without there being something that twined about their souls, in a way that 'kists full o' whistles,' or of hammers, have not surpassed."[58]

---

*These lines, by Madame Emile Girardin, better known in England as Mademoiselle Delphine Gay, will be recognized as drawn from the living subject:–

L'avez-vous entendu ce troubadour d'Espagne
Qu'un art mélodieux aux combats accompagne?
Sur la guitarre il chante et soupire à la fois;
Ses doigts ont un accent, ses cordes une voix.
Son chant est un poème harmonieux sans rime,
Tout ce qu'on éprouve, ce qu'on rêve il l'exprime.
Les cœurs à ses accords se sentent rajeunir;
La beauté qui l'écoute, heureuse en souvenir,
S'émeut, sourit et pleure, et croit encore entendre
Ce qu'on lui dit jamais de plus doux, de plus tendre.
Sa guitarre, en vibrant, vous parle tour-à-tour
Le langage d'esprit, le langage d'amour:

[55] Exiled house of Plutonia.

[56] This probably refers to Joseph Passalacqua whose collection of Egyptian artefacts was for sale in Paris in 1826. *Catalogue Raisonné et historique des Antiquité Découvertes en Égypte par Joseph Passalaqua de Trieste* (Paris, 1826).

[57] Mounted sentry.

[58] Quotation from [T. Perronet Thompson], 'The Music of Nature', *Westminster Review* 17 (1832), 345–68, at 356–58. The story of the battlefield guitars may have originated from Gilles Menage, *Menagiana ou les bons mots et remarques critiques, historiques, morales & d'erudition*, new edn, 3 vols (Paris, 1729), ii, 92. 'Les Portugais aiant perdu une bataille, on trouva quatorze mille guitares sur la place.' ('The Portuguese having lost a battle, 14,000 guitars were found on the battlefield.') Miguel was probably Miguel I of Portugal, an authoritarian absolutist monarch for whom Thompson would have had little sympathy in the radical *Westminster Review*. It is not known where the quotation 'kists full o' whistles' originated from.

Chacun y reconnait l'instrument qui l'inspire;
Pour le compositeur c'est un orchestre entier;
C'est le tambour léger pour le Basque en délire;
   C'est le clarion pour guerrier,
   Pour le poète c'est la lyre![59]

[p. 21]

THE FAREWELL GIFT.

————

I.

HE gave her at parting – ah, hapless maid! –
The guitar they both had loved:
O'er whose tuneful strings, so sweetly play'd,
His skilful hand had roved.
Her eye dwelt o'er his path afar,
Till the night-star ceas'd to burn;
And she sighed – "He has gone to that fatal war; –
"He will never more return!"

II.

A pilgrim came to her lonely hall;
He had much of woe to tell:
Her dear one pined in captive thrall, –
He had sent her his last farewell.
But her broken heart, o'er her loved guitar,
Its latest plaint had borne, –
"He is gone, he is gone to that fatal war; –
"He will never more return!"

---

[59] 'Have you heard this Spanish troubadour
Who is accompanied by a melodious art in battle?
On the guitar he sings and sighs at the same time;
His fingers have a rhythm, his strings a voice.
His song is a harmonious poem without rhyme,
Everything we feel, what we dream, he expresses.
Hearts feel rejuvenated by its chords;
The beauty that listens to him, happy in remembrance,
Moves, smiles and weeps, and still thinks he hears
The sweetest, most tender things ever said to him.
His guitar, vibrating, speaks to you in turn,
The language of the mind, the language of love:
Everyone recognises the instrument that inspires them:
For the composer it is an entire orchestra,
It is the light drum for the delirious Basque,
It is the clarion for the warrior,
For the poet it is the lyre!'

III.
Long years have pass'd; but at that still hour
When night and morn combine,
The peasant shuns that mouldering tow'r,
And makes the holy sign:
For, they say, there is heard, with that sad guitar,
Soft tones that seem to mourn, –
"He is gone, he is gone to that fatal war; –
"He will never more return!"

W. BALL.

[p. 22]

REVIEW OF MUSIC.

"Non Più Mesta," being No. 1. *of a Series of Airs; arranged as Duetts for Guitar and Piano-forte. Dedicated to* MISS JENKINS, *by* W. NEULAND.[60] Chappel.

THE above air is arranged by a gentleman, of whose abilities we augur well. This being the first number of a series of airs, we cannot fairly judge of the manner in which they will be continued; but should the same diligence and taste which we find displayed in this pervade the rest, we think the subscribers will have little cause to complain. If there is anything that we could desiderate, it is that the arranger had made the guitar somewhat more *principiale.* Mr. Neuland possess powers sufficient as a musician, both in a theoretical and practical point of view, to render anything that he touches agreeable in the form under our notice; and as we are anxious to promote the combination of the two instruments, we earnestly recommend him not to relax in his exertions, as we know of no one so fit to follow the steps and dispute the palm of excellence with Diabelli himself.[61] To those who have never heard the conjunction of these instruments, the present piece will afford them a pleasant opportunity of so doing.

1. *"Fantasia," for the Guitar, on the Air, My Lodging is on the Cold Ground. Composed and dedicated to his Friend,* FERDINAND PELZER, *by* J. A. NUSKE. Ewer.

---

60 The German musician, Wilhelm Neuland (1806–89), split his time between Calais and London in this period. Susanne Haase, *Der Bonner Komponist Wilhelm Neuland (1806–1889) Studien zu Leben und Werk* (Berlin, 1995), 11–12.

61 Anton Diabelli (1781–1858) was an Austrian composer and publisher. Alexander Weinmann and John Warrack, 'Diabelli, Anton', *GMO*.

2. *Grand Variations for Guitar. Composed and dedicated to the Hon.* GEORGIANA, LADY PONSONBY, *by* FELIX HORETZKY. Op. 20. Davis & Co.

1. This composition is excellent. The harmonies are rich and diversified, as is instanced in the introduction, and in the adagio. Mr. Nuské has long been known as an admirable composer for the guitar; and, to a skilful amateur, the above piece will be found as delightful as it is improving. It is written in Sor's best style, or rather, it is a combination of the styles of Sor and Giuliani.

2. By Horetzky. We can also recommend this to the most finished class of players, the style of which is founded in the school of Giuliani. There is always a beautiful vein of melody and good taste in this gentleman's compositions; but we must object to the great sameness of many of them. There is not sufficient variety, either in the style, fingering, or harmonies, to compensate the pupil for more than a moiety of his works, the reason of which, we take to be, arises more in a proper application of industry than in a lack of real talent. We shall rest content with this hint to him for the present.

[p. 23]

1. *Six Waltzes, for the Guitar. Composed and dedicated to* MISS THOMAS, *by* C. EULENSTEIN. Op. 16. Chappel.
2. *"Le Papillon," a Collection of easy and agreeable Airs, for Guitar, by* MAURO GIULIANI. Chappel.
3. *Twelve Easy Divertimentos, for Guitar. Dedicated to* MISS HARRIETT BRADY, *by* F. HORETZKY. Ewer.

1. The six waltzes are well adapted for beginners, and form an agreeable and easy *gradus* to the difficulties of the instrument. Mr. Eulenstein appears to us always to hit that happy medium between the simple and abstruse, which, at one and the same time, interests as well as improves the player. The waltzes 1, 3, 4, and 5, we may point out as an apt illustration of our remark.

2. There is too much sameness in these light airs of Giuliani. Apart from this objection they are instructive and pleasing.

3. Appears to be but another version of Mr. Horetzky's instructive exercises (reviewed last Number), and some of his other compositions. Whatever excellencies the studies possess, these retain, in a modified degree, – each of their divertimentos occupying only from two to four lines of music. These pieces, therefore, possess the recommendation of not fatiguing the attention of the student. No. 1 is a sweet melody – and the exquisite taste it displays, well nigh exempts it from the charge

of mannerism. No. 5 requires the bass notes to be played with great firmness. No. 7 is an agreeable pastorale.

Spanish March, with brilliant Variations for Guitar. Dedicated to
MISS T. VEA, by F. W. SMITH.[62] Chappel.

The absolute absurdity of such a composition as the one before us is so manifest, by requiring the guitar to be tuned in such a manner as merely to enable the player to finger on the first and second strings, or play *barré*, producing no other than a noisy effect, without any improvement in fingering on the left, or exercise of the right hand, that we much regret the want of taste it exhibits. It is in fact a species of charlatanism introduced from Spain, the result of the untutored attempts of the peasantry of that country; and without the compensation of either melody or harmony, it has nothing further to recommend itself than to create a noisy effect to the unlearned ear. This second version of the Spanish Retreat, we hope will be the last that we shall see in this country; and we trust our amateurs will make this hurdy-gurdy style of playing beat a retreat to the *montanas* from which it has emanated. Our English professor should discriminate – not choose the dross, when there is ample stock of much better materials submitted for his model.[63]

[p. 24]

Musical Intelligence, Chit-Chat, &c.

———

FOREIGN MUSICAL NEWS.

In VIENNA, Donizetti's opera, *Der Verwiesene* aus Rom. (L'esule di Roma) has been produced with tolerable success.[64] Die Stumme von Portici has also been brought forward, and was well received.[65] Mr. F.

---

62   Mr. F. W. Smith was a professor of dancing and music in Dorchester. 'Advertisements', *Salisbury and Winchester Journal*, 12 July 1830.
63   No copy of this has been found. It is likely that it was similar to two other contemporary editions of the 'Spanish Retreat'. Flamini Duvernay, *The Spanish Retreat* (London, 1829); Alexander Sosson, *The Spanish Retreat* (London, [1830]). (Figure 10). Both these pieces required the guitar to be tuned to a C major chord, thus facilitating the simple use of barrés for chord changes. A barré employs the first left hand finger to press several strings, sometimes all, onto the fingerboard. In spite of this writer's dislike of the piece, other arrangements were published later in the century.
64   Donizetti, *The Exile from Rome*.
65   Auber's opera *La Muette de Portici*. First performed in Paris in 1828, it was very successful and was translated and performed throughout Europe. Herbert Schneider, 'Auber, Daniel-François-Esprit', *GMO*. The content of the 'Foreign Musical News'

Figure 10. Alexander Sosson, *The Spanish Retreat* (London, [1830]). 1. The required tuning of the guitar to a C major chord is shown.

W. Pixis, the violin player, and Mademoiselle E. Barth, the pianiste, both of the Conservatoire at Prague, and Madame Podhorsky, *prima donna* at the same place, gave a concert here (Vienna) on the 22d September, and greatly distinguished themselves by a rich display of their respective talents. M. Giromale Salieri, a famous clarionet player from Venice, also gave a concert here on the 9th October. This virtuoso has attained the most perfect mastery over his instrument.

At BERLIN was performed, on 22d October, *Die Hochzeit des Figaro*, with M. and Mad. Reichel, as *Figaro and the Countess*.[66] Madame R. is spoken of as exhibiting all the qualities of an excellent singer, though not yet perfectly matured. The first winter concert here was given by Madame Milder, and took place on the 25th October, on which occasion were performed several pieces of Neukomm's.[67] M.

has largely been taken from 'Foreign Musical Report', *The Harmonicon* 11:61 (1833), 18–19.
[66] Mozart, *The Marriage of Figaro*.
[67] Sigismund Ritter von Neukomm (1778–1858) was an Austrian musician whose teachers had included Haydn. His first visit to England was in 1829. Rudolph

Felix Mendelssohn played Mozart's Concerto, in D minor. This artist is about getting up three charitable concerts during the winter, in which he will bring forward several pieces of his own. Amongst the rest a symphony in D, by Ludwig Berger, besides several other compositions.[68] The Singing Academy here proposes giving four oratorios – *Salomon and Joshua*, of Handel, *St. John the Evangelist*, by S. Bach,[69] and the fourth by Haydn. The Four Brothers, Müller, the quartett players, are expected here from Brunswick.[70] The Musical Soirées of M. Möser commenced on the 31st October, when were performed Mozart's and Beethoven's Symphonies in C major, and the overture to Euryanthe.[71]

At PARIS, at *the Theatre Royal Italian*, Bellini's opera, La Straniera (the Stranger) has been produced with success. In this, Mademoiselle Judith Grizi made her debut in the character of *Alaide*. She was supported by Rubini and Tamburini.[72]

––––––

LONDON MUSICAL NEWS.

THE second of the Vocal Concerts was attended by a numerous audience on the 21st of January.[73] The Athenæum finds fault with the "managers becoming actors," and speaks of the performances as follows:– "The descriptive cantata by Percy, was sung by Braham, without orchestral accompaniment, and, of course, did not succeed; secondly, the scena 'Col coro,' from Faust, requiring the vigour and power of a Braham, was entrusted to Mr. Horncastle, whose thin tenor voice was completely overwhelmed and lost in the 'maze' of chorus and accompaniment; thirdly, Mr. Bellamy, the ci-devant bass singer of the Ancient Concerts, attempted more than he ought, and failed to do well what he attempted; fourthly, the puny voice of Master Howe is sufficient to spoil a much better glee than 'Oh, how I long my careless limbs to

---

Angermüller, 'Neukomm, Sigismund Ritter von', *GMO*.

[68] Ludwig Berger (1779–1839) was a German composer and pianist. Richard Kershaw, revised by Michael Musgrave, 'Berger, Ludwig', *GMO*.

[69] J. S. Bach.

[70] String quartet players. Brown, *Dictionary*, 439.

[71] Weber, overture to his opera *Euryanthe*. Möser may have been Karl Möser, whose string quartet held chamber music evenings and symphony concerts in Berlin. John Moran, 'Möser, Karl', *GMO*.

[72] Giuditta Grisi (1805–40) (Judith), Italian mezzo-soprano and elder sister of the more famous soprano Giulia Grisi. Simon Maguire and Elizabeth Forbes, 'Straniera, La', *GMO*. Giovanni Battista Rubini, tenor, and Antonio Tamburini, baritone, were also leading Italian singers of the time.

[73] This was the second concert of the 'Vocal Society'. Founded in 1832, this society presented English vocal music in a series of concerts each season in the Hanover Square Rooms. It ceased after Queen Victoria stopped attending in 1838. 'Musical', *Morning Post*, 24 January 1833. 'The Commencement', *Musical World* 10:34 (1838), 61–63, at 62.

lay,' by Sir J. Rogers; fifthly, the *buffo part* in Mozart's quintetto from Zauberflöte, 'Hm Hm,' should have been given to Phillips, whose talent was entirely thrown away in Paer's duet, 'Dolce del anima', lastly, it is little short of presumption for any vocalist, with an ordinary compass of voice, to attempt the music of 'Regina' in Zauberflöte." To shew how critics (as well as doctors,) differ, the Literary Gazette applauds almost every piece that its contemporary condemns. He of the Athanæum, on the night in question, must certainly have been a little "bilious." But something must be said, and to be smart and pungent, not only carries a relish with it, but with some folks "a deal of learning" also.[74]

CONCERTS OF ANCIENT MUSIC. – It has been notified to the performers, that a reduction in the salaries in the vocal and instrumental departments of this society must be acceded to, or the Concerts will be discontinued.

Mr. ELIASON is to be the leader of the German Opera at Drury Lane Theatre. We are heartily glad of this. It is a post which no leader of the present day can fill so well. His knowledge of dramatic music, by all the best German composers, is not exceeded by any violinist of the present day.[75]

MOZART'S DON GIOVANNI will be produced at Drury Lane before our readers will have perused this Number. In this opera our old favourite, Mrs. WOOD, will make her first appearance this season.[76]

At Mr. ELIASON'S musical soirée, a very beautiful and original song, composed expressly for the occasion by M. Chelard, was admirably sung by Madame de Meric, accompanied on the violin and violoncello by

---

[74] 'Vocal Concerts', *The Athenæum* 274 (1833), 60. 'Music', *Literary Gazette* 836 (1833), 59–60. The reference to 'managers becoming actors' would have referred to Thomas Bellamy, who had been a stage manager of a theatre in Dublin and proprietor of several others. Brown, *Dictionary*, 74. Percy may have been John Percy, died 1797. Brown, *Dictionary*, 467. John Braham (1774–1856) was a leading tenor of that time. Ronald Crichton, 'Braham, John', *GMO*. Sir J. Rogers was Sir John Leman Rogers (1780–1847), an amateur composer. Brown, *Dictionary*, 518. Paer's duet 'Dolce del anima' is from his opera *Sargino*, first performed in 1803. The other singers named were less well-known. References to the 'Concerts of Ancient Music' and 'Mr. Eliason's Soirée' that follow are taken from the same article in *The Athenæum*. The former of these was a prestigious concert series founded in 1776 and managed by aristocrats. The writer, commenting on their difficulties, added that 'the old monopoly and monotony too long held sway', thus accounting for their declining fortunes.

[75] Little is known about Eliason, other than that he later organised a series of promenade concerts which failed financially. 'Musard's Promenade Concerts', *Morning Chronicle*, 4 February 1861.

[76] Mary Ann Wood, née Paton (1802–64) was a Scottish soprano. Brown, *Dictionary*, 463.

Messrs. Eliason and Lindley. The whole of the performances at this soirée went off with *eclat*.[77]

HORACE'S CITHARA OR GUITAR.[78]

––––––

IF we examine the lyrical compositions of Horace, admirable, as they are in harmony and composition, we must be sensible that they were peculiarly adapted to a musical instrument like the guitar, as those who have a nice ear for Latin verse must freely acknowledge. As an amatory poet, indeed, Horace stands in the first rank; no modern, however celebrated, can approximate to him, in point of exquisite diction, appropriate sentiment, and melody every where adapted to the sense. But it is the opinion of Quintilian,[79] a most excellent judge, and one from whose decision in Latin literature there is no appeal, that Horace is almost the only lyric poet that deserves to be read; that he occasionally rises into sublimity, abounds in every species of elegance, and is most felicitous [*sic*] in sentiment and figurative diction.[80] As for his eminence as an amatory poet, we may observe that the odes he has addressed to Roman females are among the most charming of his productions, and that his Sapphic odes are such as would be most suitable to the guitar. Horace, who like Pope, was diminutive and insignificant in person, yet frequently boasts of his success in affairs of gallantry, alluding at the same time to the powers of this instrument as being one of the most essential auxiliaries in his *Citherean* wars. When he declares in a *Farewell Ode* that he relinquishes all further amatory pursuits, he formally mentions that

77 Madame de Meric was a singer held in much esteem in London. Julian Marshall, 'Meric, Madame de', in *A Dictionary of Music and Musicians*, ed. George Grove, 4 vols (London, 1879–89), ii (1880), 313. Robert Lindley was the leading 'cellist at this time'. Brown, *Dictionary*, 387. Chelard (1789–1861) was a French musician who conducted performances by a German opera company in 1832 and 1833 at the King's Theatre. A. Maczewski, 'Chelard, Hippolyte André Jean Baptiste', in *Dictionary*, ed. Grove, i (1879), 341. Bruce Carr, 'Theatre Music: 1800–1834', in *Music in Britain, the Romantic Age 1800–1914*, ed. Nicholas Temperley (London, 1981), 288–306, at 288–89.
78 The Greek word *kithara* is the origin of the word 'guitar'.
79 Quintilian, *Institutio Oratoria*, X, 2. Quintilian (Marcus Fabius Quintilianus) was a Roman educator of the first century AD. *Horace* [online]. Chicago: Poetry Foundation, https://www.poetryfoundation.org/poets/horace [accessed 12 October 2022].
80 It has long been debated whether the ancient Roman poet Horace (Quintus Horatius Flaccus, 65–8 BC) sang his odes accompanying them himself or whether he recited them. The cithara was a lyre supported on a knee or flat surface. See Stuart Lyons, 'Singing Horace in Antiquity and the Early Middle Ages', *Early Music History* 40 (2021), 167–205, at 167–68, 175.

he will hang up his Cithara or Barbiton in the temple of Venus, as a votive offering to the goddess.[81] The lovers of music, who are generally lovers of good poetry also, will find in this poet – whom the learned Dr. V. Knox styles the best companion of a man of fashion – a great fund of truly elegant and classical entertainment; and they will meet in him what is very rarely the gift of any poet, a writer that never tires, and one who displays fresh beauties after every repeated perusal.[82] At the same time that we make these remarks, we are sensible that the classical scholar will confess that the high encomiums we have passed on this celebrated poet will not be recognised by the ordinary English reader, since the translations that have hitherto appeared, give but a faint idea of the exquisite beauties of his diction and numbers.[83] Pope we believe, in one or two instances, has approached the beauty of the original in a paraphrase of some of the odes; but as his genius was more satirical than lyrical, his imitations of the satires are fully equal and sometimes superior to the happiest efforts of this celebrated classic.[84] In justification of this opinion, which may have the appearance of novelty, we beg to quote Lord Chesterfield who expresses himself thus in one of his letters to his son: "I will venture on a little classical

[p. 26]

blasphemy, which is, that if Pope is indebted to Horace, Horace on the other hand is more frequently indebted to Pope."[85] But to return to

---

[81]   Alexander Pope (1688–1744) suffered from tuberculosis of the bone as a child and in adult life was seen as a dwarf and cripple. See Maynard Mack, *Alexander Pope: A Life* (London, 1985), 153. Horace was believed to be short in stature. Suetonius, 'The Life of Horace, believed to be an abbreviation of a Life by Suetonius', in Horace, *The Complete Odes and Epodes*, trans. David West (Oxford, 1997), xxiv–xxvi, at xxvi. There may also be here an implied reference to the relatively lowly births of both poets. Pope was the son of a merchant and Horace the son of a freedman, formerly a slave. The *Farewell Ode* referred to is Horace's *Vixi puellis nuper*, *Odes*, III, 26. In it he talks of his honours in campaigns and of his armour and lyre, whose wars have ended, and will be hung on a wall guarding the goddess Venus. Cythera (Cithera) is a Greek island reputedly the birthplace of Venus; Citherean thus refers to the goddess. The barbiton, or barbitos, was an ancient Greek instrument of the lyre family usually held against the player's body. See Jane McIntosh Snyder, 'Barbitos', *GMO*.

[82]   V. Knox edited Horace's *Odes* for use in schools. Horace, *Q. Horatii Flacci, Carmina Expurgata: in Usum Scholarum*, ed. Vicesimus Knox and others (London, 1784). Vicesimus Knox (1752–1821) was a writer, educationist, and headmaster of Tonbridge School. See Philip Carter and S. J. Skedd, 'Knox, Vicesimus', *ODNB*.

[83]   'Numbers' here means metres.

[84]   Pope wrote his *Imitations of Horace* with their epistles and satires between 1733 and 1738.

[85]   Philip Dormer Stanhope (Lord Chesterfield), 'Appendix to Lord Chesterfield's Works', in *Miscellaneous Works of the late Philip Dormer Stanhope, Earl of Chesterfield*, 4 vols (London, 1779), iv, 1–75, at 15. Philip Dormer Stanhope, 4th earl of Chesterfield,

the guitar. While we intimated to our readers that the lyrical measures of Horace were extremely apt and appropriate to an accompaniment of this instrument, yet as such a similitude is not obvious to a mere modern reader, nor is the felicity of his diction to be duly appreciated unless by persons skilled in his language – a quotation from Pope, who is allowed to be the best of translators as well as imitators, may furnish our readers with a tolerable [*sic*] just idea of Horace's mode of treating a subject of love and gallantry. It is but just, however, to observe that though our heroic measure is the best representative that affords of the Greek and Latin hexameter, yet there is no measure in the compass of our poetry that assimilates to the lyrical compositions of the ancients. The extract from Pope, however, will afford a specimen of felicitous diction which deserves to be recognized as a faithful transcript of Horace's happiest vein.

> "Then shall thy form the marble grace,
> (Thy Grecian form) and Chloe lend the face;
> His house, embosom'd in the grove
> Sacred to social life and social love,
> Shall glitter o'er the pendent green,
> Where Thames reflects the visionary scene.
> Thither the silver-sounding lyres
> Shall call the smiling loves and young desires;
> There, every grace and muse shall throng,
> Exalt the dance or animate the song;
> There youths and nymphs, in concert gay
> Shall hail the rising, close the parting day.
> With me, alas! those joys are o'er;
> For me the vernal garlands bloom no more.
> Adieu! fond hope of mutual fire,
> The still-believing, still renewed desire:
> Adieu! the heart-expanding bowl,
> And all the kind deceivers of the soul!
> But why? ah tell me, ah too dear!
> Steals down my cheek the involuntary tear?
> Why words so flowing, thoughts so free,
> Stop or turn nonsense, at one glance of thee?
> Thee, dress'd in fancy's airy beam,
> Absent I follow through the extended dream.
> Now, now I cease, I clasp thy charms,
> And now you burst (ah, cruel from my arms?)

1694–1773, is best remembered for the letters he wrote over some thirty years to his illegitimate son, Philip, who died in 1768. They were intended to equip the boy for a career in politics and were published by his widow in 1774. See John Cannon, 'Stanhope, Philip Dormer, fourth earl of Chesterfield', *ODNB*. Although the quotation here is by Lord Chesterfield it is not from any of the letters to his son.

And swiftly shoot along the mall,
Or softly glide by the canal;
Now shown by Cynthia's silver ray,
And now on rolling waters snatch'd away."

From Pope's Ode to Venus.[86]

[p. 27]

SOR.

_____

TO THE EDITOR OF THE GIULIANIAD.

SIR,

BEING a subscriber to your Monthly Guitar publication, and seeing the spirited manner in which it promises to be conducted, I sit down to write you a word or two respecting Ferdinand Sor, that excellent guitar player and composer, trusting that my humble observations with regard to the guitar, and the productions of that eminent master, may, perhaps, not prove quite unworthy of insertion in your admirable journal. It is a fact, that until the arrival of Sor in this country, which took place about fifteen or sixteen years ago, the guitar was scarcely known here, and the impression he then made on his first performance at the Argyll Rooms, which I attended, was of a nature which will never be erased from my memory; it was at once magical and surprising; nobody could credit that such effects could be produced on the *guitar!* indeed, there was a sort of a suppressed laughter when he first came forth before the audience, which, however, soon changed into the most unbounded admiration when he began to display his talents.[87] London was, at that time, not without persons who *professed* to teach the guitar; and I know that several of these guitar-quacks went there "to *scoff,* but remained to pray!" I only wish I could have had the pleasure of hearing Giuliani perform, and to be thus qualified to draw a proper comparison between him and Sor; but if, as I understand, Giuliani's tone was more powerful than Sor's, the compositions of the latter, executed by the former, must have left little or nothing to be wished for with regard to perfection on that instrument. I am well acquainted with the voluminous productions of Giuliani, and

---

86   From 'The First Ode of the Fourth Book of Horace: to Venus', in Alexander Pope, *Horace his Ode to Venus Lib IV. Ode I* (London, 1737), 5, 7. In the eleventh line 'consort' is changed to 'concert'.

87   Sor arrived in London in 1815. The first known concert in which he performed was on 20 April 1815 in the Argyll Rooms. Jeffery, *Sor*, 3rd edn, 121, 139–40. The old Argyll Rooms were in a converted mansion at the corner of Oxford Street and Argyll Street which was demolished and replaced nearby in 1819 to make way for Regent Street. Elkin, *Concert Rooms*, 115.

have learned duly to appreciate them; still, I trust it will not be considered as prejudice on my part when I say, that the beautiful compositions of Sor have touched and inspired my soul beyond all others. What wonder then that such became the chosen objects of my particular study; and if it is said of Giuliani, that "he must be considered as the inventor of a new method of *playing*"[88] – perhaps I may be permitted to say, that we ought to consider Sor as the inventor of a new method of *composing*. Let me point out to you, as a specimen, his delightful fantasia, opera 7;*[89] the introductory largo, in Comnor,[90] with its heart-thrilling combination of chords, (although rather spun out too long) which abounds

*The theme of this Opera will be found in our present number, page 31.[91]

[p. 28]

with elegance and beauty from beginning to end, leading to the tender floating theme in C major, and its variations; all these beauties must be highly relished by the proficient, as they must likewise fascinate every sincere admirer of the guitar! Allow me, especially, to draw your attention to the variations, Nos. 1, 4, and 7, and say, whether music like that is not worthy of study? I trust, Mr. Editor, that in giving some extracts of this splendid fantasia, in one of your next numbers, they will not only be welcome to those who have that instrument, but might, perhaps, do a great deal of good among a certain class of ding-dong Marsyasses, who *profess*, by their advertisements, to teach the guitar in *"Six Lessons!"* thus, by their fallacious assertions, infecting inexperienced minds with an idea that the guitar is *only* fit for an accompaniment.[92] Their assertion need excite no surprise, for as they are evidently ignorant of the capability of

---

88 Felix Horetzky, 'Preface', in Horetzky, *Instructive Exercises*.
89 Fernando Sor, *Fantaisie* (Paris, 1814).
90 C minor.
91 Fernando Sor, 'Thema', *TG* 1:3 (1833), Music 31.
92 No further extracts from Sor's opus 7 were given in later issues of *The Giulianiad*. A number of flautists taught guitar in addition to their own instrument, hence the reference to the Phrygian god Marsyas who, in Greek mythology, played the flute. Although this instrument was popular, employment teaching it may have been limited since it was not then thought suitable for women, and boys would not have learnt it in schools. Thus, there would have been more opportunities to teach the guitar because it was played by women and taught in numerous girls' schools. A number of teachers claimed in advertisements to teach the basics of accompaniment in a specified number of lessons. For example, Napoleon Gould advertised to teach pupils to accompany songs in six lessons. *Morning Post*, 12 April 1842. Mr. Stiegler promised that if a pupil had not acquired the skill of 'universal accompaniment' in three to six lessons, no payment would be accepted. *Morning Post*, 23 October 1837. This might have been a tempting proposition, although what constituted 'universal accompaniment' may have been difficult to define.

the instrument, they cannot, of course, be competent to teach what they themselves do not understand. Thus, then, their *"Six Lesson' Pupils"* remain for ever standing, as it were, upon one leg, with the other lifted up to step into the vestibule that leads to the sanctuary of the guitar, but prevented by their *excellent* masters from venturing farther, for fear of both master and pupil breaking their necks. If such pupils ever have the chance of hearing a superior performer on the guitar, and possess, perhaps, taste and judgement to appreciate it, (an effect not to be expected from their masters), they would naturally exclaim, "Is it possible! we had no conception of such brilliant effects from the guitar."

But the guitar, as a classical instrument, would be exploded for ever, had it the misfortune to depend on the mercy of such quacks. I really think, the idea would not be a bad one, to have a college established, where pupils (on all instruments) should undergo suitable examinations, like surgeons, to prove that they are skilful, before they are permitted to practice, such a regulation would speedily banish these pretenders and imposters (these "Six Lesson" gentry), and thus leave the field open to unpresuming merit, that would rest solely on its own talents and attainments.[93]

However, I trust, Mr. Editor, that your valuable journal will essentially contribute to raise the guitar in the estimation of those whose ideas have hitherto suffered under wrong representation by worthless charlatans, and that the instrument in question will universally obtain the patronage to which it is so justly entitled.

I have the honour to be, Sir, your's obediently, N.

[Our obliging correspondent N. appears to us to assign too much importance to these arrogant pretenders. Their very insignificance sinks them to their proper level; and although the English public have been, and still are liable to be duped, yet, when once the test of real merit is exhibited to them, they immediately discard the meretricious pretensions of combined incapacity and presumption. Music, like other departments of art and science, is infested by a swarm of shameless sciolists, but such tribes are naturally evanescent, and sink gradually into their native obscurity at the approach of superior light and information. With regard to the compositions of Sor, we are warm admirers of them, and shall, of course, extract from them in our future numbers. A critical analysis of his performance will likewise be given in an early number.] – ED.[94]

---

[93] The Royal Academy of Music in London had been founded in 1822 with ambitions to train professional musicians. However, guitar was not offered there until 1959. Efforts to give professional status to music teachers continued throughout the century. Rosemary Golding, 'Music teaching in the late-nineteenth century', in *The Music Profession in Britain, 1780–1920*, ed. Rosemary Golding (Abingdon, 2018), 128–48, at 128.

[94] No analysis of Sor's performance was later published.

[p. 29]

"SING TO THY GUITAR."

———

1.

I'VE listen'd to the sweetest songs
That ever wanton'd by,
Where pleasure led her courtly throngs,
And festal joy was high;
The nightingale in bow'ry shade,
The gondolier afar, —
But none like thine, O lovely maid!
When sounds thy sweet Guitar.

11.

There is a murmur'd soul-felt sigh,
That trembles through the lay,
Before whose charm my sorrows die,
Like morning dews, away:
Oh! ere the kind illusion fade,
Invoke some pitying star; —
Renew, renew the spell, dear maid!
Sing to thy sweet Guitar.

W. BALL.

[p. 30]

THE FANCY BALL.

A FRAGMENT.

BY MRS. L. MILES.[95]

———

"There is a festival, where knights and dames,
And aught that lofty lineage claims,
Appear."[96] ——

A CONFUSED sound of revelry, mingled with the dull rolling of
carriages over pavements; – then the stunning knocker shook my nerves; –

---

[95] A later version of this story was published in 1838 under the pseudonym 'Azelmisia'.
See Azelmisia, 'The Fancy Ball', *Monthly Magazine* 26:151 (1838), 63–64.

[96] George Gordon Byron, 'Lara: a Tale', in *The works of Lord Byron, A new, revised
and enlarged edition, with illustrations*, ed. Ernest Hartley Coleridge and R. E.
Prothero (New York, 1898), 321–71, at 338. Two words are omitted here from the
second line, which reads: 'And aught that wealth or lofty lineage claims.'

wherefore was I here? Lady L., in the ceremony of receiving her guests, had forgotten her friend; I was alone, and, to avoid observation, leaned over a vase of flowers; already they drooped, and, hanging their pale heads, methought they sighed for the dews of the evening – for the song of the nightingale. Another attracted my attention – strange! every flower was bright, every stem unbent; I approached wondering; no perfume was emitted from their sapless leaves lovely imposters! Alas! the sense of earth, and earthly things comes back, and I indulged an awakened train of reflections – even in a ball-room.

My meditations were suddenly interrupted, – a glittering form stood beside me – it was ROSALIE, the admired daughter of my inattentive hostess, who, in the costume of an eastern princess, was every where anxiously seeking her rustic friend. "If I may guess your thought," said she, as we walked towards the saloon, "confess, were you not (in Fancy's elysium) borne away by the enchanter, memory, to your own sylvan scenes? and were not those superban bowers transformed into flower beds? and the garlands wreathing round marble pillars – did they not resemble –" Thus rallied the playful girl in the mirth of her heart.

We have reached the saloon; the light of a thousand lamps seemed to illumine the spacious apartment, which terminated in a vista, where fanciful temples, grottos and pagodas, amid embowering trees, were revealed by an expansive arch exhibiting hues of the rainbow. Towards this attractive spot the motley crowds were all hastening, while the waving of plumes, the bending of heads, slight, – reverent, – or most obedient, formed an intelligent pantomime of the costly pageant. Rosalie in fashion's mystic mazes was perfectly initiated; the hours glided insensibly away – nor were we reminded of their lateness, till the "hum" of preparation, announced the meeting of scattered groups. Here a Turkish pacha offered

[p. 31]

his arm to a veiled nun; there an oyster-girl was escorted by a Hindoo chief; the soldier and necromancer departed together; and drowsy bacchanals, dreading the night-chill, tarried not behind; a troop of flower-girls and Swiss peasants closed the cavalcade; the farewell compliments were spoken; the last chariot rapidly whirled from the door, and we were again alone.

"'Tis thus the play ends," said Rosalie, turning languidly to me, "'Nature resumes her empire,'[97] and we will visit her in her solitude; for, although fatigued and oppressed, I feel little inclined for repose." The

---

[97] William Smellie, *The Philosophy of Natural History*, 2 vols (Edinburgh, 1799), i, 448. He writes of boys in Scottish schools who are unnaturally confined in classes and taught Latin. He says 'nature [...] during the hours of recess [...] resumes her empire, and [...] obliges the children to frisk and romp about.'

delicious coolness of the air was reviving, and we wandered towards a distant arbour, when the plaintive tones of a guitar softly stole upon the stillness of night; we listened, and ere the first strain was concluded, I felt the susceptible Rosalie tremble, as her arm rested upon mine. A voice, full of melody, accompanied the instrument with the following words:–

> "The world in its coldness is sleeping,
> The lovely and mirthful are gone,
> While I my lone vigil am keeping,
> Forsaken, but never alone.
>
> The friend of my bosom is leaning,
> (Where oft it has leant) on my breast,
> From my sorrow all others are waning,
> But this is the truest and best.
>
> Its touch has a power beguiling
> To call from the dreams of repose,
> The spirit that long hover'd, smiling,
> And sooth'd, with her softness, my woes.
>
> Though friendship and feeling may perish,
> And beauty, and truth are afar;
> Still fondly this bosom will cherish
> The gift of my love – her GUITAR."[98]

The minstrel ceased, and a moment more brought him to our view, dressed in a Spanish costume; Rosalie quickly recognised him, whom she had mourned as a wanderer in another land, returned with unshaken fidelity – her *betrothed*. The clouds of adversity, which darkened their early prospects, had passed away; and, like the faint streaks of sunrise, which now gleamed in the horizon, the dawn of future happiness smiled above them.

[p. 32]

INTERESTING MUSICAL FACTS.
(From Gardiner's Music of Nature.)

———

FORMATION OF A MUSICAL EAR. – The formation of a musical ear depends on early impressions; – infants who are placed within the constant hearing of musical sounds soon learn to appreciate them, and nurses have the merit of giving the first lessons in melody; for we learn

---

98   This ballad may be the same as one published later in America. 'The World in its coldness is Sleeping', no. 5 in *Anguera's Collection of Popular Ballads Composed and Arranged for the Guitar* (Boston, c.1849). No copy of this has been located.

from the lives of eminent composers that their early fondness for the art may be traced to the ditties of the nursery.[99]

A FINE EAR. – Mr. Darwin informs us in his Zoonomia, that the late Justice Fielding walked for the first time into his room when he once visited him, and after speaking a few words, said "This room is twenty-two feet long, eighteen wide, and twelve high" – all of which he guessed by ear.[100]

SYMPATHY OF MOTION. – It has been found that in the watch-maker's shop, the time pieces or clocks, connected with the same wall or shelf, have such sympathetic effect in keeping time, that they stop those which beat in irregular time; and if any are at rest, set agoing those which beat accurately.[101]

POWERFUL TONE OF BIRDS. – It is difficult to account for so small a creature as a bird making a tone as loud as some animals a thousand times its size; but a recent discovery has shown, that in birds the lungs have several openings communicating with corresponding air bags or cells, which fill the whole cavity of the body, from the neck downwards, and into which the air passes and repasses in the progress of breathing. This is not all, the very bones are hollow, from which air passes are conveyed to most parts of the body, even into the quills and feathers. This air being rarified by the heat of the body, adds to their levity. By forcing the air out of the body, they can dart down from the greatest heights with astonishing velocity. No doubt the same machinery forms the basis of their vocal powers, and at once solves the mystery.[102]

BARKING OF DOGS THE RESULT OF CIVILIZATION. – Dogs in a state of nature never bark, they simply whine, howl, and growl, – this explosive noise is only found among these which are domesti-cated. Sonnini speaks of the shepherds' dogs in the wilds of Egypt as not having this faculty; and Columbus found the dogs which he had previously carried to America, to have lost their propensity to barking.[103]

---

[99] Gardiner, *Music*, 3.
[100] Gardiner, *Music*, 5. Gardiner discusses how nature compensates for the loss of sight by sharpening the senses of hearing and touch. Erasmus Darwin, *Zoonomia; or the Laws of Organic Life*, 2 vols (London, 1794–96), ii (1796), 486–87. Sir John Fielding (1721–80), who became blind in 1740, was a reformer and a justice of the peace for Westminster. Philip Rawlings, 'Fielding, Sir John', *ODNB*.
[101] Gardiner, *Music*, 179.
[102] Gardiner, *Music*, 226–27.
[103] Gardiner, *Music*, 199. He refers to Sonnini: 'J'observai que les habitans de ces contrées élevées de l'Egypte nourrissoient une espèce de chien assez approchante de celle du chien de berger. Leur voix est extrémement affoiblie; ils peuvent à peine aboyer.' C. S. Sonnini, *Voyage dans la haute et basse Égypte*, 3 vols (Paris,

[p. 33]

REVIEW OF MUSIC.

———

Quatre Variations avec Introduction et Finale pour la Guitarre. Composées et dediées à CAPITAINE GEO. H. PHILLIPS, *par* F. HORETZKY. Op. 22. Aldridge.[104]

Variazione Concertante sopra un Tema originale di Rossini per Chitarra; e dedicate alla CONTESSA DI GUILPORT, *da* L. SAGRINI e G. OSBORNE. Aldridge.[105]

The first of these compositions, by Horetzky, displays, as do most of his writings, great taste, with little originality or invention. The higher attributes of writing, this composer does not appear to possess; or if he possess them, lacks the industry of properly appropriating them. Horetzky's playing, on the contrary, is of the very first description; every thing that he attempts on his instrument is agreeable, and in the highest degree finished. That he is not an original composer, therefore, is a fact which may be soon proved by the great uniformity of the majority of his compositions. Take either of them singly, and you will be highly delighted; and the one under review is one of the most delightful; but play several of them one after the other, and you will find one so much resembles the other – so much sameness – so much tautology – that they in time become tiresome and insipid. The present composition is,

[1799]), iii, 166. Christopher Columbus, on his voyages to America in the late fifteenth century, encountered mute dogs in the Caribbean. He also took dogs to use militarily with him from Spain. John Ensminger, 'From hunters to hell hounds: the dogs of Columbus and transformations of the human-canine relationship in the early Spanish Caribbean', *Colonial Latin America Review* 31:3 (2022), 354–80, at 366. It is unclear where Gardiner's notion that the dogs from Spain lost their bark originated.

104   Captain Phillips was an amateur player who, according to Giulia Pelzer's 'Memoirs', helped the Pelzer family find somewhere to live when they first arrived in London. Pelzer dedicated his *Instructions for the Spanish Guitar* [1830] to his 'friends Captain G. H. Phillips and John Hodgson'. It is not clear who John Hodgson was. Pelzer also dedicated his *Introduction and Palacca from Caraffa* for two guitars (London, n.d.) to his 'friend Capt. G. H. Phillips'.

105   The Italian guitarist Luigi Perret Sagrini (1809–74) first came to London with his father in 1829. He stayed and became a naturalised British citizen in 1845. George Alexander Osborne (1806–93) was an Irish pianist and composer; he gave concerts with Sagrini in Belgium in 1828–29. The publication reviewed here is the only known one for which they collaborated. Bernard Lewis and Robert Codwell, *In Search of Sagrini* (n.p., 2021), 49, 132, 304–5.

however, an excellent specimen of Horetzky's style; and it is dedicated to a gallant captain, whom we have heard can do justice to its difficulties.

The Concertante Variations for Guitar and Piano, by Messrs. Sagrini and Osborne, are exceedingly showy and effective, when in the hands of first-rate players. But it is the sort of music which must be played well, for in the hands of even tolerable players its best effects will be marred; such is the difficulty of surmounting its niceties.

Before we conclude our notice of these compositions, we wish to remind the publisher of the inconsistency of affixing titles in foreign languages to productions destined for the use of English people, who naturally wish, at the first glance, to discover the nature of what is offered to them for their approbation.[106]

[p. 34]

Six Rondeaux Progressifs pour la Guitarre. Composées et Dediées à MR. FRANCOIS LANGER par MAURO GIULIANI. Davis.[107]

These progressifs rondeaux (we wish that Mr. Davis would give us English) are admirably calculated for those amateurs who like to be pleased with little exertion. This is in fact real amateur music; easy, agreeable, and in a style at once familiar and natural. Who, that plays these little pieces, will stop at the threshold – or, as our correspondent "N," more classically says, at the vestibule of the guitarist's sanctuary; and who, that thus finds his way to the door of the temple, will not strive to take a peep at the inside? These pieces should be in the hands of every master, and every pupil should ask his master for them.

Fantasia for the Guitar, introducing "God Save the King." Dedicated to LORD SALTOUN *by* I. [*sic*] R. NUSKE. Boosey & Co.

Next to Sor there is, perhaps, no guitar composer who can better display his musical lore than Mr. Nuské. He is a writer for whom we have a great respect; and were he to cultivate the great talent that he undoubtedly possesses, he would, we feel confident, soon rank among the first benefactors of the instrument. The present piece will gladden the eye and ear of the first connossieur [*sic*]. The introduction, as a piece of music, is admirable, but it wants that great desideratum in an

---

[106] This may seem a strange comment given that there was a distinct preference for foreign musicians by the upper-class English at the time.

[107] This was an edition of Giuliani's opus 14, first published in Vienna c.1811. Mauro Giuliani, *Six Rondeaux Progressives pour Guitarre*, iii, *Complete Works in Facsimiles of the Original Editions*, ed. Brian Jeffery (Vienna [1811]; facs edn, with introduction by Brian Jeffery, London, 1984). The publisher Davis was probably Richard and William Davis. No copy of this edition has been located.

introduction – a few notes, like the theme, to prepare the ear for it, when it is afterwards introduced. The modulation which precedes the theme, however, is indeed masterly, and it is a fine study to those who wish to dive a little deeper into the beauties of the instrument than a mere superficial attainment. The variations are all excellent.

————

FOREIGN MUSICAL NEWS.

CONSTANTINOPLE.

————

THE reform, which the Sultan has been so industriously and zealously promoting in the manners and customs of the Turks, promises to be soon as complete in musical, as it is already in military affairs. The Turkish or rather Arabic music has given way to that of Europe, and scarcely any thing of melody or harmony is now heard in Constantinople that has not been imported from Italy. At four o'clock in the afternoon, at the moment of Gindy, the time when the public functionaries among the Ottomans retire from business a band of wind instruments is daily heard traversing the interval between the courts of the new palace. This band is called the 'Band of the Agas of the Seraglio,' and consists entirely of young Turks who have become able performers, under the instruction of M. Donizetti, brother of the composer. At first the combinations and harmony, and the overtures of Rossini, were too base for the ears of all good Musselmen; but they begin, at length to be somewhat reconciled by use, and their holy horror at whatever proceeds from the Giaours of the West is not proof against the charms of 'Di Tanti Palpiti,' and numerous other melodies of Rossini, &c.[108] Mr. Slade in his 'Travels in Turkey, Greece, &c,' just published, gives us a curious account of the knowledge of the Turkish *Capitan Pacha*, or High Admiral, in musical affairs. This officer had been a shoemaker, and knew as much of

---

[108]   Quoted from 'Foreign Musical Report, Constantinople', *The Harmonicon* 11:62 (1833), 41. Here the word 'Gindy' replaces the original 'Yindy'. The sultan, Mahmud II (1789–1839), reformed the Turkish army and was himself a musician. Among Italian musicians arriving in Constantinople was Giuseppe Donizetti (1788–1856), brother of the famous opera composer, who was appointed music instructor to the imperial band. Italian operatic culture was introduced and Western music (of non-muslims, Giaours) became accepted by Muslims (Musselmen). Vittorio Cattelan, 'The Italian Opera Culture in Constantinople During the Nineteenth Century', *Annali di Ca'Foscari* 54 (2018), 621–56, <http://dx.doi10.30687/AnnOr/2385-3042/2018/01/028>. 'Di Tanti Palpiti' was a popular aria from Rossini's opera *Tancredi*.

[p. 35]

naval matters as of the fine arts. Mr. Slade visited him on board his ship, and among other amusements got up for the English traveller, was a concert which he thus described: "In the middle of the day he (the Capitan Pacha) crept into the kennel abaft the mizen-mast, and reposed for some hours, an example which was followed by all the officers, who were stretched out on the quarter deck and covered by flags to keep off the sun. On awaking, coffee and chibouques were served. Water was then brought with a complete change of garments! and in the same narrow box, six feet by three, by two high, he washed and dressed; then came out and enjoyed the cool of the evening on his quarter deck couch, always doing me the honour to place me beside him with a chibouque, and no doubt it was a droll sight to the crew, who all gathered round to see the *Pacha* and me thus cheek by jowl. His band, consisting of as many drums and cymbals as could be collected, with two clarionets and one fife, made a noise for our benefit. It played the Hunters' Chorus in 'Der Freitschutz [*sic*],' 'Zitti Zitti', and 'Malbrook' over and over again until I fairly wished it at the bottom of the sea. I not only could not stop my ears, but was obliged to applaud liberally. Thinking that its style was more adapted to Turkish music, at the same time intending a compliment, I asked the Pacha whether it could perform any Turkish airs? "Turkish airs," he repeated with astonishment; "*Marshallah!* have you not been listening to them these two hours?" I bowed, and took refuge in ignorance.[109]

PARIS.

THE new opera, by Bellini, entitled *I Capuleti ed I Montuchi*, lately brought out here, has been attended with great success. The "*Revue Musicale*," edited by M. Fetis, thus speaks of it:– "Few operas have been more favourably received in Italy (where it was first produced). The most brilliant portion of the first act is the *cabalette* of the finale; it excited enthusiastic plaudits, and decided the success of the opera. The second and third acts consist each of only one scene, but these scenes are well conceived, and full of powerful situations. In the second act, *Romeo* challenges his rival, *Tebaldo*; both are on the point of drawing

---

[109] This is taken from: 'Diary of a Dilettante', *The Harmonicon* 11:62 (1833), 36–39, at 36–37. This, in turn, was taken from: Adolphus Slade, *Records of Travels in Turkey, Greece etc. and a Cruise of the Black Sea with the Capitan Pasha in the years 1829, 1830 and 1831*, 2 vols (London, 1833), i, 193–94. The original spelling of 'Pasha' is changed to 'Pacha'. The 'Hunters' Chorus' is from Weber's opera *Der Freischütz*. 'Zitti Zitti' is a trio from Rossini's opera *Barber of Seville*. 'Malbrook', or 'Marlbrough', was a popular French song. Pelzer's daughter, Catharina, composed a set of variations on it later in the century.

their swords. Such a situation would have inspired Rossini with one of his finest *morceaux*. Just as the rivals are about to fight, Juliet's funeral procession appears at the back of the stage. This incident might have been rendered productive of powerful effect; but here Bellini's inspiration has failed him, and there is more of declamation than real expression. In the music that is allotted to Romeo and Tebaldo, however, at the close of this scene, there occurs a passage of admirable beauty. The scene between the two lovers, after the revival of Juliet, was very fine. *Julia Grisi* was, by turns, graceful and energetic in the part of Juliet. This young lady is making rapid and extraordinary progress; her acting was exceedingly pathetic in the scene in which she throws herself at her father's feet, to implore his pardon. Rubini sang, in his usual superior style, the cavatina, which, together with the duo in the second act, contributes all that is remarkable in the part of Tebaldo."[110]

[p. 36]

Musical Intelligence, Chit-Chat, &c.

KING'S THEATRE, FEB. 16. – As we are anticipated by all the daily and weekly papers, in giving an account of the opera and the drama, we shall not be guilty of the bad taste of giving lengthened details on subjects, which, to our readers, at least, must of course be notorious, and therefore stale and unprofitable. We are further anxious to beat out a new path for ourselves, choosing rather to be *alone* in the opinions that we may venture, than to follow in the wake of those, who, having set up their idol in some particular performer, worship it to the exclusion of all other just claimants. But when we have no novelty of this description to lay before our readers, we intend giving, in an abridged form, the various and oftentimes contradictory opinions of the public press, imagining that our readers, like ourselves, will sometimes relish a dish, which, like many in the culinary art, is the more piquant for the very reason of containing many opposite ingredients. The horizon of the musical critic is not very limited, particularly if he include the thousand-and-one semi-public concerts which take place in a single season in this great metropolis. But the real musical

---

[110]   This is taken and translated from extracts in: François Joseph Fétis, 'Nouvelles de Paris, Théatre Royal Italian, Première Représentation de e Capuleti ed i Montecchi', *Revue Musicale* 50 (1833), 397–99. The Belgian, François Joseph Fétis (1784–1871), was an influential critic and founder of the Parisian *Revue Musicale*. Bellini's opera *Il Capuletti ed i Montecchi*, first performed in Venice in 1830, was received with less enthusiasm in Paris and London in 1833 than it had been in Italy. Julian Marshall, 'Bellini', in *Dictionary*, ed. Grove, i (1879), 212–14. Giulia (Julia) Grisi (1811–69) was an Italian soprano. Elizabeth Forbes, 'Grisi, Giulia', *GMO*.

critics themselves are truly circumscribed in numbers; if we say there are a dozen good ones, we are really overrating their numbers. How frequently these "doctors" disagree, it will be our future province to show; at the same time, we will, without any arrogant presumption, endeavour to put the reader right, by showing the fallacy or truth of the opinions of all parties. In announcing this intention, we shall only give it its own due importance, and not encroach on space, that we may be more profitably employed. At the opening of the King's Theatre on the 16th was performed Rossini's Cenerentola, on which occasion Madame Boccabadati (a long name, but very short personage), made her *debut* as Prima Donna.[111] Most of the daily papers awarded her a very qualified degree of praise. The Literary Gazette says – "With respect to her musical accomplishments, their display on Saturday evening induced a comparison far from favourable, with those whom we have been accustomed to hear in this opera: her voice appear to be of a thin, weak quality; pretty in its softer tones, but decidedly ineffective where power, either of execution or sustension is required. The opening ditty was feebly given."[112] The Athenæum's opinion is, that "her voice, like most flexible voices, is of a thin quality: her intonation is generally perfect, and her style is purely Italian, rather meretricious in ornament perhaps, but expressive. Her species of voice is properly denominated, *voce di testa*,[113] and it has little power below F; and we observed that some melodies were not only transposed, but disguised by inversion. However, altogether it was a respectable performance, and her reception was very flattering."[114] To these accounts we may add, that Madame Boccabadati is a lady of rank, and a very estimable private character. All the papers seem to have discovered simultaneously, that De Begnis is getting old: for example, Times – "De Begnis played admirably, but he is no longer young."[115] Athenæum – "De Begnis is no longer young; but his acting is always good."[116] Turn to the Literary Gazette, and we read – "De Begnis is a funny fellow, but he did not make a hit in the *Magnifico*. He is growing old"![117]

KING'S THEATRE, FEB 26. – Rossini's opera, "La Donna del Lago," has been played here this evening, De Meric sustaining the character

---

[111] The Italian soprano, Luigia Boccabadati (1800–50), took the role of Angelina. Elizabeth Forbes, 'Boccabadati, Luigia', *GMO*.

[112] 'Drama', *Literary Gazette* 840 (1833), 123–25, at 124.

[113] Head voice, singing high notes that are not strained.

[114] 'Music', *The Athenæum* 278 (1833), 124.

[115] Giuseppe de Begnis (1793–1849) was an Italian bass who had created the role of Dandini in Rossini's opera *La Cenerentola*. Elizabeth Forbes, 'Begnis, Giuseppe de', *GMO*. This quotation has not been found in *The Times*.

[116] 'Music', *The Athenæum* 278 (1833), 124.

[117] 'Drama', *Literary Gazette* 840 (1833), 123–25, at 124. The reference to De Begnis growing old is not in the original review in the *Literary Gazette*. The sentence has been added here.

of *Elena*, and Donzelli that of *Roderic Dhu*.[118] The former was not in excellent voice; she sung too flat throughout the night. Her best effort was the *finale*, which afforded the opportunity of displaying her power in her favourite syncopated passages. Donzelli sang with great care, and was repeatedly honoured with applause. Arigotti, whom we remember last season in very trifling parts, was tried this evening in the character of James or Hubert; he was considerably improved in his singing, and if he would only open his mouth, so as to render his articulation louder and more distinct, and endeavour to throw *some* animation into his acting – for at present he gives it none whatever, he might be of use in the general cast of operas.[119] Mademoiselle Schiasetti, from the Theatre Italien, Paris, made her first appearance here in the character of *Malcolm Græme*.[120] To a thorough acquaintance with her profession in all its essentials of acting, stage trick, &c., this lady adds the possession of a good voice. Her style, however, is bald and disjointed. She has a knack of overcoming any difficulties, by manœuvring through, rather than singing them. Her figure is very small; her face possesses much animation, and her acting, on the whole, is easy and graceful. The opera, with the exception of the spirited scene, "the gathering of the clans," went off rather tamely. The ballet of *Faust* closed the performances, *somewhere about two o'clock*.[121]

[p. 37 – Issue 4, April 1833]

OBSERVATIONS ON THE MUSIC OF

THE FIRST NUMBER OF THE GIULIANIAD.

As the Guitar is still in its infancy in England, the great object of the Editor of this work has been to select Airs, which, whilst they are easy, are also good practice from their correct harmonies. The Giulianiad indeed may be resorted to, the instant a pupil has gone through an instruction book, many of the airs being expressly adapted for this purpose. The First Number contains:– 1. A March, extremely easy, in

---

[118] Domenico Donzelli (1790–1873) was an Italian tenor. Elizabeth Forbes, 'Donzelli, Domenico', *GMO*.

[119] Arigotti was a tenor who at this time performed with De Begnis's Italian Opera Company. 'Death of Signor de Begnis', *Musical World* 24:34 (1849), 529.

[120] Mademoiselle Schiasetti was a mezzo soprano and was probably Italian. 'King's Theatre', *Morning Advertiser*, 27 February 1833. The only references to appearances in London are from the early part of 1833.

[121] It was usual for operas to be followed by ballet performances, making for a long evening. In addition, on some occasions ballet performances were inserted in the operas. Jennifer Hall-Witt, 'Representing the Audience in the Age of Reform: Critics and the Elite at the Italian Opera in London', in *Music and British Culture 1785–1914*, ed. Christina Bashford and Leanne Langley (Oxford, 2006), 121–44, at 142.

imitation of a band heard at a distance. 2. An easy Waltz. 3. A Tyrolienne Air. 4. A Landler (also easy). 5. A Rondo, by a Lady. 6. A pretty Theme, played by Paganini, (easy); and, 7. The Favorite Waltz of the Queen of Prussia ;– these occupy four pages. Page 5 commences with an extract from Giuliani's 3rd Concerto, which, as a composition has elicited the praise of Hummel and Czerny, which latter composer has adapted the whole of the Concerto for the Piano-Forte. Pages 6, 7, and 8, are also filled with some Classical Music by Giuliani. Pages 9, 10, 11, and 12, contain a Song, (with English words), which has become very popular.

THE MUSIC OF THE SECOND NUMBER.

The 1st Air of this number is a Polish quick March. 2. and 3. French Airs. 4. A Swiss Air. 5. A Waltz by Giuliani. 6. My Lodging is on the cold ground, newly arranged. 7. Rousseau's Dream. 8. The Captive Knight to his Guitar ;– these occupy four pages, and are all easy. The three next pages are occupied with Classical Music by Sor. The 1st. (page 17), an Andante Maestoso, with some beautiful harmonies. Pages 18 and 19, a delicate Theme, Andante Pastorale, inserted by permission of Mr. Welsh of the Argylle [*sic*] Rooms, whose copyright it is. Pages 20 and 21 are occupied by a lively French Song, with words; 22 and 23, a German song by Weber, with English and German words, written expressly for this work by Mr. Ball; and the last page contains a very beautiful Waltz by Sor.

THE MUSIC OF THE THIRD NUMBER.

The first four pages of this Number are also easy, containing six pieces. Page 29 contains a little German Song, with English words written expressly for this work. This Song is very pretty, and really so easy that the accompaniment could be played by a person who has only taken up the Guitar for a week. Pages 30 and 31 contain some Classical Music by Giuliani and Sor. Pages 32 and 33, Song, with English words, written expressly for this work, entitled, "The captive Knight to his Guitar." An Italian Song, with Italian and German words, occupies pages 34 and 35, and the Music concludes with an easy German Song and words. Each of the three first Numbers contains 12 pages of letter-press, which it is presumed the professed Guitarist will find instructive as well as amusing.

OBSERVATIONS ON THE MUSIC OF

THE PRESENT NUMBER (FOUR).

Page 37 contains an Andantino and Larghetto (the latter in A minor) both by Sor, extracted from Sor's 24 Exercises, Op. 35, published by Johanning and Co. The whole of these Exercises we can strongly recommend. They are, as our extracts will show, easy and progressive; but although easy, the harmonies are correct and classical. Page 38 contains a Swiss Waltz, a Galopade, and a German Air. The Swiss Waltz contains harmonics in imitation of the peasants' pastoral music. Page 39 contains two Movements by Giuliani, each of which, whilst they are easy, will be found to exhibit his peculiar taste for melody. Page 40 contains an extract from Kreutzer's Fantasia of God save the King. The harmonies of the Theme will be found excellent, without being difficult, and the variation brilliant and easy. Page 41, a German Song with English words. This pensive and plaintive Air will be found to require much expression, and the melody to be sung slow. The *Tempo di Minuetto* of page 42 has been sent us by an amateur of Jersey, who, we hope, from the specimen sent us, will prosecute his studies on this instrument. The remainder of this page is occupied by the original Air of "The Alpensanger," which has become so popular in London. The two Waltzes in page 43 require great taste and expression in their execution. The French Song, with words, "Le Souvenir du Pays," is extremely easy and beautiful. "Le Petit Tambour," which occupies pages 46 and 47, we have never seen arranged for the Guitar in this country, and therefore have introduced it as being a very popular melody. The music closes with a Serenade by Weber, with English words by Mr. Ball.

––––––––

Number 5 of this work will contain original compositions by many of the first professors now resident in London.

[p. 38]

ON PUBLIC PERFORMANCES ON THE GUITAR.

––––––––

PEOPLE hearing a performance on the guitar in a large room, for the first time, are generally disappointed. The reason is obvious: not taking into consideration the limited powers of the instrument, so far as loudness is concerned, they misdirect their attention from the merits of the instrument, and fix it on its want of power, which is its greatest defect. The merits of the guitar to the ear, are like those of a miniature to the eye, they both court the most searching scrutiny and minutest examination. Heard or held afar off, where the nicest delicacy of shade and tint are not discoverable, they both lose their greatest charm. The resemblance is really so true and striking between them, that with the assistance of a very little imagination, we may pursue this likeness in almost every direction. The delicate touches of the miniature are as delicately produced by the fair guitarist. The tint that is so beautifully shaded, and imperceptibly blended with the other colours, is like the last sweet gentle chord, produced by her taper fingers, gradually dying into silence.

From the striking similitude we may, as the Westminster Review expresses it, as well line the stage with miniatures, and view them from the upper boxes, as condemn an instrument that possesses every variety

87

and gradation of shade, because it is not equal in noise to a full orchestra, or to Mr. Bochsa and his twelve pupils on thirteen harps.[122] This is so unfair in musicians, that for the sake of analogy, we will compare a miniature, exquisitely painted, to a fine oil painting by Raphael or Rubens. Suppose, if we were to say of Rubens, this picture is very fine at a distance, but come to minutely examine it, we find that it is not at all comparable to our miniature. Suppose, on the other hand, we were to view the miniature at a distance, and see nothing of those innumerable beauties which can only be seen by a close inspection, what would be said of such a critic, were he to make such a comparison? Why, to make such a blunder as to compare the two, he would be deservedly laughed at for his pains. And yet such, unaccountably, is the conduct of the musical critic with regard to the guitar. He compares the miniature to the oil painting; he judges of the guitar by a piano-forte, or church organ! We marvel at the bad taste so often exhibited by these gentlemen, and the only excuse we can make for them, is that they have never heard the instrument well played, or never saw any excellent guitar composition.

[p. 39]

It is the high test and proof of the genius of the guitar, that in all ages it has been regarded with partiality and even affection. This instrument possesses that genius, or it would long since have ceased to charm; and is an instrument then that is capable of every possible variety of tone, expression, and modulation; an instrument that for more than three thousand years (for we have good authority for this fact from Egyptian antiquities) has held an uncontrolled dominion over the best feelings of human nature, and that now reigns favourite over the greater part of Europe. Is the instrument of which old Macedonius, in the Greek Anthology, with an undying fire, thus speaks, to be consigned to oblivion by modern vulgar criticism?

> There hang my lyre! this aged hand no more
> Shall wake the strings to rapture known before.
> Farewell, ye chords! *ye verse-inspiring powers,*
> *Accept the solace of my former hours!*
> Be gone to youths, ye instruments of song!
> For crutches only to the old belong.*
>
> *Bland's Translation.*[123]

---

[122] [Thompson], 'Musical Periodicals', 472. The harpist Nicholas Bochsa (1789–1856) organised a concert on 21 February 1823 which included a performance by thirteen of his pupils playing thirteen harps. The item was criticised for the inordinate amount of time spent arranging the instruments. 'Drury Lane Theatre', *Caledonian Mercury*, 24 February 1823.

[123] Macedonius, 'The Poet's Offering', in *Collections from the Greek Anthology*, ed. Robert Bland (London, 1813), 424.

Is, we ask, such an instrument to be decried in the estimation of our fair countrywomen, by the irony, envy, or ignorance of the mere spiniteer?[124] We say the *mere spiniteer*, for the true piano-forte player, the real musician, will ever speak with respect of the peculiar properties of an instrument: as well may we find fault with the piano-forte for not producing those nice gradations of sound which the guitar possesses, as with the guitar for not expressing the strength and force of the piano-forte.

It is from the cause of imagination being stronger developed (as the phrenologists would say) in woman than in man, that the guitar has been regarded with so much affection by ladies in all countries.[125] The instrument is so obedient to the expression of their feelings,– it echoes their sportive gaiety, their little griefs, calm tranquillity, and noble and elevated thoughts, with such nice precision, that it would seem to be a natural appendage and true barometer of the state of their own fair bosoms. An instrument seems fully conscious of the difference between struck by the hammer, or a maiden's fingers. In the former, as on the piano-forte, the effect is produced at second or third hand. The hand touches the keys – the keys the hammer, and the hammer the wire. In the latter, as on the guitar, the feeling is instantaneous and electrical; the string is touched by the finger, and

*The coincidence of the sentiments here expressed to Pope's Translation of Horace's Ode to Venus, inserted in our last number, will hardly fail to strike the reader.[126]

[p. 40]

simultaneously conveys the true impression of the heart. Who that has once felt the true sentiment of love, but does not know the impression of the mind in the mere touch of the beloved object? Who that has thus felt will readily comprehend the meaning, when we attribute to the strings of the guitar the agent which receives and conveys with

---

[124] A spiniteer was probably a spinet player. The word is not in the *Oxford English Dictionary*. A spinet was a small harpsichord used in domestic settings.

[125] The pseudo-science of phrenology was popular in the 1820s and 1830s. It put forward the belief that the intellect of women was inferior to that of men because their brains were thought to be generally smaller. M. T. Parssinen, 'Popular Science and Society: The Phrenology Movement in Early Britain', *Journal of Social History* 8:1 (1974), 1–20, at 7. It was suggested that this lower intellect of women meant that their 'powers of reflection were not so great; they do not extend their reasonings beyond the range of the visible world, nor make any great or daring excursions into the regions of fancy'. 'Of the Female Character', *Phrenology Journal and Miscellany* 2 (1824–25), 275–88, at 278. The writer in *The Giulianiad* may have misunderstood the idea.

[126] 'Horace's Cithara or Guitar', *TG* 1:3 (1833), 25–26, at 26.

unerring fidelity the state of the performer's feelings. The taper fingers of the lady too are admirably adapted for this instrument; those of a man being larger and more clumsy, he finds a difficulty in introducing them between the strings, and hence the effect of jarring, and sometimes an indistinctness in the production of chords. The diminutive size in general of the fingers of a lady allows her never to feel this obstacle: they find a ready ingress and egress, although the finger board may be narrower, and the strings consequently closer together,– and all these matters contribute to a clear and perfect performance.

But in public exhibitions on the guitar there is one great fault in which performers generally indulge, and of which they appear to us to be wholly unconscious. Playing generally in a large room they naturally wish that every part of the audience should hear, and in doing this they wholly mistake the manner in which it can be successfully effected. They pull the strings with so much force, for the purpose of producing a *loud* tone, that, although they produce more noise, they, in fact, lessen the real tone of the instrument. Their want of knowledge in acoustics is here verified. It is not the *largeness* of tone that travels furthest and quickest, it is the *quality* of it. A mere whisper, if the tone be sweet and compact, will find its way to every corner of a large theatre, while an overstrained string will produce a tone which will fall, so to speak, dead and lifeless.* By these observations we would have performers fully conscious of the powers of their instrument – for, of course, some have a greater tone than others – and not to tax it beyond its strength. On the other hand, an audience must not expect too much; they must not expect to hear from our little instrument, a tone as large as that produced by the discharge of the monster mortar at Antwerp.[127] Let them be as critical as they like on its quality of tone and expression, but expect not the roar of the lion when the dove puts forth its plaintive voice. Expect not the force of an oil painting when a miniature is shown you. The guitar, as we have before said, may be regarded as a miniature, which the more we scrutinize and examine,– the more we listen and attend – the better we can judge of its sweetness, its unerring intonation, and its heart-thrilling pathos.

*Take, for instance, Paganini's tone on the violin, which is by no means large, but earnest, intense, and searching. – Hear again, Madame Stockhausen's voice, which, although delicate, is every particle of it, real tone.[128]

---

[127] A large mortar was used by the Belgians in the siege of Antwerp in 1832 during the war of Belgian independence. 'The Monster Mortar of Antwerp', *The Mechanics' Magazine, Register, Journal, and Gazette* 18:500 (1833), 374–78, at 374.

[128] Madame Stockhausen (1803–77) was an Alsatian soprano. Robert Pascall, 'Stockhausen [née Schmuck], Margarethe', *GMO*.

[p. 41]

REVIEW OF MUSIC.

Fantasie pour la Guitarre, Composée et dédiée à MADEMOISELLE EMELIE DUBONT, *par* W. NEULAND. Op. 5. Joanning [*sic*] and Co.

Introduction et Variations pour la Guitarre, sur un Motif de l'Opera, "La Famille Swisse de Weigl." *Composées et dédiées a son Ami* F. PELZER, *par* W. NEULAND. Op. 7. Duff and Co.[129]

As long as Mr. Neuland writes for the guitar, so long shall we have fine music. Contrary to the opinion which Englishmen in general have formed of foreigners, (and with some of them a foreign name denotes musical abilities) this talented man is rather under-rated than sufficiently appreciated. It is true, he has not been a long time in this country, but the impression he has made to every musician with whom we are acquainted, is, that his genius is applicable to the composition of any kind of music, and universally adapted for every instrument. The Fantasie now under notice is alike creditable to the composer and to the little instrument which can produce such effects. Let the piano-forte player cast his eye over this composition, and if, after he has examined it, he is still of opinion that an instrument capable of pourtraying, with ease, such harmonies, is "trifling and superficial," we will forego all future pleasure in its performance. Let him look at the first eight bars of the introduction, and the third variation, and ask himself if he can write his opinion in the words of his label, "trifling and superficial."

The introduction and variations on an air from "The Swiss Family," are not so difficult as the preceding. The *fantasie*, we take it, was written for professors – this for the select class (we wish they were more numerous) of experienced amateurs. We may point out the introduction and *sixth* variation as exhibiting a combination of good taste and judgement. The *finale* produces some effects, purely dramatic, (see the last two lines) a quality which we should like to see more fully displayed and amplified by this gentleman's pen.

———

THE MINSTREL'S LAY.

The following verses should have been inserted in the last Number of the Giulianiad, as they were written expressly for the little Song at page 29 of our Music. They will be found in a second edition of the Number; but as the majority of our readers are not in possession of them, we here reproduce them.

[129]   No copies of either of these pieces of music have been located.

I.
Lightly and cheerily,
Singing right merrily,
I, a poor minstrel gay,
Through the world find my way.

II.
Sweet is my shelter free,
Under the greenwood tree;
Sweet is the draught I take,
Fresh from the silver lake.

III.
Sunshine and friendly cheer,
These all my toils endear;
Oh! and all else above,
Smiles from my own true love.

[p. 42]

Musical Intelligence, Chit-Chat, &c.

Madame de Meric no longer forms one of the opera company. This is a serious loss to the manager, as well as to the public, by whom she is deservedly admired.

Captain Polhill comes into a fortune of £80,000 by the death of his mother. His loss at Drury Lane Theatre, for the last three years, has been about £30,000.

Planché is now writing words to the last of Chelard's operas, for Drury Lane.

The Drury Lane German company begin their season shortly after the Easter holidays.[130]

Miss Mounsey's concert takes place at the City of London Tavern on the 19th of April. The bill announces some attractive names; for example, Miss Paton, Miss Inverarity, Phillips, Wilson, and some others, among

---

[130] These news items were reported in both *The Standard* and the *Morning Post* on 26 March 1833. The singer De Méric appears to have had a difference of opinion with Pierre Laporte, the manager of the King's Theatre, in late March which was soon resolved. 'King's Theatre', *Morning Chronicle*, 25 March 1833; 'Musical', *Morning Post*, 9 April 1833. The playwright James Planché (1796–1880) translated into English Chelard's opera *The Students of Jena*. 'Fashionable World', *Morning Post*, 26 March 1833. Chelard conducted German operas at Drury-lane Theatre with singers from the German opera company. 'Gossip on Musical Matters', *Court Magazine and Belle Assemblée* 2:5 (1833), 258.

the vocalists; and Mori, Dressler, Wilman, and the Miss Mounseys will perform on their respective instruments. Mr. Nelson Weippert leads.[131]

A concert also, of great attraction to the guitarist, will take place at the Opera Concert Room on the 15th of May. Mr. Dressler, the celebrated flutist, and Mr. Pelzer, the guitar player, will give it conjointly.

Miss Bruce, a lady of great musical talent, and who is patronised by many of the musical aristocracy, intends giving three musical soirées, at her residence in Great Marlborough Street. They take place May 9, 20, and June 3. Many other concerts are announced, but we must leave them all till our next.[132]

KING'S THEATRE.– As nothing in the shape of novelty has taken place in the Italian Opera since our last, we shall not take up the time of our readers by the mere recapitulation of opinions which they are already in possession of. We regret to add that the German company, at this theatre, will not bear a comparison – in point of first-rate singing – with that of last season. The loss of Haitzinger and Madame Devrient is most sensibly felt. Neither can we call it prudent management of M. Laporte, that he produced "Der Freizchutz [*sic*]" for the five hundredth time, as the opera for the opening of his campaign. "Beethoven's Fidelio," if he had singers to do it justice, which, we doubt, and which an English audience, last season, was just beginning to understand and appreciate, would have been infinitely more attractive.

The King and Queen honoured the performance of "Der Freizchutz" with their presence on Thursday, the 21st March. His Majesty was strictly incognito, and sat at the back of the box. The Queen was loudly cheered, and acknowledged the tribute by repeatedly bowing. The house was respectably filled, but not crowded.

DRURY LANE THEATRE. – A sort of half-balletic, half operatic performance took place here on Saturday, the 17th March, which has

---

[131] The first Miss Mounsey named here was Ann (1811-91) who was a composer and organist. See Jane Bernstein, 'Mounsey, Ann', *GMO*. Her younger sister, Elizabeth Mounsey (1819–1905), also took part in this concert and was also an organist; she held the post of organist at St Peter's Church, Cornhill, from 1834 until 1882. Frederick George Edwards, 'Elizabeth Mounsey', *Musical Times* 46:753 (1905), 718–21. In addition, Elizabeth played the guitar and was a pupil of Ferdinand Pelzer. The singers listed were all well-known. Nicholas Mori (1796/7–1840) was a leading violinist of the day. Keith Horner, revised by Christina Bashford, 'Mori Family', *GMO*. Rafael Dressler (1784–1835) was a Hungarian flute player. Richard Rokstro, *The Flute* (London, 1890), 578–79. He also taught guitar. Thomas Willman (1784–1840) was a clarinet player. Pamela Weston, 'Willman, Thomas Lindsey', *GMO*. Nelson Weippert (d.1834) was a pianist. 'Mr. Nelson Weippert', *The Standard*, 12 August 1834. The City of London Tavern was in Bishopsgate and was sometimes used for concerts. Alec Hyatt King, 'The London Tavern: a Forgotten Concert Hall', *Musical Times* 127:1720 (1986), 382–85, at 383.

[132] Miss Bruce, not her real name, was a soprano who made her debut in London in 1830. 'Theatres', *Morning Post*, 1 February 1830.

been christened by the designation of a "Ballet Opera," and further called "the Maid of Cashmere." The plot, taken from Goethe's well-known poem, which is again founded on the original eastern legend of a god sent to wander on earth, until he finds a beautiful girl who loves him with pure and devoted affection.* The music is by Auber, and is better known to us by the title of "*Le Dieu et la Bayadère.*"[133] It is light and pretty, but certainly not equal to former efforts of this original composer. The singing, however, in "the Maid of Cashmere," is a secondary affair, Mademoiselle Duvernay's dancing occupying almost undivided attention. She alone can be pronounced perfectly successful.[134]

*Miss Landon has beautifully poetized this subject in her Improvisatrice. The following passage will be agreeable to those who have seen Madame Duvernay as the Maid of Cashmere.

> "But there was one who 'mid them shone
> A planet lovely and alone –
> A rose, one flower amid many,
> But still the loveliest of any!
> Though fair her arm as the moonlight,
> Others might raise an arm as white:
> Though light her foot as music's fall,
> Others might be as musical;
> But where were such dark eyes as hers?
> So tender, yet withal so bright,
> As the dark orbs had in their smile
> Mingled the light of day and night.
> And where was that wild grace which shed,
> A loveliness o'er every tread,
> A beauty shining through the whole,
> Something which spoke of heart and soul."[135]

[p. 43 – Issue 5, July 1833]

TO THE EDITOR OF THE GIULIANIAD.

SIR,

I beg to enclose you the annexed little piece,* which I trust will prove acceptable to your numerous Subscribers.

---

[133] Auber (1782–1871) was a French composer; the opera was first performed in Paris in 1830. Herbert Schneider, 'Auber, Daniel-François-Esprit', *GMO*.

[134] Pauline Duvernay (1813–94) was a French ballet dancer.

[135] Letitia Elizabeth Landon, *The Improvisatrice; and other Poems* (London, 1824), 163–64.

Nothing, I assure you, will give me greater pleasure than to see THE GIULIANIAD successful – a work, that must eventually, as well as beneficially, be in the hands of every lover of the Guitar.

I have the honour to be, Sir,

Yours obediently,

J.A. NUSKE.

26th April, 1833.

54, WILLIAM STREET, REGENT'S PARK.

* At Pages 56–7 of our Music.[136]

––––––––

THE ΚΙΘΑΡΑ[137] OF THE ANCIENTS – THE MODERN GUITAR.

TO THE EDITOR.

SIR,

Dr. Burney, in noticing the representation of a musical instrument of two strings, with a neck to it, (much resembling the Calascione still in common use throughout the kingdom of Naples) which is to be found upon an Egyptian obelisk lying broken in the Campus Martius, at Rome, whither it was brought by Augustus – observes that "this instrument seems to merit a particular description, not only from its great antiquity, but from its form." He adds, "indeed, I have never yet been able to discover, in any remains of Greek sculpture, an instrument furnished with a neck; and Father Montfaucon says, that, in examining the representations of near five hundred ancient lyres, harps, and citharas, he never met with one in which there was any contrivance for shortening strings, during the time of performance, as by a neck and finger-board."[138]

Of the first mentioned instrument, indeed, Dr. Burney gives another representation from an antique painting in a sepulchral grotto, near the ancient Tarquinia; and Colonel Thompson in his admirable "Instructions to my Daughter for playing on the Enharmonic Guitar," chap. 28, says, "instruments of the guitar kind with necks, are found represented in the tombs at Thebes, on the Egyptian obelisk at Rome, and in various other remains of remote antiquity."[139] But he does not invalidate the statement of Dr. Burney and Montfaucon as to the absence of the representation of any instrument with a neck and finger-board in Grecian sculpture.

---

[136]   J. A. Nuske, *Thema by Mozart, arranged for the Guitar with Variations*, *TG* 1:5 (1833), Music 56–57.

[137]   Kithara.

[138]   Charles Burney, *A General History of Music*, 4 vols (London, 1776–89), i (1776), 205. Bernard de Monfaucon was a Benedictine monk and scholar. A calascione was a guitar with two or three strings found in southern Italy.

[139]   [T. P. Thompson], *Instructions to my Daughter for playing on the Enharmonic Guitar* (London, 1829), 22. An enharmonic guitar allows for notes that are enharmonically equivalent, such as C♯ and D♭, to be played with slightly different pitches.

Colonel Thompson, indeed, adds, "and what was known in Egypt must have been conveyed, along with other knowledges, to Greece and Rome." The truth of this, however, rests on something else than such induction and conclusion: Montfaucon and Dr. Burney, it will now appear, merely overlooked such representations in Grecian sculpture; for in No. 35 of the Fifth Room of the Townley marbles in the British Museum – a sarcophagus on the front of which various figures of Cupid and Psyche are represented – may be seen a figure, not of the Dichord, like that alluded to by Dr. Burney and Colonel Thompson, but of a five or six-stringed guitar, in which the length of the body is equal only to about one-third of the neck, and its breadth rather less, in which five or six strings may be traced on the finger-board – though there appears to be something like four pegs at the end of the neck, and in which the hands are applied very beautifully to the strings.[140]

As this is probably a correct representation of the κιθάρα of the ancients, it cannot be uninteresting to the readers of THE GIULIANIAD, to have it pointed out to them.

DONALD WALKER.

[p. 44]

GUITAR PROFESSORS, AND GUITAR MAKERS AND SELLERS.

───────

As this work was commenced with the avowed intention not only to disseminate, as widely as possible, the capabilities of the guitar, but also with a view to benefit the player of every description, whether amateur, professor, or music-seller, we shall take an early opportunity of giving our readers some information on the subjects which head the present article. We shall have a little to say to each of these personages; and, in giving a word or two of advice touching certain matters, shall, perchance, suggest a few alterations, whereby *they* will, most certainly, not be injured, and the public, for whom we write, and to whom we address ourselves, be materially benefited.

---

[140]   Many of the antiquities of the collector Charles Townley (1737–1805) were sold to the British Museum after his death. They were housed in a new wing of Montagu House, the British Museum. This new wing was named the 'Townley Gallery' and was opened to the public in 1808. Montagu House and the Gallery were demolished in the mid nineteenth century and replaced by the Museum building that stands today. The sarcophagus, Museum number 1805.0703.132, depicts a winged female figure playing a pandurium, or guitar-like instrument. It is not currently on display. B. F. Cook, *The Townley Marbles* (London, 1985), 60–62. *Sarcophagus*, https://www.britishmuseum.org/collection/object/G_1805-0703-132. [accessed 1 August 2023].

Our correspondent "N," in the 3d Number, complains, with some truth, of the "quack masters" of the guitar; the gentry, as he terms them, who profess to teach the instrument in half-a-dozen lessons![141] The inference from which he would deduce, is, that these quack masters being more numerous than the genuine guitar teachers, they consequently infect a large portion of would-be-players with the idea, that the guitar is merely fit for an accompaniment to a song, and nothing more. This is, to a certain extent, true, but there is one portion of the subject which he entirely overlooks. He does not take into consideration that the quack is generally the active, plodding, persevering man of business; and the man of talent and genius — the true professor, too often possesses the reverse of these qualities.

It is *Addison*, in his "Spectator," we believe, who tells the story of the progress through life of a great genius; and one of those heavy, stupid dunderheads, whose only merit is that of a steady and constant application. They were both barristers; and the sequel and merit of the story is, to shew that the snail-like, plodding, stupid fellow was a more successful man of the world than the bright idle wit. "The race is not always to the swift."[142] It is not enough, therefore, that the man of talent and education should be a man of genius; he must also be active and indefatigable in his profession, and never think his time misspent or ill employed, when conveying his instructions to his pupils. How often is it the case, that the finest player on an instrument, is the worst possible teacher? And what is the reason — but that he does not possess patience, and give a proper direction to his

[p. 45]

knowledge. There cannot be a question, that were the man of talent as industrious and persevering as the quack, the latter would stand no chance in the field of competition. But as long as the charlatan is *active*, and the man of genius *passive*, so long shall we hear similar complaints to those of our correspondent.

There is another way, also, in which the public are cozened with regard to their masters and their instruments; and that is by music-sellers. A lady wishes her daughter to learn the guitar, and forthwith proceeds to a music-shop to purchase an instrument. Ignorant as she must be of the nature of its construction, she relies solely on the probity of the music-seller, who sells her an instrument which he calls a very good one. He is asked for a master; the seller, of course, recommends a master who will

---

[141] Anon, 'Sor', *TG* 1:3 (1833), 27–28.

[142] The Bible, Ecclesiastes 9:11. This is quoted in [Joseph Addison], 'Untitled', *The Spectator* 293 (1712), 587. It is not clear where the story of the two barristers originated.

praise his guitar; and thus, by connivance, the master, in return, completes the obligation; and it generally happens the guitar is worth as much as the master, and the master as much as the guitar – just nothing. The consequence of this is, that the daughter is merely shewn a few chords, and not finding in the instrument the beauties and capabilities she expected, throws down the instrument in disgust, and straightway forms one of those who cry out that "she does not like the guitar."

How different is the proceeding of a respectable professor. In the very first lesson he seldom fails to make his pupil in love with her guitar. The master has chosen an instrument from some respectable seller or maker, and has consequently adopted that one which is best adapted to his pupil's fingers. The aptitude of the player, therefore, in the first starting, is materially facilitated. Where, as in the other case, all was awkwardness and difficulty, here is (if not grace) ease and facility. At every lesson she finds greater beauties, until at length, when a little execution begets confidence, and her feelings expression, she feels a delight which no other instrument is capable of eliciting in so short, or retaining for so long, a time. A guitar ought to suit the hand, as a shoe does the foot; and the master who sets no value on such a trifle, does not yet possess the secret of inspiring the pupil with a love for this peculiar sort of music.

The English guitar makers have yet a vast deal to learn in the construction and finishing of their instruments. All beginnings are rude and unpolished; a few years ago there was not a guitar manufacturer throughout London. There are many now, and some of them deserving of attention and recommendation. We shall take an opportunity of speaking of these, and recommending those makers, those sellers, and those professors, in whose respective abilities confidence may be placed.

[p. 46]

PUBLIC CONCERTS.

———

It would far exceed the limits of this Magazine, were we to detail the merits of all concerts which take place at this season of the year. We must leave that to our piano-forte contemporaries, in whose more peculiar province it would appear to be.*

It will be meeting the demand of our readers, we believe, if we give a slight sketch and account of those concerts wherein the guitar has formed a principal feature; but we must, nevertheless, not be misunderstood in even mentioning these. The guitar has many claims to the patronage of the musician; and we wish to advocate those claims, not on slippery and meretricious grounds – not on a foundation of sand – but on grounds of a firm and substantial nature – on such a foundation that the candid musician shall give his hearty and willing sanction to.

In one word, then, the guitar, as an instrument for public performance in a large concert-room, is seen and heard to great disadvantage; and, so far as its capabilities are then and there heard and seen, – coming immediately in contact and contrast, as it there does, with more powerful instruments, – it a poor and sorrowful idea of many fascinating qualities which it possess gives but when otherwise employed.[143]

A professor of the guitar, no doubt, is as anxious to display his abilities on this instrument as the violinist or flute player; and so far as the right goes, he has an equal pretension. If he were to be prohibited entirely from exhibiting its capabilities before the public, how are the public to judge? and how are pupils to be made? But it is precisely these that make our argument. It is because these capabilities are *not* displayed, and because the public consequently can *not* justly judge of its powers, that we object to its display in a large theatre or room. A performer may possess sterling abilities, and two-thirds of an audience, who are too distant to hear, not be able to appreciate them. Yet, with all these objections (which, as truth is our only object, we have stated frankly and candidly,) it would appear a most cruel *dictum* to exclude for ever the guitarist from the public. We will conclude this part of our subject, therefore, with recommending all those who are really lovers of the instrument, to attend as early as possible at any concert where the guitar is to be played, and obtain as near a seat to the

*The PHILHARMONICON, a monthly piano-forte work, is the only one we have seen that gives a full detail of concerts.[144]

[p. 47]

orchestra as possible. This is the only way to obviate all inconvenience of the nature alluded to.

It may be added also, that as the audiences at concerts are at present composed in London, – where they frequently resort for any purpose but for that of hearing, – there is generally as much noise as sound, and the audience part is heard as loud as the singer or orchestra.

---

[143] This should probably read: 'it gives but a poor and sorrowful idea of many fascinating qualities which it possesses when otherwise employed.'

[144] *The Philharmonicon, A Periodical of Piano-forte and Vocal Music [Part IV:] A periodical of Musical Literature and Piano-forte and Vocal Music*, London, 1–4 May–August 1833. Langley, 'Musical Journal', 552. Only four monthly issues are known of.

Of this class are a species of opera-goers, who *chatter* through the opera, and *listen* to the ballet. In such noisy scenes as these, the poor guitar player has no chance whatever.

Having stated where the guitar should *not* be heard, we will now throw out a hint or two to our readers, and suggest a few situations where no other instrument can be so characteristically employed. At this season of the year, when the buds and blossoms of flowers are breaking, or have already broken, into freshness and beauty, what instrument can discourse so blandly and bewitchingly in the embosomed and fragrant arbour? Here, it is not only romantic, but reasonable and seasonable – here, it is the true poetry of music – here, we can fancy that Raphael and Salvator Rosa embodied it in their pictures to heighten their scenes of wild picturesque beauty.[145]

It lies in so small a compass, and its portability is so easy, that from the drawing-room to the arbour, or from the arbour to the drawing-room, it may be conveyed as easily as a *bouquet* of flowers. So rich, indeed, and gay and graceful is the appearance of a beautiful girl with her guitar, in an arbour where the foliage is full and luxuriant, that we wonder, the architect, as well as the painter has not turned the figure to some advantage in his art. That this is no frivolous or presumptuous idea, we need only recall to mind the origin of the Corinthian style of architecture, which Vitruvius informs us sprung out of the following circumstance:

"A Corinthian virgin, who was of marriageable age, fell a victim to a violent disorder. After her interment, her nurse collecting in a basket those articles to which she had shown a partiality when alive, carried them to her tomb, and placed a tile on the basket for the better preservation of its contents. The basket was accidentally placed on the root of an acanthus plant, which, pressed by its weight, shot forth towards spring in stems of large foliage, and in the course of its growth reached the angles of the tile, and thus formed volutes at the extremities. *Callimachus*, who was a man of great ingenuity and taste in sculpture, happening to pass the tomb, observed the basket, and the delicacy of the foliage which surrounded it. Pleased with the form and novelty of the combination, he took the hint for inventing

[p. 48]

these columns, and used them in the country about Corinth, regulating by this model the manner and proportion of the Corinthian order."[146]

---

[145] The artists Raphael (Raffaello Santi) (1483–1520) and Salvator Rosa (1615–73) included musical instruments in a few of their works.

[146] This is largely taken from: Marcus Vitruvius Pollio, *The Architecture of Marcus Vitruvius Pollio*, trans. Joseph Gwilt (London, 1826), 101–02.

But to return to the guitar. On occasions of boating, while sailing in calm tranquility on the silvery bosom of some quiet or rippling lake or river, whilst the moon may lend its mild rays to the scene, – at such a moment, what so sweet and touching as the music from this instrument? In a gipsy party, also – where there must be a sprinkling of romance, and an oblivion of the dull cares of the world – where, we say, there must be these, or the very appellation of gipsying would be a fraud on the intention – what instrument can be listened to with so much reverence and buoyant pleasure? The blockhead who would not, or *could* not then feel its influence, must be one of those of whom Shakspeare speaks, when he describes a being not fond of music, as fitted only for "stratagems and spoils," and who concludes the exordium by saying,

"Let no such man be trusted."[147]

In all such situations as these, where you would as much think of wishing for a street in London, as for the piano-forte, or where if you had a piano-forte, it would be out of all character and place – in all such situations of festive mirth and convivial recreation, the guitar is the instrument of joy and gladness. No pleasure party of the young and the buoyant, of the "thoughtless and the free" ought to omit this little talisman, which awakens at its touch, the kindest and most amiable of human emotions. Another valuable acquisition, also, on such occasions, is a flute. There are no two instruments so well fitted for each other as these: the guitar lending its harmony (in which the flute is deficient) to the flute: and the flute its *sostenuto* tones (which is a deficiency in the guitar) to the guitar. With these two instruments – to play Giuliani's compositions, (and he has written a great many for the two) you may enjoy a concert, and no mean one either, in a wilderness.[148] Inanimate nature you might not move, as did Orpheus the trees and mountains: but from experience, we know, that the birds are moved, and make a willing and happy audience. Having gone a little out of our way to make these observations we will now resume our plain matter-of-fact duty, and briefly allude to those concerts where guitar performances have been introduced.

MISS MOUNSEY'S CONCERT,
CITY OF LONDON TAVERN.

THIS concert, for the benefit of Miss Mounsey, an excellent piano-forte player, was patronised by a very numerous audience, notwithstanding it was given at an early period of the season, when the *influenza* might have been supposed to *influence* many in stopping away. There was a duett for guitars, admirably composed by Neuland, performed by Mr. Pelzer and his pupil,

---

[147] William Shakespeare, *The Merchant of Venice*, v. 1. 97.
[148] Twenty-two duets for flute and guitar by Giuliani are known. 'The Compositions of Mauro Giuliani: A Checklist of the Earliest Editions', in Heck, *Giuliani*.

[p. 49]

Miss E. Mounsey.* Of the playing of this duet, we shall merely say, that it gave general satisfaction to the audience as well as the composer.

Mr. Pelzer's pupil, Miss E. Mounsey, is already a good performer, and it may be mentioned that she is the first female player that has yet been brought before the public.[149]

MESSRS. DRESSLER AND PELZER'S CONCERT,

CONCERT ROOM, KING'S THEATRE.

THAT the guitar possesses admirers – and numerous admirers too – this concert was a convincing proof; for one of the principal features in the programme was guitar playing; first as a solo, second as a duet, and third as as [*sic*] a trio.[150] Mr. Pelzer, a second time, brought forward his clever pupil, Miss E. Mounsey, and another in the person of his daughter, a child of some eight years of age.[151] The latter performed with all the *nonchalance* of a veteran, and displayed excellent tact for so young a creature. Her playing was much admired by the juvenile part of the audience. Miss E. Mounsey again improved upon her former efforts; her tone was rich and harpy, and her style elegant and expressive. She is a great credit to herself and master. Of Mr. Pelzer's public performances we shall merely say, that we like his ideas, better than his execution. He has a fine tone, and a just idea of expression, with those branches of expression – grace and elegance; but his nervousness in a large room, renders those qualities ineffective. In private – in a small room – he is distinguished for his good taste, and his complete mastery over the instrument. He has evidently drank deep of Giuliani, whose style he emulates, and possesses a greater and more comprehensive knowledge of music than usually falls to the lot of guitar players.

The vocal portion of this concert was well sustained by Madame de Meric, Miss Bruce, Madame Pirscher, Miss Bellchambers, and two

---

149   This concert, which took place on 19 April, was given advance notice in Issue 3, p. 42 of *The Giulianiad*. It was claimed at the time that around 40,000 people had had influenza in London and, although painful, few cases terminated fatally. 'Varieties', *Literary Gazette* 849 (1833), 268. It is not known which of Neuland's duets was performed on this occasion. Elizabeth Mounsey was not the first female guitarist to perform in public; Emilia Giuliani played duets with her father, Mauro Giuliani, at the Teatro Nuovo in Naples in 1828. Nicoletta Confalone, 'Emilia Giuliani (1813–1850)', in *Great Vogue*, ed Page, Sparks, and Westbrook, 237–50, at 240.

150   For the full programme of this concert, which took place on 15 May 1833, see 'Public concerts', *The Philharmonicon* 2 (1833), 1–3.

151   Pelzer's daughter would have been Catharina.

Catharina Josepha Pelzer   Ætat nine years

Geo. Brown delt   C E Wagstaff Sc

Figure 11. Catharina Josepha Pelzer, aged nine years, engraved by C. E. Wagstaff, after George Brown.

Misses Dressler; by Messrs. Wilson, Morley, (an excellent bass), Master Dressler, Mr. Stretton, and the German chorus.[152]

Mr. Dressler's flute-playing was, as it generally is, much admired. His compositions, with us, have always been much esteemed; and the facility of imparting his musical knowledge was well illustrated in the persons of his three children (one of whom was a boy of the tender age of six) who sung, and were encored in Mozart's trio from Zauberflöte. Mr. Wolf, (a pupil of Mayseder) performed a fantasia on the violin with the most touching expression and brilliant execution.[153] There was a sad disappointment in the absence of Mr. Nelson Weippert, from indisposition, who was to have played a solo on the piano-forte. His place was supplied, at a moment's notice, by Miss Mounsey,[154] who, to do her justice, played with great precision and judgment, considering the moment she was called on to perform. Mr. Eliason led, and Mr. Neuland conducted – both with great precision.

The crowded state of the large room in which this concert was held is the best possible refutation that the guitar is not patronised in this country. It was a great treat to us, also, to see that two-thirds of the audience were composed of ladies; a proof, if any were wanting, that they are beginning to discover, they are more admired in the graceful and easy attitude as performers on the guitar, than they are in the constrained position at a piano-forte.

*The same young lady who presented us with a song, inserted in our first number.[155]

[p. 50]

MISS BRUCE'S SOIREES.

THIS lady gave a series of three concerts, at the residence of J. Taylor, Esq. which were attended with fashionable audiences of nobility and gentry.[156] Nearly all the talented vocalists now in London, both foreign and native, were present: nor were the instrumentalists forgotten,

---

152 Master Dressler was aged five or six. 'King's Concert-room', *The Times*, 17 May 1833. It is not known what age the Dressler girls would have been. Miss Bellchambers was probably Juliet Bellchambers, who composed some ballads. The other singers named would have been well-known at the time. The German chorus would have come from Chelard's German opera company.

153 Wolf may have been Ludwig Wolf. Sainsbury, *Dictionary*, ii, 546. Joseph Mayseder (1789–1863) was an Austrian violinist. Brown, *Dictionary*, 421.

154 This would have been Ann Mounsey.

155 'Fair evening Star', music by Elizabeth Mounsey, words by E. J. J. *TG* 1:1 (1833), Music 9–11.

156 The three concerts took place on 9 May, 20 May, and 3 June. 'Advertisements', *Morning Post*, 6 May 1833.

Moschelles, Nelson Weippert, Holmes, Dressler, Nicholson, Mori, Wolf, Blagrove, and Pelzer, exhibited their abilities on their respective instruments.[157] MISS BRUCE is a singer of great perseverance and merit. She has a voice of good quality, and her taste is improving every hour. Her talent has secured her a vast host of patronage, and it is to the credit of that patronage that it is bestowed on native talent. Of the piano-forte players a few words must be said – Moschelles is well known, both here and on the continent, as a man of extraordinary ability; but Nelson Weippert, a player of no less excellence, is not yet (for his opportunities have been few) so highly estimated: this gentleman's playing is of a splendid description – it is feeling, delicate, vigorous and precise. In fact, it has all the character of first-rate, and we predict the time when he will be as great a favorite as Cramer or Moschelles, in whose combined styles he has individualized his own.

MR. SCHULTZ'S CONCERT.

THERE are no musicians in London who have, by their talents, raised themselves patrons, more deserving of admiration than the brothers of this name: the one a piano-forte player of great genius, the other a guitarist who has laid all the difficulties of his instrument under complete subjection. As an executionist he is perhaps unrivalled; the only deficiency of his playing lies rather in the hurried manner of commencing a subject than in his after treatment of it. A riper judgement will teach him due caution on this point. It ought to be added that these clever performers are pupils of their father, Mr. Schultz, a man who possesses a true, sound, and varied knowledge of the means of imparting musical instruction. This concert took place under the patronage of His Grace the Duke of Devonshire.[158]

MR. SAGRINI AND SIGNOR GIUBILEI'S.

THIS was one of the best concerts of the season, and took place at the residence of Sir J. de Beauvoir, Connaught Place, Edgware Road. M. Sagrini's performance is an excellent specimen of guitar playing – uniting a good harpy tone with much feeling, and brilliant execution. Nothing can be more dexterous than his fingering – it is clean, clear, and unerringly

---

[157] Holmes may have been the pianist William Holmes (1812–85). Charles Nicholson (1795–1837) was a flute player. Nicolas Mori (1793–1839) was a violinist. Henry Blagrove (1811–72) was one of the most distinguished violinists in London at the time. Brown, *Dictionary*, 329, 444, 433, 97.

[158] Leonard Schulz's elder brother was the pianist Eduard (c.1812–76); both brothers were child prodigies. They first visited London with their father, Andreas Schulz, in 1825 and returned in 1832. Leonard's guitar playing received great acclaim, although his performances became less frequent in the 1840s. Stenstadvold, 'Schulz', 9–16. The concert took place on 17 May 1833 in the Hanover Square Rooms. 'Advertisements', *Morning Post*, 15 May 1833.

exact. We were greatly pleased with this gentleman's performance, the more so as he perseveres, and knows that there is something beyond his present playing worthy of acquirement: this is a sure test of capacity and judgement. His brother, also (who is only ten years of age) displayed much precocious talent for this instrument. His playing was full of promise, and elicited the spontaneous applause of a very crowded audience. In taking a retrospect glance at the concerts of this season, we have every reason to congratulate the lovers of the guitar, on the patronage which has been bestowed on its professors. On a general average the guitar players can boast of as full an attendance as those professing any other instrument – a clear proof that the guitar is progressing onwards.[159]

MISS FANNY WOODHAM'S.

THIS precocious little lady gave her benefit concert on Monday, the 17th June, on which occasion the Marchioness of Salisbury generously opened her spacious mansion in Arlington Street. The young vocalist was assisted by much talent both vocal and instrumental. Madame Pasta, in addition to the *aria* announced for her, kindly supplied the place of Mademoiselle Pixis in a duet with Miss Woodham, as also did Miss Inverarity that of Madame Schrœder Devrient, by singing the scena from *Der Freischutz*, in a manner that elicited applause. A new and beautiful ballad, sweetly sung by Mr. Roche, "Adieu then every blessing," (Neuland), excited much attention and enquiry; and Mendelssohn's First Grand Concerto for the piano-forte, was played by Mr. G. F. Kiallmark in such a style of brilliancy, that the author, who happened to be in the room, commended the ability and taste displayed in terms of the highest admiration. Miss E. Mounsey again exhibited her talent on the guitar, in a duet with her master, Pelzer; and the progress of Miss F. WOODHAM in the science to which she is devoted, since her appearance, last season, was spoken of as reflecting the greatest credit on her master, Sig. Lanza, who, it may be recollected was the musical preceptor of that delightful vocalist, Miss Stephens, perhaps the most universal favorite of our time.[160] The attendance at this concert

---

159 The concert took place on 3 June 1833. Sagrini's brother mentioned here was Italo Augusto Sagrini (b.1822). Augustus Giubilei (c.1812–51) was a singer. Lewis and Coldwell, *Sagrini*, 57, 87, 295–96.

160 Little is known about the singers Fanny Woodham or Mr Roche. Francilla Pixis, also a singer, was referred to as 'one of the novelties of the season'. 'Music', *Literary Gazette* 858 (1833), 413. George Frederick Kiallmark (1804–87) was a pianist. James Brown and Stephen Stratton, *British Musical Biography* (Birmingham, 1897), 230. Mendelssohn's presence would have added significantly to the prestige of the event. He visited London ten times between 1829 and 1847; he was enormously popular and became very influential. Colin Eatock, *Mendelssohn and Victorian England* (Farnham, 2009), xi. Catherine Stephens (1791–1882) was a soprano; in 1838 she

was distinguished by the presence of many families of the first rank and fashion.

MISS F. HEALY'S.

THIS Concert took place at Willis's Rooms, on Friday, the 28th June, and was very fully attended. Miss HEALY met with the most enthusiastic reception, and more than realised the expectations of the numerous professors and amateurs present, by the display of an extraordinarily fine and flexible voice, by the delicacy and justness of her execution, and by the tasteful and elegant character of those embellishments which betoken at once the science of the master, and the industry of the pupil. Miss Bellchambers evinced talent and ability which places her high in the rank of English singers. Madame de Meric, whose high and various accomplishments cannot but receive from us a passing meed of admiration, bore a conspicuous part in the attractions of the evening. Haitzinger sang with all his wonted excellence. Chatterton's performance on the harp was as usual, good; the guitar trio, by Miss E. Mounsey, and Messrs. Pelzer and Neuland, was a good composition; and, for the piano-forte, it is enough for us to say that it was in the able hands of Mr. Kiallmark. Signor Lanza, as the instructor of Miss F. HEALY, was frequently greeted with applause.[161]

[p. 51 – Issue 6, October 1833]

Instructions to my Daughter for playing on the Enharmonic Guitar, by a Member of the University of Cambridge. Goulding and D'Almaine.

This is a work of such great ingenuity and erudition – so much time, labour, and talent have been employed in its concoction,* that it will hence-forward – so important do we consider it – form much of the ground-work of the Giulianiad; that is, in so far, that frequent reference will be made to its contents in future Numbers.[162]

This book must not be superficially studied, nor be spoken of as a work of every-day performance; it must be a text-book for every professor in the kingdom, wherein each will find a mass of information of such a nature as will, if he be a thinking man, give an impulse and direction to the whole of his practical knowledge. This will be the

married the earl of Essex. Gesualdo Lanza (1779–1859) was a singing teacher from Naples who lived in London. Brown, *Dictionary*, 375, 576.

[161] Miss F. Healy was a singer who was to make her debut in opera in London in 1834. 'The English Opera House', *Literary Gazette* 913 (1834), 501. John Chatterton (1804–71) was harpist to Queen Victoria. Brown, *Dictionary*, 154.

[162] This promise remained unfulfilled; no subsequent edition of *The Giulianiad* contained a 'text' section.

good it will effect. It will give a more theoretical, or rather a more philosophical turn of thought to the study of the guitar, now that first causes and their effects are so amply, lucidly, and so ingeniously laid out for examination.

We cannot as yet enter into its contents; we wish we could: it will require an almost undivided attention for the next three months. As well might an optician offer his *dictum*, after a slight reading of Newton's Elucidation of the Principles of Light, as us, with the slight acquaintance of the book, attempt to analyse this, which takes upon itself to explain, philosophically and mathematically, the first principles of sound. Not only this either – it furthermore practically points out the application of its calculations to the guitar, and proposes, in that operation, to perfect that instrument; or, in other words, has attempted on it the discovery of the ENHARMONIC of the ancients.

To give an opinion on the contents, with our present imperfect, crude, and undigested reading, therefore, would be premature and abortive. We beg now only to draw the reader's attention to the author's introduction, which will give a good idea of what he may expect in the body of the work:–

"The following pages had their origin in a desire to abate the untuneableness of the common guitar – which, though an instrument possessed of many agreeable qualities, has the defect of being out of tune to a greater extent than any other that is played by means of either strings or keys. For the other instruments – as the piano-forte, harp, and organ – are, at all events, capable of playing in some keys, with something like an approach to correct harmony; while in the guitar, the errors, instead of being collected into some particular keys, are disseminated as widely as possible among all, in consequence of the octave being divided into twelve equal intervals, which is, in fact, necessary, as long as the frets on the different strings are to form continued straight lines, in order to cause the octaves, and the representatives of the same sound in different parts of the instrument to be in tune with each other. And besides this, the instrument has two other sources of inaccuracy – namely, the errors caused by the increase of tension, produced on pressing a string down to the fret, and those arising from irregularities in the string itself, or what is called the string being *false*; either of which, if not remedied, would be fatal to the attempt at correct harmony.[163] So that it is quite true, according to the observation of *Pere Mersenne*, that in its ordinary state *'le luth est le charlatan de la musique, parce qu'il fait passer pour bon ce qui est mauvais, sur les bons instrumens.'*[164]

---

[163] There is evidence in method books that gut strings could be a problem; they broke easily and could be 'false', in other words out of tune, and therefore unusable.

[164] F. Marin Mersenne, 'Nouvelles Observations physique et mathématiques', in *Harmonie universelle, contenant la théorie et la pratique de la musique, seconde*

"It will, however, be recollected that the guitar is the representative of the *Kithara* or *Cithara* of the ancients; and that the ancients had a kind of musical division under

---

*The author, in a postscript, states, "On the magnitude of the concluding chapter, it may be some excuse to say, that the work has been five years in hand, and upwards of fourteen months in the press."

[p. 52]

the title of *Enharmonic*, which they applied to their principal instrument, the cithara or lyre, and considered as more perfect than the other modes of division which were in use at the same time. What this enharmonic was to do, nobody has seemed able to tell; and since the ridicule thrown about the subject in the 'Memoirs of Martinus Scriblerus,' it is hardly safe to desire to know.[165] The account given by the moderns appears to be, that the artificial and difficult enharmonic was lost soon after Alexander the Great;[166] yet there exist numerous works of the ancients upon the subject, from Aristoxanus and Euclid down to Ptolemy and Capella. The first inference from these remains of antiquity is, that the musical string was divided into a very great number of parts; and it appears from a passage preserved by Photius, that a philosopher of the fifth century, in an endeavour to recover the enharmonic genus, carried the divisions to as many as 220, but without success. One thing, however, is clear – that the ancients attempted to improve the cithara by means of a complicated scale of division; and if the improvement, which was the object of their search, can be recovered upon the instrument, where from circumstances it appears likely to be easiest of access, it may be found capable of extension to others where the application is less obvious.[167]

partie (Paris, 1637), 20. 'The lute is the charlatan of music because it passes off as good what is bad on good instruments.'

[165] Alexander Pope, *Memoirs of the Extraordinary Life, Works, and Discoveries of Martinus Scriblerus* (Dublin, 1741), 47–48. The memoirs of this fictional scholar were written by members of the Scriblerus Club, which included Pope and Swift, and attacked the pedantic approach of some contemporary scholars.

[166] A reference for this notion is given in the original book. 'The artificial and difficult Enharmonic however, seems to have been lost soon after the time of Alexander the Great.' Charles Burney, *A General History of Music from the Earliest Ages to the Present Period*, 2nd edn, 4 vols (London, 1789), i, 425.

[167] Ancient Greek writers used the tetrachord (a group of four notes) as the basic unit for music. There were three types: diatonic, chromatic, and enharmonic. The last of these necessitated the use of quarter tones. R. P. Winnington-Ingram, 'Greece; Ancient', in *The New Grove Dictionary of Music and Musicians*, ed. Stanley Sadie, 29 vols (London, 1980), vii, 659–72, at 663–64.

"The object in what follows will be, first, to show how the guitar may (with some trouble, indeed, which 'the gods have attached to everything good') be made to produce correct harmony, or, in the language of musicians, be a perfect instrument; and afterwards, to present the reasons for believing that the lost *Enharmonic* aimed at neither more nor less than this, and, in fact, meant nothing but playing in *harmony*, or, in other words, *in tune*. How far the other modes of division are from being in tune, will be best collected subsequently from comparison.

"It will be taken for granted that the reader knows the places of the notes on the common guitar, and can read music; with which provisions, it is apprehended that nothing will be met with in the sequel, but what with moderate application will be easily understood. It may not be necessary actually to go through the whole of the calculations described, unless for the purpose of examining their correctness; but to go through them, in imagination at least, will be found the most effectual way of keeping pace with the subject. Those who are not familiar with the rules of proportion and the use of decimals, must be content to take the arithmetical operations upon trust. A little should be read at a time, and anything that is not understood on the first reading should be marked for the purpose of referring to it at a future period, when it is probable that increased acquaintance with the question will have removed the difficulty. In return for all which, it is hoped that the scholars in the language of *Mersenne*, recommending his *clavier*, *'feront quantité de beaux passages et de gentilesses, qu'ils ne peuvent trouver sur les claviers ordinaires,* '[168] and will find their information usefully extended upon what is apt to be considered as abtruse [*sic*] and unapproachable branches of the history of musical sounds."[169]

There is always good effected by enquiry, even if it fail in the first intended or avowed object: there is always something found out – if not in the immediate – in a collateral branch of the subject, which leads to a discovery of something else more important. All that tends to keep the mind on the *qui vive*[170] is at once wholesome and ultimately beneficial. It must sometime or other bear and produce its fruits.

---

[168] Mersenne, *Harmonie universelle*, 357. 'Will make a number of beautiful passages and niceties which they cannot find on ordinary claviers'. He advocated the construction of a clavier with many extra keys that would facilitate performance in all three of the ancient Greek tetrachords. Thompson himself designed and had built an enharmonic organ which was on display at the Great Exhibition of 1851. Johnson, *Thompson*, 158, 259. Peter and Ann Mactaggart (eds), *Musical Instruments in the 1851 Exhibition* (Welwyn, 1986), 56–57.

[169] [Thompson], *Instructions*, 1. This lengthy quote consists of Thompson's entire introductory chapter minus his detailed notes on sources.

[170] alert.

The author has boldly met and grappled with his subject, and, with singular ability and clearness, has thrown a light upon its abstruse nature. At all events, he writes in better times than when the Memoirs of Martinus Scriblerus was penned in ridicule of a similar inquiry.*

The price of the book puts it in the power of every description of amateur and professor to have it in his possession: thirty large folio pages of closely printed matter, with scales, tables, and illustrations, *for four shillings!*[171] As

---

*The "Spectator" and "Harmonicon," both good critics, not to speak of the "Westminster Review," have all recorded their favourable opinion of the ability displayed: there was not one Scriblerus amongst them.[172]

[p. 53]

much of what we shall write in our next number will not be understood, unless the book be laid before the reader, we invite him to procure, and give it a few perusals previous to reading our observations.

On the whole, although we will not anticipate an opinion, which might, after all, be at variance with our present impression – and although some positions of the writer may not be found tenable, or be brought into immediate practical operation, still the field for reflection which he has opened for guitarists is so extensive, that we confess, with all our enthusiasm for the instrument, we have not till now given it credit for the wide arena of discussion it embraces. The author is understood to be Colonel Thompson.*[173]

---

[171] Four shillings was a low price; detailed method books at this time had cover prices of twelve shillings whilst less detailed ones ranged from four to twelve shillings. Clarke, 'Instrument', 130, 149.

[172] 'Mathematics of Music', *The Spectator*, 21 November 1829. 'Instructions to my Daughter', *The Harmonicon* 8 (1830), 35. [T. P. Thompson], 'Enharmonic of the Ancients', *Westminster Review* 16 (1832), 429–79.

[173] Although this book has the title 'Instructions' it is not a tutor; it is a lengthy and detailed mathematical treatise on the enharmonic guitar. For a full description of Thompson's plan for an enharmonic guitar and a surviving example of one made by Louis Panormo in 1833 in London, see James Westbrook, 'General Thompson's Enharmonic Guitar', *Soundboard* 38:4 (2012), 45–52.

REVIEW OF MUSIC.

PELZER'S *Instructions for the Guitar.*[174]
CHAPPELL, Bond Street; EWER, Bow Church Yard; BOOSEY, Holles
Street, Oxford Street; DUFF, 65, Oxford Street; and JOHANNING and
Co., 6, John Street, Oxford Street.

The didactic part of this work is very brief – too brief indeed for
such a man as Pelzer, whose authority is justly held in respect by the
leading guitarists of the day. This brevity must doubtless be attributed
to his being a foreigner; although we could have borne with greater
prolixity of detail, had he conveyed his sentiments in such language as
the introduction exhibits. From this we shall make an extract:–
"The guitar, when introduced amongst the Spaniards, was a simple
instrument with four strings: two others have since been added, by
which it is rendered capable of expressing those concords and discords
which constitute the light and shade of music, and of producing the
most intricate modulations through all the keys of the musical scale.
Independently of its merit as an accompaniment to the voice, every
species of composition may be played upon it, when taught by an able
master. With such powers, added to its lightness and small dimensions, it
may well claim and receive admission in situations from which the harp,
piano-forte, and other large instruments must be excluded. It has, in fact,
from the earliest times been the favored companion of the accomplished
of both sexes. In the solitary hour, in the closet, and in the camp, it
has been the delight and solace of the beautiful and the brave; and it
is no small recommendation of it, that in situations, in which louder
instruments might be an annoyance to others, the performer may, from
the most gentle vibrations of its strings, enjoy every combination of
musical sounds which can gratify a cultivated ear."[175]
In a clear and perspicuous manner – although too briefly as we before
said – the author then introduces and explains the rudiments of music,
and its proper application to the guitar. The few first lessons are easy,
progressive, and in point of harmony – no small advantage to a beginner
– is unexceptionable.

---

*At least our esteemed correspondent, Mr. Donald Walker, thus
entitles him. In a short preface, remarkable for its declaration of previous

---

[174] This review probably relates to the second edition published c.1833 and not the
first edition of 1830.

[175] Pelzer, *Instructions*, 4. In the sixteenth century there were guitars in Spain with
four courses, or pairs of strings. The first three were tuned in unison and in the
fourth the two strings were tuned an octave apart. James Tyler, 'The Guitar in the
Sixteenth Century', in James Tyler and Paul Sparks, *The Guitar and its Music*
(Oxford, 2002), 5–45, at 5.

Figure 12. Ferdinand Pelzer, *Instructions for the Spanish Guitar* (London, [1830]), Title Page. The picture pasted onto the front was used for the first edition and for the first printings of the second. It conveys a romantic image of a fretted string instrument with what appears to be a well-dressed woman with a minstrel. Later printings of the second edition replaced this with an image of a girl playing a guitar.

slight acquaintance with the subject undertaken, the name is "T. Perronet Thomson."[176]

[p. 54]

A prelude, consisting of the common chord, is prefixed to the beginning of every new key; and it seems to have been premeditated that every prelude should be precisely alike. By this means, the pupil, knowing by heart one of them, must infallibly be acquainted with the common chord in every mode, and thus never be at a loss for a few notes as a prelude, prior to the performance in any key.[177] This is certainly a practical method of fixing this important point on the mind and fingers of the pupil, and we see no objection to its use, unless, perhaps, that it may tend to engender a mannerism, which the author in another part of his instructions, seems so anxious to avoid.

The author has been extremely diligent, and almost too pedantic, if we may here use the term, in showing those musical heretics, who doubt the fact, that the guitar is capable of being played in every key, making no exception whatever. A little of this display could well have been spared; unless the author meant by this that the pupil should take a bird's-eye view of the whole elements of modulation. The best portion of the book, next to the few first progressive lessons, is that from pages 33 to 53, wherein those finishing touches, so entirely indispensable to an accomplished guitar player, are finely explained and illustrated. It is this part of the book which has made it such a favorite with teachers. In the rules here laid down the well-taught professor will perceive many of those secrets which have been ridiculously withheld from the public, and, until this work made its appearance, the means of acquiring them were entirely unknown in England: the merit of first divulging them must, therefore, be awarded to the author.

"It has been," as the writer observes, "usual with masters in writing instructions for the guitar, to teach it according to their own style of playing, or, in other words, in that style which their own continual practice had rendered most easy to themselves." We agree with him also "that this, as in painting, produces a mannerism which cannot fail to be tiresome."

The principal object which the author had in view, and which, we admit, he has fully realised in his pages, he briefly announces thus: "My object is, after leading the beginner by the most simple and easy progress to the

---

[176] Donald Walker's publications included *Exercises for Ladies* in which he discusses how to hold the guitar and praises Mr. Schulz; he would have been referring to Leonard. Donald Walker, *Exercises for Ladies*, 2nd edn (London, 1837), 38–41.

[177] Performances of improvised introductory preludes before pieces were common in the eighteenth century and the practice continued to a lesser extent into the late 1800s. Valerie Woodring Goertzen, 'By Way of Introduction: Preluding by 18th- and Early 19th-Century Pianists', *Journal of Musicology* 14 (1996), 299–337.

finger-board of the instrument, to teach him every position of the fingers of the left hand, and every mode of striking the strings with those of the right, which can be required in the execution of any compositions for the guitar, whether by Giuliani, Carulli, Sor, Aguado, Legnani, or any other master.[178] By thus combining all the different modes of fingering, that distinction between them, which ought never to have existed, will be done away with, and the pupil will acquire a more thorough knowledge of the instrument, and a greater facility in executing whatever music may be set before him."[179]

This Instruction Book on the whole displays an intimate acquaintance with all the best masters; unfolds what the instrument is really meant for; and exhibits a soundness and ripeness of judgement which will act as an antidote against the nostrums of charlatans. In a word, they are sound, practical instructions, based on a legitimate experience of many years, and calculated to effect much good amongst amateurs in this country. And as such we recommend it.

[p. 55]

"*'Twere vain to tell thee all I feel.*" *No.* 3, *of a Series of Airs, arranged as Duets for Guitar and Piano-forte. Dedicated to* MISS WILDE, *by* W. NEULAND.
"*L'Or est une Chimère,*" *from Meyerbeer's Opera of "Robert." No.* 4 *of a Series of Airs for ditto. Dedicated to the* MISSES MAY *and* ELIZABETH DAVIES, *by* W. NEULAND, Op. 12.
"*Jadis Regnait en Normandie,*" *from Meyerbeer's Opera of "Robert." No.* 5 *of ditto for ditto. Dedicated to the* MISSES ANDERDON, *by* W. NEULAND, Op. 13. Chappel.[180]

These are a continuation of those arrangements for guitar and piano-forte which we noticed in the 2nd Number of "THE GIULIANIAD."[181] To go into details upon their merits is unnecessary, the same careful attention in arranging – the same happy distribution of parts to both

---

[178] Dionisio Aguado (1784–1849) was a Spanish guitarist whose influential method book remains in use today. Luis Briso de Montiano, 'Dionisio Aguado', in *Great Vogue*, ed. Page, Sparks, and Westbrook, 221–36. Luigi Legnani (1790–1877) was an Italian guitarist. Douglas James, 'Luigi Rinaldo Legnani' (unpublished doctoral dissertation, University of Arizona, 1994). There is no evidence that either musician visited England.

[179] Pelzer, *Instructions*, 4.

[180] All three pieces were published by Chappell in 1833. The first of his *Series of Airs, arranged as Duets for Guitar and Piano-forte* was reviewed in *TG* 1:2 (1833), 22. Meyerbeer's opera *Robert le Diable* was first performed in Paris in 1831 to great acclaim. Julian Marshall, 'Meyerbeer', in *Dictionary*, ed. Grove, ii, 320–26, at 323. Arrangements of arias from the new opera were popular; the British Library catalogue lists eighteen published in London in 1832 and 1833. Editions from abroad would also have been available.

[181] The first of this series was reviewed in the second issue, page 22.

instruments – each bearing a due proportion of interest, has been bestowed on these as in No. 1. If there be any living composer who is familiar with the genius of the guitar, and can combine its effects with those of the piano-forte – that man is Neuland. A clever pupil, who has previously known nothing of the guitar, will be able to play these duets in three months – supposing always a good master.

Fantasia on the most favourite Airs in Der Freyschutz; composed for Guitar, and dedicated to A. T. HUERTA, Esq., *by* S. PRATTEN.
The last Waltz of Weber's, and Mozart's favourite Waltz; arranged for Guitar, and dedicated to MISS JANE JOHNSTONE, *by* S. PRATTEN. Both published by Metzler and Son.[182]

It is with no small degree of pleasure that we find an Englishman's name attached to these excellent arrangements; it is at once a proof of his zeal in studying, and good taste in the style of treating his subject. It shows also that some able heads exist, exclusive of foreign masters, capable of displaying this instrument to advantage. We trust that Mr. Pratten will continue to consult the pages of Giuliani and Sor, as models of guitar compositions; for, he may be assured, that the time is now arrived when they can be appreciated in this country. We heartily recommend both these pieces to the notice of master and pupil; but, at the same time, express a wish that the author will attentively examine the proofs, which are sadly defective as the engraver has left them. Many errors of harmony, from this cause alone, are left uncorrected.

1. *Six German Waltzes, with Introduction and Finale, arranged by* W. F. KUCZYNSKI. Purdy and Fendt.
2. *Duet for Guitar and Flute, or Violin, composed by* GIULIANI. Metzler.

No. 1. These waltzes are exceedingly pretty, and one or two of them approach to elegance.[183]
No. 2. The duet for flute and guitar is easy for both instruments, but pleasing and effective. This is one of the pieces respecting which we said a few words in our last number.[184]

---

[182] Stephen Pratten (1799–1845) lived in Bristol and was a pupil of Huerta. He was a flautist, guitarist, and singer, and was the father-in-law of Madame Sidney Pratten. Britton, 'Guitar', 229–35.

[183] Vincent Kuczynski was a Polish refugee who was probably exiled from the Polish November uprising of 1830–31. He took part in concerts to raise funds for Polish exiles. 'Sheffield, Feb. 15.', *Sheffield Independent*, 5 February 1834. No copy of the *Six German Waltzes* has been located.

[184] Comment is made on page 48 on how 'well fitted' the two instruments are. This duet is almost certainly Giuliani's opus 77.

FOREIGN GUITAR MAKERS AND ENGLISH MUSIC SELLERS.

————

To put the reader in possession of sound and authentic information on this subject, we shall commence with giving him the names of those foreign guitar makers whose names are celebrated in some of the principal towns on the Continent and Peninsula. SOR, whose authority must be allowed to have great weight in this matter, thus speaks of guitar makers:—[185]

"The manner of constructing the body of the instrument is almost everywhere understood extremely well, and most Neapolitan, German, and French guitars, leave, in this respect, very little superiority to the Spanish. In the goodness of the body or box, the Neapolitans in general long surpassed, in my opinion, those of France and Germany; but that is not the case at present; and, if I wanted an instrument, I would procure it from M. Joseph Martinez, of Malaga, or from M. Lacote, a French maker, the only person who, besides his talents, has proved to me that he possesses the quality of not being inflexible to reasoning.[186] The guitars to which I have always given the preference are those of *Alonzo*, of *Madrid*; *Pagés* and *Benediz*, of *Cadiz*; *Joseph* and *Manuel Martinez*, of *Malaga*; or *Ruda*, successor and scholar of the latter; those of *M. Lacote*, of *Paris*; and *M. Shroeder*, of *Petersburgh*.[187] I do not say that others do not exist; but never having tried them, I cannot decide on that of which I have no knowledge. I ought to repeat, that the faults which I have found in several guitars, I have not always attributed to the ignorance and folly of the makers. These defects are frequently acquired by the guitarists, who, instead of blaming their own way of touching the

[185]   This quotation is taken from the English translation of 1832 with some corrections and minor changes. Ferdinand Sor, *Method for the Spanish Guitar*, trans. A. Merrick (London, [1832]), 9.

[186]   José Martinez (b.c.1772) worked in Malaga. José Romanillos and Marian Harris Winspear, *The Vihuela de Mano and the Spanish Guitar, a Dictionary of the Makers of Plucked and Bowed Musical Instruments of Spain (1200–2002)* (Guijosa, 2002), 237. René Lacote (1785–1871), of Paris, was one of the most important luthiers of the nineteenth century. For a full account of his life and work see Bruno and Catherine Marlat, *René Lacote, Luthier à Paris* (Paris, 2022).

[187]   Alonzo would have been Lorenzo Alonso Esteban (d.1796). The other Spanish makers were better known. Juan Pagés Garcia (1741–1821) and Josef Sebastián Benedid Díaz worked in Cádiz. Manuel Martinez (b.c.1774) worked in Malaga. It is not clear if he was related to José Martinez. Ruda would have been Fernando Rada (b.c.1785). Romanillos, *Dictionary*, 12–14, 281–83, 36–37, 238, 317. Shroeder was probably J. H. Schröder. Willibald Leo Freiher von Lütgendorff, *Die Geigen und Lautenmacher vom Mittelalter bis zur Gegenwart*, 2 vols (Frankfurt, 1922), ii, 453.

strings, blame the instrument, and would have it accommodate itself to their play, instead of the performer accommodating himself to its nature. For my own part, when I have heard a string jar, I have examined, first, whether the fault proceeded from the bad conformason[188] of the ins trument [*sic*], or from my ignorance in using it; secondly, whether the false direction which I might have given to the ply of the right hand finger was the cause of it, or whether, by pressing that string with the left hand, the force of the arm might not have added to that produced by the pressure of the fingers against the thumb, and, in consequence, the finger-board or neck having yielded backwards, brought the string too near the frets. Very frequently I have found it proceed from one of these causes, and I have endeavoured to correct myself accordingly."

The superiority of Lacote's guitars consists in their symmetrical proportions, in the quality of the wood, in the mathematical exactness of the frets, neck, and head, and in their general workmanship. A proper regard seems to be paid also to the thickness, or rather thinness of the wood, and above all, that this wood shall be well seasoned. The pains Lacote takes in superintending his manufactory has finally gained for him the reputation of being one of the first, if not the very first, maker in Europe. Add to this the inspection and examination which these instruments undergo by such men as Sor, Carulli, &c. before they are finally sent from his workshop.

Experience is often more available than genius, and in mechanics often supplies its place. Genius makes a discovery, and experience improves and perfects it. Colonel Thomson, the inventor of the Enharmonic guitar, is assuredly one of the former; and years of practice will, it is hoped, enable Mr. Panorma [*sic*] (the manufacturer) to profit by the ideas which he has communicated to him. It is to be hoped also, that professors will *examine* the construction of this instrument, not in a vein of querulous captiousness, but in a spirit of emulation and inquiry. To condemn it merely because it is new, and because the frets deviate from the regular distances of those in a common guitar, will

[p. 57]

show that teachers are impervious to improvement. If it were only that it set professors *thinking*, it will have done some good; but that, if being found impracticable in its present state, it should lead to improvement either on this guitar or the guitar generally in use, it will have pointed out the way for important changes, the advantages of which it is as yet impossible to foretel or appreciate. We see much difficulty to overcome when the instrument is required to modulate; but surely practical men may suggest a remedy for this. In the mean time, it is but justice to the

---

188   Conformation, or structure.

inventor to state, that the harmony procured on this instrument in the key in which it is made mathematically perfect, is so charming to the ear, that, as one of the oldest and best judges of the guitar we know, said on hearing it – "It reminds me of the perfect harmony produced by four good players in a quartett on two violins, tenor, and bass."[189]

We invite professors and makers, and all those who are practical judges, to a serious consideration of this subject.

The quantity of didactic books, and of classical music for the guitar published in England by the London music sellers is greater than may be imagined. The following list shews that there must be some good amateurs amongst us:–

Published by

Instructions to my Daughter for playing on the Enharmonic
    Guitar .... GOULDING and Co.[190]
NUSKE'S Fantasia on an Irish Air, dedicated to CAPTAIN
    PHILLIPS .... CHAPPEL.[191]
NEULAND'S Duet for Piano and Guitar, dedicated to GIULIO
    REGONDI .... Do.[192]
PELZER'S Divertimento .... Do.[193]
——— Instruction Book for the Guitar .... Do.[194]
GIULIANI'S Ops. 1 and 40. .... Do.[195]
EULENSTEIN'S Two Fantasias, introducing Weber's and
    Beethoven's Waltzes .... Do.[196]
SOR'S Method for the Guitar .... COCKS.[197]
GIULIANI'S Three Rondos for two Guitars. ....
                                     PAINE and HOPKINS.[198]
NUSKE'S Arrangement of Beethoven's Adelaide .... Do.[199]

---

[189] It is not known where this quotation is from.
[190] [T. P. Thompson], *Instructions*.
[191] J. A. Nüske, *Fantasia on a Celebrated Irish air* (London, [1831]).
[192] Wilhelm Neuland, *Introduction and Variations on a Favorite Waltz by Himmer for the Spanish Guitar with an accompaniment for second Guitar, or the piano forte, composed for the Celebrated Giulio Regondi, op. 16* (London, 1833). Giulio Regondi (1822/3–72) was a guitar and concertina virtuoso. In the 1830s he attracted attention as an accomplished child prodigy. The publisher was Chappell.
[193] Pelzer published at least fourteen Divertimenti.
[194] Pelzer, *Instructions*.
[195] Copies of these editions have not been located.
[196] Charles Eulenstein, *Introduction and Variations for the Spanish Guitar on Weber's Last Waltz, op 12* (London, [1832]). Charles Eulenstein, *Introduction and Variations for the Guitar on Beethoven's Celebrated Waltz* (London, [1832]).
[197] Sor, *Method*.
[198] Mauro Giuliani, *Giuliani's Three Rondos for two Guitars*, rev. G. H. Derwort (London, n.d.).
[199] No copy of this has been located.

SOR, Op. 6. ....CLEMENTI.[200]
KREITZER'S God Save the King, varied ....EWER.[201]
NUSKE'S Fantasia (My Lodging). ....Do.[202]
KNIZE'S Rondo..Do.[203]
HORETZKY'S Modulations...Do.[204]
—— Exercises, in two Books ....BOOSEY and Co.[205]
PELZER'S Fantasia (Op. 8) ....Do.[206]
NUSKE'S Two Fantasias, introducing God Save the King, and
    German Air .... Do.[207]
NEULAND'S Duet for Two Guitars ....METZLER.[208]
HORETZKY'S Divertimento ....Do.[209]
—— Modulation .... Do.[210]
PRATTEN'S Divertimento from Der Freischutz .... Do.[211]
GIULIANI'S Six Rondos .... DAVIS.[212]
HORETZKY'S Fantasia, dedicated to LADY PONSONBY .... Do.[213]
SOR'S Fantasia, Op. 9.....................................WELSH.[214]

[200] No copy of this edition has been located.

[201] Joseph Kreutzer, *God Save the King arranged with Variations for the Spanish Guitar* (London, n.d.). Kreutzer published much for the guitar in the years 1822–28. Josef Zuth, *Handbuch der Laute und Gitarre* (Vienna, 1926), 163–64. The theme and first variation is included in the music section of the fourth number of *The Giulianiad*, page 40.

[202] For a review see 'Review of Music', *TG* 1:2 (1833), 22.

[203] No copy of this has been located. Franz Max Kniže published music for guitar in Prague and Vienna in the early nineteenth century. Josef Zuth, *Handbuch*, 158.

[204] No copy of this has been located.

[205] For a review see 'Review of Music', *TG* 1:1 (1833), 11.

[206] No copy of this has been located.

[207] For a review see 'Review of Music', *TG* 1:3 (1833), 34.

[208] This is probably: Wilhelm Neuland, *Andantino and Rondo for Two Guitars* (London, c.1832).

[209] No copy of this has been located.

[210] Felix Horetzky, *Preludes, Cadences, and Modulations in every key for the Guitar, Op. 21* (London, [1833]).

[211] This is probably *The Fantasia* by Stephen Pratten reviewed earlier. 'Review of Music', *TG* 1:6 (1833), 55.

[212] No copy of this edition has been located. It was probably Giuliani's *Six Rondeaux, op. 14*.

[213] No copy of this has been located.

[214] Fernando Sor, *The Favorite Air, "Oh Cara armonia", from Mozart's Opera Il Flauto Magico, Arranged with an Introduction and Variations for the Guitar* (London, 1821). This would refer to the edition that was published in London by the Royal Harmonic Institution which was taken over by Welsh and Hawes in 1825. These partners separated in 1828 leaving Welsh in business alone. Jeffery, *Sor*, 2nd edn (London, 1994), 153. John Parkinson, *Victorian Music Publishers* (Michigan, 1990), 231, 285. An earlier edition was published in Paris in 1819. Erik Stenstadvold, 'Introduction', in Fernando Sor, *The Collected Works for Guitar*, ed.

—— Divertissement, Op. 13. .... Do.[215]
—— Ops. 1 and 2, (which we particularly recommend)..... MONZANI.[216]
NEULAND'S Fantasia ....DUFF and Co.[217]
HORETZKY'S Fantasia, dedicated to CAPTAIN PHILLIPS.........
                 ALDRIDGE.[218]
SAGRINI and OSBORNE'S Duet for Guitar and Piano............... Do.[219]
GIULIANI'S Third Concerto: the master-piece of all compositions
 for this instrument .... JOHANNING.[220]
SOR'S Twenty-four Exercises, Op. 35.. Do.[221]
NEULAND'S Fantasia, dedicated to EMILY DUBOUT .... Do.[222]
GOMEZ' Waltzes .... Do.[223]
A. SHULTZ'S Air with Variations .... Do.[224]

In this list there is nothing but sound classical music. Such music in fact as a real musician would be delighted with; and such as a connoisseur may study with advantage. That we have omitted some pieces published in London which may come under the denomination of "classical" there is no doubt; but the error is one of omission, not intention, and one that we shall be happy at any future opportunity to rectify.

English guitar-makers will form a separate article.[225]

Erik Stenstadvold, 2nd edn, 14 vols (Heidelberg, 2022), iii, 14. The piece was one of the great works from this period and remains in the concert repertoire today.

[215] Fernando Sor, *Six Divertimentos for the Guitar* (London, 1819). Jeffery, *Sor*, 2nd edn, 154. This edition, like the previous one, was first published by the Regent's Harmonic Institution.

[216] Opus one: Fernando Sor, *Six Divertimentos, for the Spanish Guitar* (London, c.1815). Opus two: Fernando Sor, *Six Divertimentos for the Guitar* (London, c.1815–19). Jeffery, *Sor*, 2nd edn, 149. Both these editions were first published by Monzani and Hill.

[217] It has not been possible to identify this piece.

[218] No copy of this has been located.

[219] L. Sagrini and G. Osborne, *Variazione concertante sopra un tema di Rossini, per chitarra e piano forte* (London, n.d.). Lewis and Coldwell, *Sagrini*, 147. It was reviewed in *The Giulianiad*, 'Review of Music', *TG* 1:3 (1833), 33.

[220] Mauro Giuliani, *Third Grand Concerto for the Guitar, with a separate accompaniment for the Piano Forte, op. 70* (London, [1833]). This edition is advertised on an unnumbered page at the beginning of this volume.

[221] Fernando Sor, *Vingt Quatre Exercises* (London, [1830]). Jeffery, *Sor*, 2nd edn, 161.

[222] Wilhelm Neuland, *Fantasie pour la Guitare* (London, c.1832). For a review see 'Review of Music', *TG* 1:4 (1833), 41.

[223] This piece has not been identified. The composer may have been Francisco Gómez, who published some songs with piano or guitar accompaniment in the 1820s in London.

[224] This piece has not been identified. Andreas Schulz, father of Leonard and Eduard, was a guitarist. Eight of his compositions were published in Vienna, 1811–24. Stenstadvold, *Schulz*, 9.

[225] This proposed article was never published.

[p. 58]

Musical Intelligence, Chit-Chat, &c.

FEMALE COMPOSER. – MISS LINWOOD, of Birmingham, has entirely written and composed an Oratorio, called "David's First Victory;" of which, upon its first performance at St. Paul's Chapel there, the provincial journals speak in terms of very high admiration.[226] It is certainly a great work for a female musician, and the first of the kind we remember to have heard of. MISS MOUNSEY and MISS BELLCHAMBERS should turn their attention to this high class of composition.

DEATH OF SIR JOHN STEVENSON. – This ancient musician and composer died at his daughter's, the Marchioness of Headfort, Meath, on Saturday, at the age of seventy-four. His share in producing the Irish Melodies in conjunction with Moore, will cause him to be long cherished in the popular memory of his country: while some of his more elevated and sacred compositions remain to stamp his name among the foremost we can boast in this delightful science. Only a few years ago his appearance was wonderfully juvenile, and his conversation and manners as sprightly as his looks. He was most agreeable and entertaining in society, and seemed almost to have discovered the secret of perpetual youth. But we now find the *elixir vitæ* is a phantom.[227]

WORCESTER MUSIC MEETING. – This grand musical festival has just terminated, beneficially we are happy to say for the funds of the several charities. MALIBRAN, DE MERIC, MISS H. CAWSE, and BRUCE among the ladies; and DONZELLI, HORNCASTLE, HOBBS, and PHILLIPS among the gentlemen were the principal vocalists. They all acquitted themselves with much applause, especially MISS BRUCE, who is represented as having been a great favorite.[228]

MR. MORLEY, the bass singer of Covent Garden, joins the Victoria. The managers ought to procure a good prima donna for this house, in which they are sadly deficient.[229]

---

[226] Mary Linwood (1755/6–1845) was known for her embroidered pictures as well as her musical compositions. Sophie Fuller, *The Pandora Guide to Women Composers* (London, 1994), 189–90.

[227] John Stevenson (c.1761–1833) was an Irish composer. Brown, *Dictionary*, 577.

[228] The Three Choirs Festival, dating from the eighteenth century, was based in turn in the cathedrals of Gloucester, Worcester, and Hereford. See Watkins Shaw, revised by John Phillips, 'Three Choirs Festival', *GMO*. Musicians from London, such as the singers named here, would take part.

[229] The Victoria was probably the Royal Coburg Theatre in Lambeth which was renamed the Royal Victoria Theatre in 1833. Jim Davis and Victor Emeljanow, *Reflecting the Audience, London Theatre Going 1840–1880* (Hatfield, 2001), 8. It is now known as the 'Old Vic'.

C. Eulenstein

Engraved by G. Adcock from a Drawing by S. Branwhite.

Figure 13. Karl Eulenstein [1833], engraved by G. Adcock from a drawing by Branwhite.

LAPORTE is in treaty with M. BOILIEU, the French composer, for a new opera, which will form one of the novelties of the ensuing season at the King's Theatre.[230] As soon as M. LAPORTE has found guarantees for the payment of rent required by the assignees of MR. CHAMBERS, they will make a reduction to him in the rent of the house of £2000 per annum. Should M. LAPORTE fail to meet this condition he will still be the lessee of the Opera House upon his present agreement, three or four years of which are unexpired. It will, however, be at the present rent of £13,000 per annum, which, in the present depressed state of theatrical affairs, is enormous.[231]

DRURY LANE, COVENT GARDEN, OLYMPIC, STRAND, ADELPHI, and other theatres are now on the point of opening their campaigns: while the HAYMARKET continues its season to an unprecedented late period.[232]

MADAME DE MERIC, with other excellent vocalists, have been on a provincial tour, without, however, meeting with brilliant success. Not so with MR. and MRS. SEGUIN, who, with YATES of the Adelphi, have made good hits in almost every in town [*sic*] which they have exhibited.[233]

MUSICAL EARS OF THE BLIND,– "The accuracy of the ear gives to blind persons a very great advantage in music: they depend entirely upon it; and hence they harmonize so well together, and keep such perfect accord in time, that Paganini, after listening to some pieces performed by pupils of the Institution for the Blind in Paris, declared that he never before had an accurate notion of what harmony was." – *North American Review*.[234]

CURIOUS EFFECTS OF MUSIC. – Rousseau speaks of a lady of rank, upon whom the effect of music produced involuntary fits of laughter.[235] Mankind, however, are not the only beings subject to its influence. It has been remarked, long since, the excitement produced

---

[230]   This report was in several newspapers, including 'M. Laporte', *Morning Post*, 28 September 1833. The French composer François-Adrien Boieldieu (1775–1834) did not provide the work hoped for.

[231]   Pierre Laporte, a French actor, managed the King's Theatre from 1828 until 1842. He inherited debts with a mortgage to the bankrupt banker Mr. Chambers. Daniel Nalbach, *The King's Theatre 1704–1867* (London, 1972), 97–100. £13,000 would be equivalent to nearly two million pounds today.

[232]   These were the main theatres in the West End of London.

[233]   Arthur Seguin (1809–52) and his wife Anne (d.1888) were singers; in the late 1830s they moved to America and established their own small opera company, the Seguin Troupe. Nicholas Tawa, 'Seguin, Arthur', *GMO*.

[234]   Anon, 'Education of the Blind', *North American Review* 37:80 (1833), 20–58, at 26–27.

[235]   Jean-Jacques Rousseau, *Dictionnaire de musique* (Paris, 1768), 315. '& je connois à Paris une femme de condition, laquelle ne peut écouter quelque *Musique* que ce foit sans etre saisie d'un rire involontaire & convulsif'.

on horses by the sound of horn or trumpet. Bernardin de Saint-Pierre observed that spiders in the corner of rooms, where *music* was being performed, never failed of approaching the place occupied by musicians; and that they never returned to their webs until the sounds of the instruments had ceased.[236] Sir Everard Home had studied the effect of a piano upon a lion and elephant; and he found that the attention of these animals was completely fixed by the higher notes of that instrument, and that their fury broke out from the moment the lower notes were touched.[237] An experiment of a similar nature was made at Paris upon two young elephants, male and female; an orchestra, composed of eleven musicians, executed various pieces of music. The first effect produced upon the animals was that of astonishment; but they very soon shewed by their motions the pleasure they felt. M. Fetis, the present organist of the Royal Chapel of the King of Belgium, has made some very curious experiments upon various kinds of animals.[238]

[236] Variations of this story were given in several publications in the eighteenth and nineteenth centuries. The version by the French writer Bernardin de Saint Pierre (1737–1814) has not been located.

[237] Everard Home, *Lectures on Comparative Anatomy*, 6 vols (London, 1814–28), iii (1823), 283–84.

[238] François-Joseph Fétis, 'De l'action physique de la musique', *Revue Musicale* 4 (1829), 97–110. Fétis describes the effect of music on several animals and includes an account of an orchestral performance to two elephants.

THE MUSICAL HERALD

THE
MUSICAL HERALD,
A Journal for the Diffusion
OF
VOCAL AND INSTRUMENTAL MUSIC
AMONG THE PEOPLE.

———

No. I.[1] GRATIS PRICE, 0d.

———

PROPOSALS

FOR ESTABLISHING A SOCIETY FOR THE DIFFUSION OF MUSICAL KNOWLEDGE.

MR. FERDINAND PELZER having been long desirous that a Society might be formed upon principles of mutual benefit, for the purpose of spreading the knowledge of Vocal and Instrumental Music amongst all Classes of the People, in which unity of design and interest would be the actuating principle, and conceiving that none are better qualified for such purpose than men of experience in the art, he is anxious that the Members of the Society should be composed of established Professors, who, by forming a Committee of Twelve Directors from among themselves, should consult and devise the best means for carrying out such measures as the majority in a general assembly should decide upon.

Such an Association, by establishing a more extended intercourse amongst its own Members, would bring a communion of ideas, originating from experience and talent to combine in effecting that great and desirable good, for which the true philanthropist has so long struggled: – namely, the regeneration of the people from debasing habits, and which the British Government has recently shown itself so desirous of promoting, by the formation of Musical Classes,[2] by which, means of enjoy–

---

[1] The addresses on the twelfth page suggest that this was published between late 1841 and late 1843. Metzler & Co. moved to Great Marlborough Street between September and December 1841. On 18 September they were in Wardour Street, 'Advertisements', *Leeds Intelligencer*, 18 September 1841. They had moved to Great Marlborough Street by 25 December, 'Books and Periodicals', *London Phalanx*, 25 December 1841. The Pelzers left 47, Poland Street in the autumn of 1843 as confirmed in the rate books.

[2] These would have been Hullah's classes in Battersea and at Exeter Hall.

[p. 2]

ment is provided, to fill up those hours which would otherwise be passed in indulging vicious propensities, or wasted in vacant idleness.

The success which has already crowned this laudable attempt, demonstrates what might be done, if, instead of individual efforts, a combined plan of operations were to spread in all directions, from one common centre, a sufficient provision to meet the universal demand for moral and religious improvement through the Agency of Music.

A few Sketches for Rules are submitted to form the basis for future consideration:–

FORMATION OF CLASSES.

Each Class to consist of at least 200 pupils, and to comprise from that number up to 600.

At the opening of every Class the First Lesson to be given gratis.

TERMS.

Sixpence per four lessons, one lesson per week, for which an admission ticket will be given.

TIME OF MEETING OF THE CLASSES.

Eight o'clock in the evening.

REMUNERATION TO THE PROFESSOR.

Half of the funds formed by the subscription of the classes will go to remunerate the Professors, the other half for expenses of the room, bills, printing, advertisements, and any surplus to the benefit fund.

Other classes will be formed at one shilling, two shillings and sixpence, and five shillings, the four lessons, in proportion to the expenses incurred.

A Professor will be considered a Member of the Society who devotes the time of one class lesson per week. A Member will be at liberty to form private classes on terms agreeable to himself.

BENEFIT FUND.

It will be a principal object to form a fund from the surplus proceeds of the public performances of pupils for the benefit of professional members of the society when disabled by illness or other misfortune from following their profession.

COMMITTEE OF MANAGEMENT.

After the classes have gone through the seven parts,[3] into which this system is divided, a Committee of twelve Professors to be held for con-

[p. 3]

sulting on the best description of Music for the carrying on a more complete development of their pupils' abilities, and other matters of interest.

JOURNAL.

This Journal will be published Monthly, containing Reports of the Proceedings of the Society, of its progress, and treating of all transactions affecting its immediate or future prospects, and the best endeavours of the Editors will in every respect be given to the advancement of the general interests of the Musical Art.

———

Every possible publicity will be given to the plans and objects of the Society by means of advertisements, placards, reviews, &c.

———

ADDRESS TO THE CLERGY, HEADS OF PUBLIC SCHOOLS, ETC.

To assist in furthering the objects of this undertaking, the Clergy, Heads of Schools, Managers of Societies of all denominations, are hereby respectfully appealed to, and their support solicited in forming classes amongst their respective Congregations, Establishments, and Fraternities. – The use of their School Rooms and other localities is also earnestly requested for the classes; for whose instruction competent Professors will be supplied on application to the
Office of the Society, No. 47, Poland Street, Oxford Street.

———

To Colonels of Regiments, and other Military Authorities, facilities will be afforded for teaching Soldiers in barracks.

Charity Schools and others will be taught gratuitously upon their forming classes of two hundred – and if not sufficient number in one establishment, two or three may unite to make up the complement.

———

---

3   For full descriptions of the seven parts see Ferdinand Pelzer, *Music for the People, on Universal Principles Practically Arranged by F Pelzer and Theoretically Explained by H Doherty*, 2nd edn (London, 1858).

FRIENDLY HINTS TO THE MUSICAL PROFESSION.

IT is the intention of this Journal to promote the general interests of the Musical Art; and being persuaded that this object will be most surely attained by unity of purpose, we are particularly anxious that the numerous and influential body of Professors should examine the present state of musical instruction in order to come to some conclusion upon the question whether the recent innovation of teaching in classes be totally

[p. 4]

opposed to their own established method, or whether an approximation might not be just and good policy, and adopted with benefit to all parties.

Some discussion is certainly imperatively demanded, and an eclaircissement[4] necessary in order that they may not appear opposed to the public voice, in which false position they ought not to stand for a moment.

A very sensible writer has truly said: "The art of instruction depends to a very secondary extent upon methods; the secret of success lies in sympathy with the pupil, a thorough mastery of the subject, delight in the art, and extreme patience."[5] If this be true, systems on the railroad principle of making short work of it, cannot maintain their ground much beyond the mere elementary part, and the thorough musician will eventually be required to carry on and complete what they have begun.

However, besides the question upon the merits of different modes of instruction we would wish to call the particular attention of Professors to the new honours which have been recently claimed for Music by those who attribute to it a moral agency, which may be made materially to assist in forwarding the best objects of education; from this, therefore, arises an additional spur to enquiry, for if music is destined to become an aid to moral instruction, the Professor will naturally reflect on how much this circumstance, which increases its importance to society, will contribute to raise his own – for music must in some measure be identified with the musician.[6] The relative tie approaches to that of a mother and her children, who have been nourished at her bosom – educated in her precepts; in their early years she has encouraged their hopes, and allayed their fears – and in maturity has rewarded their exertions – and they, in their turn, have imparted to others the feelings of their common nature.

---

4   explanation.
5   [W. E. Hickson] *Part Singing, or Vocal Harmony for Choral Societies and Home Circles*, quoted in [W. E. Hickson], 'Art VII,—. Part Singing', *Westminster Review* 38:1 (1842), 153–67, at 159.
6   The good influence of singing on moral education was referred to by many choral teachers at this time. However, Pelzer may have particularly had in mind Mainzer's view that the moral influence of singing was a source of elevated sentiment and refinement of manners. Mainzer, *Singing*, xii.

But it will be demanded, what is the import of this moral agency? Our reply is, that as far as we can judge, it consists in a proper application of its effects on the feelings and passions, so as to regulate and give them a right direction, by exciting good and subduing evil inclinations.

[p. 5]

Whether this moral agent be of certain or uncertain power remains for future consideration. The duty of a Professor has hitherto been to teach music as an elegant accomplishment – a necessary part of a liberal education, and as a delightful recreation. These are the traits of music in its social character, and in that character it has been the care of the Professor to make it as attractive as possible, with what success the daily records of music – the echoes of the hall, the boudoir, and the parlour, from thousands of hearts rejoicing in the re-union of the evening hour will abundantly tell! These happy effects, so creditable to both master and scholar, have resulted from the long and frequent attendance of the former, at particular hours, devoted exclusively to the cultivation of the talent of one individual. This exclusive mode of instruction it will not be possible to alter in numerous instances, since the individuals themselves would not like it altered, or to join in a class. How far private teaching of individuals will bear a further reduction of terms, which have in general been already much reduced, is uncertain; but the change for which the Professor should be prepared is that inevitable one – the demand for class teaching from numbers (above the poorer sort of people) who will resort to it for the sake of economy, and who would have learnt as individuals, but that the eclat given to the class system by government patronage and public performances, has induced them entirely to abandon private instruction.[7]

ON MUSIC,

As it may influence the Moral and Religious feelings.

THE rapid spread of the desire for Musical Instruction in public schools and among the people, through the facility of learning according to the new systems of teaching in classes, renders it not only a matter of mere curiosity or speculation, but of practical importance to examine

---

[7] There is conflicting evidence that music teachers' charges for lessons fell at this time. Rohr, *Careers*, 136. Evidence of guitar teachers' fees is very limited; however, examples of two teachers who reduced their fees have been seen. Ventura advertised one guinea for four lessons in 1835 and then three pounds for twelve lessons in 1836. Sola advertised fifteen shillings in 1828 and two shillings and sixpence in 1840. Clarke, 'Instrument', 115. The government patronage probably refers to the support given to Hullah for his choral teaching of classes by the Committee of Council on Education.

what kind of influence Music is likely to exert on the mind, beyond its powers of affording mere

[p. 6]

amusement. This we shall endeavour to do, and while unfolding the observations of science, shall quote practical illustrations, with the view of not only rendering the whole subject better understood, but of enforcing its truth.

Though the facts resulting from this examination are expressly intended to show how Music may be made an agent in forming the character of the child, and regulating the disposition of the man, still they can only be considered as rough materials collected in readiness for the use, and placed at the disposal of the moral and religious guardian, to be moulded by them into rules suitable to the principles of the establishment to which they may belong, and applied in accordance to the various tempers and dispositions of the individuals under their care.

In order to put Music as a moral agent on a durable basis, that it may be productive of lasting good, it seems evident that its properties should be better understood than they are at present, to avoid their misapplication. We shall, therefore, subject it to a kind of analysis by classing it under three heads :–

The power to amuse – to excite – and to subdue; this classification will assist both the reasoning facilities and the memory.

The pleasure derived from sweet sounds through the sense of hearing is of itself a great blessing bestowed by the benevolent Deity to contribute to our happiness. The moral and religious Addison has said, that Music is the only pleasure that may be indulged in with total impunity, and that even if enjoyed to excess it leaves no stain.[8] Therefore its powers of amusing may be advantageously employed as a relaxation from business – to relieve the dryness of study – or to lighten the toil of labour – and herein may be traced an indirect moral agency; – those hours engaged in this innocent recreation being, perhaps, so much time redeemed from vicious pursuits.

Tunes of a light, cheerful, and joyous nature, therefore, should be taught, as well as ballads of a gay and lively cast of thought and sentiment, in order that the face of youth may be suffused with the glow of healthful merriment, and the domestic circle sparkle with the smiles of gladness and content.

---

[8]   This is most likely a paraphrase of a remark attributed to Johnson: '[music] is the only sensual pleasure without vice.' William Cowper, 'Johnsoniana', *The County Magazine* 1:18 (1787), 282.

[p. 7]

A spirit of hilarity breathes through many of the Irish and Scotch airs which is truly delightful, while others for pathos and deep, yet natural feeling, are unsurpassed by those of any other nation. There is a wholesome vigour in this music collectively which will recommend it to all admirers of the natural and unsophisticated, therefore we need not illustrate this part of our subject by particular examples.

To proceed with the second branch of our subject – Music has the power of exciting us to noble deeds, of raising in our breasts patriotism and loyalty, of which our national anthems of "God save the Queen," and "Rule Britannia," are memorable and distinguished illustrations – also of inspiring us with courage, fortitude, and perseverance; witness the powerful effect of the sea songs of Dibdin during our long struggle against the enemies of liberty in the war which ended so gloriously for Great Britain.[9] The power of this species of Music likewise in rousing and bracing the nervous and physical energies, is practically illustrated by the use of drum and trumpet in battle, and by sailors singing their "Yo, heave ho!" in a kind of rhythmetical accompaniment to some of their nautical duties. In Naval and Military Schools, Music possessing the above characteristics is, therefore, peculiarly applicable.

The ancient Greeks, our predecessors, and instructors in the arts of civilization, no doubt made much use of this kind of music in their exercises for strengthening the body, as well as in exciting the soul to noble deeds.

We come now to Music of a subduing character. There is a soothing power in music which even the infant feels while being lulled to slumber by the mother's lullaby; – and observations may show the careful disciplinarian how to apply it in correcting the asperities of temper in the child. Perhaps, wilfulness – petulancy – sudden gusts of anger – sullenness and obstinacy might be overcome, if, instead of coercion, the offender was brought to listen to the performance of a melody of a soothing character with appropriate words until the evil feeling had passed.

[p. 8]

Songs expressing penitential sentiments might be employed advantageously to subdue the unruly disposition into gentle emotions of obedience and contrition.

In subduing worldly thoughts, in kindling devotional feelings, and in adding a deeper solemnity to its holy rites, Music has been for ages a handmaid to religion.

---

9   Charles Dibdin (1745–1814) was regarded as a respectable entertainer whose sailor songs were popular during the Napoleonic wars. He was given a government pension between 1803 and 1806. Derek Scott, *The Singing Bourgeois* (Aldershot, 2001), 32–33.

The expressive composition of Handel, "The Dead March in Saul;" usually performed at military funerals, is a sublime illustration of the solemn and pathetic; its deeper tones subduing the soul to a reverential awe, or its plaintive chords causing the heart to wail, as we are reminded, that it is but dust which we are consigning to its kindred earth, for that the spirit has departed.[10]

This subject so fruitful in interesting hopes, and opening a new field for physical, moral, and spiritual agency, cannot but prove an attractive theme for future discussion to ourselves and others.

———

THOUGHTS ON THE NECESSITY OF UNION,

IN PROMOTING BENEFICIAL PURPOSES.

Unity is strength! In this age of general enlightenment, too little consideration has been given to a sincere and permanent practical union between classes whose interest directs them to the same object; this, however, does not proceed from want of feeling its paramount importance in carrying on the business of life, nor from ignorance of how much it contributes to give energy to individual exertion, whilst bringing in a valuable accession to the common stock of usefulness; since in religion, in social, domestic, and political economy, in all arts, sciences, trades, crafts, and professions, its beneficial influence is acknowledged. Why then do we not more firmly adhere to the principles of unity? The cause of its frequent failure may be traced to the failings of human nature; for

[p. 9]

though the social feelings of man lead him to seek for sympathy and support, in the hours of trial and weakness, yet selfishness and pride of heart again isolate him from his fellow-creatures, and in proportion as he wishes his own opinions alone to prevail, regardless of the feelings of others, he becomes anti-social; and, as in the pursuit of his unreasonable ambition, he, naturally enough, meets with resistance, thus the seeds of dis-union are sown: his bad example, perhaps, creates imitators, the fruits are contentions! – feuds! – jealousies! – the evil passions are unchained! – society is split – divided and subdivided into parties full of animosities towards each other – the bond of union is dissolved, and the good purposes for which it was instituted perish with it.

———

[10] Handel's *Dead March* from the third act of his oratorio *Saul* (1738) was performed at the state funerals of Lord Nelson (1806) and the Duke of Wellington (1852). 'British Library Collection Items: The *Dead March* from Handel's oratorio *Saul*', https://www.bl.uk/collection-items/handel-dead-march. [accessed 5 August 2023].

MUSIC FOR THE PEOPLE,

ON UNIVERSAL PRINCIPLES.

Practically arranged by FERDINAND PELZER, *and theoretically explained by* H. DOHERTY, Esq.

In the pursuit of beneficial discoveries, the active spirits of the present age have not been idle, and in bringing Music to the aid of moral cultivation they hold out a new land of promise to the world of civilization; for the idea that the human heart and understanding may be profitably wrought by means of the natural affinities of musical sounds with the suggestions of thought and feeling, there is much reason to believe is a great truth: – and, since it has been made known that statesmen have recommended Music as a branch of national education, an eager desire has been manifested to test its value, by putting it into immediate operation in all description of places devoted to educational purposes, whether of children, or adults.[11] One cause of this universally favourable reception, at the present juncture, may possibly arise from the hope, that Music will become the harbinger of peace and social order.

[p. 10]

From a tacit acknowledgment, therefore, of its expected advantages, has resulted numerous enquiries after the best method of instilling the first principles of Music into minds hitherto unprepared for their reception.

In aspiring to forward this meritorious object, it was but natural that those individuals who had made it their peculiar study, should each take his own view of the best means of effecting it; thus has arisen several systems of instruction, which, though alike in the chief point of bringing the uninformed together in numbers, in order that information might be imparted at the smallest expense, and with the least loss of time to the teacher and the taught; yet, differ in the medium through which that instruction should be conveyed: this difference, however, lies chiefly in a trial of skill, as to who can most divest the art of technicalities and of all extraneous matter, without injury to essentials; and by reducing it to its simplest state, render its rules, as far as possible, easy and intelligible to all. This is more necessary from Music being a complicated art, inasmuch as it requires not only the faculty of memory, (which in itself is sufficient for many studies,) but the skilful use of peculiar functions of the ear, voice, and touch, which are rarely called into use by the common business of life. The musical faculties, therefore, not having been

---

[11]   This refers to James Kay and the Committee of Council on Education.

brought into exercise, cannot be supposed to be in readiness at the first call, and although their occasional use cannot give us a perfect command over them, neither will such be expected, except from the professional musician; and to whom that advantage is the reward only of a long and careful cultivation by art, of those gifts bestowed by nature. Keeping, therefore, this fact in view, this work – "Music for the People" – has been written upon the principle, that every one shall be enabled to perform his part with ease and credit to himself, and satisfaction to others; for, whatever be our ability, if what we do is well done, our efforts are meritorious, and the individual who thus contributes his share to the general fund of recreation is fulfilling a pleasant duty, which ought to be the object of every society, and is entitled to the

[p. 11]

praise and consideration of every friend to humanity. Let none, therefore be discouraged by the fear of wanting the necessary qualifications, as the progressive rules and lessons, of which this work is composed, will furnish the means of improvement to all without distinction.

> Not by a bound the mountain top is gain'd,
> But step by step the height may be attain'd.[12]

———

As the remarks in the preceding article touch only upon the general tendency of "Music for the People," considered as an elementary work, and as many may be desirous of forming some farther idea of it from a detailed account of its contents; our endeavour shall be to give as circumstantial and explanatory a description as the limits of our pages will admit.

"Music for the People" has been written throughout (as the title-page expresses it) upon "Universal Principles" – meaning that it is so constructed that Music may be understood – practised – enjoyed and appreciated by all without distinction – by individuals of every rank, condition, taste, and capacity; step by step leading them through each successive rule, and making the mastery of one rule a stepping stone to the next. The lessons by which this is effected being explained in a simple, definite and attractive manner, the pupil will encounter no strange and discouraging terms or technicalities of art, no puzzling theory, difficult of comprehension, and though occupying much time and attention, yet producing no practical result. Plurality of clefs is

---

[12]   The source of this quotation has not been found.

dispensed with,[13] and, in short, all unnecessary barriers to his progress have been removed, and something will be constantly gained either in the shape of an useful exercise, or a pleasing melody.

Harmony, always indispensable to good music and a good musician, has received due attention; and in order to enable the pupil to take an early share in part singing, a part for a second voice has been harmonized to the first lessons, which will besides form an exercise for either the first or second voice; and

[p. 12]

which will be taken into practice after some necessary knowledge of intervals has been acquired.

The author's plan will also facilitate the learning of any military instrument, by which bands may be formed for recreative assemblies, professional meetings, or parties of pleasure. Soldiers will also be enabled to sing choral melodies, with or without the regimental band, either in barracks, in the camp, or on a march.

The sound method of instruction which this work inculcates, offers to members of the Profession an opportunity of acquiring private pupils well grounded in the first principles of music; and to the pupils themselves it will afford the satisfaction of reflecting that their acquirements are of a solid nature, and that they are properly prepared, should inclination or circumstances incite them to dive deeper into the treasures of the art.

The great advantage of the method consists in the union of practical simplicity and lucid theory.

TO THE PROFESSION.

Anxious to promote the general interests of the Musical Art, the pages of this Journal will be freely open to discussion on any subject connected with it, which may appear likely to lead to a favorable result. The interest of the Art being identical with that of its Professors, we invite them to contribute (through the medium of literary correspondence) the aid of their talents and experience to that desirable end; at the same time earnestly requesting that their attention may be directed only to such measures as may be practically useful, accompanied, if possible, by some suggestions as to the most ready means for their accomplishment.

"In the multitude of counsellors there is wisdom."[14]

---

[13]   Pelzer advocated the replacement of standard five-line clefs with one clef of twelve lines. Pelzer, *Music for the People*, 2nd edn, 132–53.

[14]   The Bible, Proverbs 11:14: 'in the multitude of counsellors there is safety'.

LONDON: Published at the OFFICE, 47, Poland Street, Oxford Street; where all communications for the Editor are to be addressed; and Sold by METZLER & Co., 37 Great Marlborough Street.

[First Leaflet]¹

PELZER'S
UNIVERSAL SYSTEM OF INSTRUCTION
IN MUSIC.

———

ADDRESS TO ESTABLISHED PROFESSORS.

MR. PELZER wishes to call the attention of the Established Professors of Music to the importance of CLASS-TEACHING, and having written a Method entitled "Music for the People," by which he will qualify any Professor in "two hours" (without fee) to teach from two to four hundred pupils with the same facility as one, he respectfully invites them to an interview, at his residence, 47, Poland Street, Oxford Street, London.

———

N.B. – Orphans and Charity Schools taught gratuitously, and Classes immediately opened on application to Mr. PELZER, as above; or to METZLER and Co., Music Warehouse, 37, Great Marlborough-st. London.

———

Opinions of the Press.

MUSIC FOR THE PEOPLE. – "To simplify musical education of the many is a very important object; and nothing can be more politic than to facilitate the study of an art which can give rational enjoyment at a small expense. There are no royal roads to learning by which that which can delight for years can be acquired in a few hours; but the way may be very much shortened; and class-teaching has become the fashion. Mr. Pelzer, who has written a very able work on the best method of conveying instruction, proposes to teach professors the means of instructing hundreds with the same facility as they could instruct one or two individuals; and his plan, on which he intends to lecture in public, seems simple and yet very comprehensive." – *Saunders' News-Letter, September* 1842.²

MUSIC AND SINGING FOR THE PEOPLE. – "It is highly gratifying to find every moral, social, and scientific improvement following in the march of Temperance. I must refer with gratification to the lessons which have been gratuitously and most kindly given by Mr. Pelzer, assisted by

---

¹   This probably dates from 1842.
²   'Music for the People', *Leinster Express*, 10 September 1842. The review has not been seen in *Saunders's News-Letter*.

Mr. Searle and other professors, in the large school-room, Essex-street, under the Rev. A. O'Connell, and St. Peter's School, Aungier-street, under the Very Rev. Dr. Spratt.[3] At two o'clock yesterday the lessons were given in the latter; and at seven o'clock yesterday evening in the former, at which several clergymen and a large number of gentlemen and ladies attended. In the course of about an hour and a half each time, nearly five hundred boys thus derived a knowledge of music and singing, which could not otherwise be communicated to even a few individuals in several months. The peculiar merit of the system is its simplicity, and, at the same time, its extension, conveying the largest portion of scientific and practical knowledge in the shortest possible time, and to the greatest possible number of persons who can be brought together. It is, we understand, Mr. Pelzer's determination to give these lessons gratuitously to the children in all free schools, and to others, who may desire it, on reasonable terms, in select classes, to be formed immediately." – *Freeman's Journal, September 1st*, 1842.[4]

MUSIC FOR THE PEOPLE – "We had the pleasure of attending Mr. Pelzer's first meeting for Popular Vocal Instructions in classes, at the Teetotal-hall, French-street, on his plan, and we must say that we were pleased and astonished. The persons who

[p. 2]

attended to receive instruction were chiefly composed of working classes, to the number of one hundred and fifty. Mr. Pelzer commenced his lessons by explaining the nature of the clef-line in music, time &c. &c. and afterwards made the pupils sing a single note, and led them on by degrees to sing a melody, all in the first lesson! But they did not merely sing, they understood what they sang! Mr. Pelzer has, since his arrival here, given instructions gratis to upwards of six hundred children in the several charitable schools of the city. We have had classes amongst us on the Wilhem method for the last nine months, and we will venture to say, that they are not competent to sing the German air as it was sung by Mr. Pelzer's class on Tuesday." – *World, September* 10, 1842.

"The Right Hon. the Lord Mayor having kindly granted the use of the Round Room in the Mansion-house to Mr. Pelzer, for last Thursday evening, that gentleman exemplified the great facility of his method by demonstrating how much may be done with a large number of

---

3   These two schools in Dublin would have been the school of St Peter's Orphan Society in Aungier Street and the St Michael's and St John's Free Schools in Essex Street. *Thom's Irish Almanac and Official Directory* (Dublin, 1850), 653, 655.

4   Mr. Searle was probably a music teacher who continued to teach according to Pelzer's system in 1842. 'Advertisements', *Freeman's Journal*, 25 January 1843.

individuals in a single lesson, when the fundamental principles of music are treated simply and scientifically, and without wasting time in tedious explanation. The company, which was highly respectable, testified its approval by the greatest attention during the lesson, and by an unanimous shower of applause at its conclusion. Among those present we observed several of our first-rate professors, most of whom lent their aid on the occasion." – *Freeman's Journal, September* 10, 1842.[5]

MUSICAL INSTRUCTION FOR THE PEOPLE. – "On Thursday evening last, Mr. Pelzer gave a lesson on his system at the great room at the rear of the Mansion-house, in which he was assisted by several eminent professors, to a highly respectable auditory, including many amateurs, who unanimously expressed themselves highly gratified at the simple method by which the delivery of the notes upon the voice correctly in tune and in strict time was accomplished in the short space of time allotted to the first lesson." – *The Evening Packet, September* 10, 1842.[6]

MUSIC FOR THE PEOPLE. – "Amongst the most remarkable characteristics of the present age in Ireland, there is no one more striking than the rapid spread of those sciences which directly tend to soften, to harmonise, and to beautify the domestic habits, and the social intercourse of the heretofore rude and untutored millions. A quarter of a century since, a taste for reading was looked upon as little better than a token of confirmed idleness; yet now, go which side you will, you find the peasantry able to read and to converse with you on the current events of the day. Thanks to the system of national education, the rising generation, the future labourers, and operatives and traders – those who will constitute the people – will have laid a foundation of arithmetical, geographical, and historical knowledge, sufficient to make them hereafter a more useful and more powerful body of men than their fathers. But as, without habits of temperance, these additional lights would serve but to lead the possessor into the ways of mischief, a new grace was bestowed, and intemperance was banished from the land. With temperance came a love for those more rational pleasures which can relax and gratify the mind, and thereby render unnecessary those stimulants which almost invariably drove pleasure into a wicked and painful excess.[7] Instrumental music begun to be very generally taught,

5   In the newspaper Pelzer is spelt Peltzer. The Round Room, attached to Dublin's Mansion House, was built in 1821 in honour of the visit of King George IV. It can accommodate around 700 people.
6   The newspaper adds: 'Mr. Pelzer intends to give a *second* lesson at the same place on Monday evening next, at eight o'clock.'
7   There are parallels between the singing class and Temperance movements. Theobald Mathew (1790–1856), a Capuchin friar, was a leading figure in the latter. Large numbers flocked to take the pledge (to abstain from alcohol) in the very late

and must do much to banish rudeness from society. But far greater and more rapid means of advancing the beauty and the harmony of society is to be found in the newly adopted plan of teaching the millions to use their voices musically. Every human being possessing a voice has provided for him by nature, in a certain degree, the faculty of singing. This faculty is susceptible of a higher or lower degree of development, by means of instruction, and more or less practice being afforded to the ear and voice. There are very few indeed to whom nature has not given the means to become, by instruction, imitation, and practice, pleasing singers. This truth has been long known in Italy and Germany: there is nothing to a foreigner more agreeably surprising than to hear the common rowers in the Venetian gondolas sing with exquisite skill the sweet music of their native land, whilst they ply their ordinary labours. In Germany, too, the practice of singing in bands is the general amusement of the people; and latterly, the same delightful source of pleasure has been cultivated with equal success in Holland, Prussia, and France. A simple and successful mode of enabling every person to improve the vocal powers has been very recently introduced into this country by M. Wilhem, M. Mainzer, and M. Pelzer, professional instructors. The latter gentleman gave

[p. 3]

instruction in the Mayoralty-rooms, in this town, on Wednesday and Thursday evenings. On the first, about forty gentlemen and a few highly respectable ladies attended; but so highly did they report of the gratification afforded them, that, on the second night, the room was crowded to excess. We had the pleasure of attending both nights, and have no hesitation in expressing our conviction that the system can be carried into the most extensive practice. *We were very agreeably surprised to find that there was no attempt at charlatanism, no pretence to new theories, no whimsical assumption of originality. The whole secret of success lies in the simplicity of the mode of teaching – in beginning at the beginning – and leading the pupils on step by step; nor did the lecturer waste any time in tiresome harangues or explanations, further than was necessary.* It is as easy to teach ten hundred as it is to teach ten. The mode is this: At one end of the room is placed a black board with the ordinary music lines, and on this the instructor marks the notes and explains the name and value of each. He gives a clear and concise explanation of the musical sounds, and of the manner in which they

1830s and early 1840s in Ireland. The Temperance societies that were established organised, among other things, social meetings and reading rooms for members. The movement led to reductions in alcohol consumption and crime. Colm Kerrigan, 'Mathew, Theobald', *ODNB*.

are represented in musical writing. This exercise has the double object of cultivating the voice and preparing the eye for musical reading. He commences with one note alone. This is the middle note *g* or *sol*, which is to be found in every voice. After having executed a few of such exercises, a music book is placed in the hands of each pupil; a second note is practised in connection with the first; then a third, and so on. After having obtained certainty and facility in the execution of these notes, and singing them in every possible combination of time, little melodies of three notes are practised, and then of four; so that speedily, pleasantly, and almost imperceptibly, the pupil is led to be able to perform the most difficult. Not the least agreeable part of the pleasure is the consciousness which the pupil feels that he is making certain progress. Mr. Pelzer has left town; but we feel much pleasure in stating, that our talented, scientific and musical professor, Mr. Crofton, has already made arrangements to give instruction upon precisely the same system which Mr. Pelzer has demonstrated to be so perfect, so simple, and so well adapted to the object in view." – *The Drogheda Argus, September* 24th, 1842.[8]

MUSIC FOR THE PEOPLE. – "A very simple and successful mode of enabling every person to improve the vocal powers has been introduced into this country recently by M. Mainzer, M. Wilhem, and M. Pelzer, professional instructors. The latter gentleman gave instructions in the Mayoralty-rooms, in this town, on the evenings of Wednesday and Thursday last, which delighted the fashionable and crowded houses that attended. M. Pelzer has since left town; but it affords us much pleasure in stating that our talented townsman, Mr. V. Crofton, has entered into arrangements for continuing a course on the system." – *ConservativeJournal* [*sic*]*, September* 24th, 1842.[9]

MUSIC FOR THE PEOPLE. – "Mr. Pelzer, whose successful efforts in the diffusion of musical knowledge have been repeatedly brought before the public by our brethren of the metropolitan press, has been, during two evenings of the present week, engaged in this town in imparting to a very large class of pupils instructions in vocal music, by a mode of teaching, the simplicity of which seems to be only equalled by the great proficiency which a few lessons produce. The effects of music, whether in a moral, physical, or spiritual view, are too universally accredited to require more than a reference from us; and we therefore feel much pleasure in calling the attention of those who have not already

[8] No copy of this newspaper has been found. It is not clear who Mr Crofton was.

[9] 'Singing for the Millions', *Drogheda Conservative Journal*, 24 September 1842. The title has been changed here; the original newspaper title of 'Singing for the Millions' would have alluded to the title of Joseph Mainzer's book *Singing for the Million*.

attended Mr. Pelzer's lectures, to the means by which they can, in a very short period, acquire a perfect knowledge of a science as delightful as hitherto difficult of attainment. We understand that a professional gentleman of this town will continue, in public classes, the 'musical education of the people,' on the same system which Mr. Pelzer has so successfully commenced." – *Drogheda Journal, September 24th,* 1842.

CLASS-SINGING FOR THE IMPROVEMENT OF THE PEOPLE. – "On Monday evening last, Mr. Pelzer, the celebrated German Professor of Music, assisted by Mr. J. C. Rogers, gave a lecture on his excellent system of class-singing in the Court-house of Navan. There were present on the occasion – the Pastor of the Parish, Dr. O'Reilly, the venerated Archdeacon of Meath, the Rev. P. Keely, the other parochial clergymen, and the Rev. and learned Professors of the Navan College, together with several highly respectable ladies, and about 150 other persons. The success was most striking: before the conclusion of the lesson, the pupils had become acquainted, not only with the names of the notes, &c. the value of them as respecting time, but were able to sing at sight a little

[p. 4]

German air with great precision and accuracy. It is true that the people of Navan were well prepared to receive such a system, having had their musical taste highly cultivated by their experienced and talented organist, Mr. J. C. Rogers, whose choir is now said to be the best amateur one in Ireland, as they execute with ease the most sublime and difficult compositions of Handel, Beethoven, Haydn, and Mozart. The Very Rev. Dr. O'Reilly, who, from residing a long time on the Continent, has seen the working of several systems for teaching music, has expressed his conviction of the superiority of Mr Pelzer's plan, not only for its great simplicity and clearness, but also for the practicability with which it can be carried into effect for the great body of the working people. Choirs and choral societies shall spring up among the people, and music shall be as the language of the land; where the discord of strife and faction-fighting formerly wounded the ear, there in future shall be heard either the song of social happiness, or the hymn and thanksgiving to the Lord! On the following day (Tuesday) Mr. J. C. Rogers, accompanied by Mr. Pelzer, proceeded to Kells, and opened a class in the School-rooms in that town, which were kindly granted by the very Rev. Mr. M'Evoy for the occasion, who, with his usual anxiety for the public good, and especially for the advancement of intellectual pursuits, not only afforded every facility to Mr. Pelzer and Mr. J. C. Rogers, but prefaced the lectures in his own peculiar style of brilliant eloquence, by proving the great moral and religious advantages to be derived from the cultivation of vocal music. Several fashionably dressed ladies were present, who expressed their entire approval of the system. The members of the Teetotal band, by the direction of their able President, Dr. Bennet, kept order in the room, which was crowded to excess. Mr Pelzer and Mr J. C. Rogers proceeded to Dublin on Wednesday, to open Mr. Rogers's Dublin class, in the great lecture-room, Abbey-street; which class, together with those in Kells and Navan, will here-after be continued by Mr. Rogers.

In Drogheda, Mr. V. Crofton commenced his classes on Wednesday evening with decided success, and will continue on each succeeding Monday night – *The Drogheda Argus, Oct.* 1, 1842.[10]

DINNER TO MR. PELZER – Mr. Pelzer, the celebrated German musician and lecturer, was publicly entertained by the members of the profession at Gilbert's hotel, Westland-row, on Saturday.[11] The dinner was served in a style of elegance which did credit to the establishment, and consisted of every delicacy which the season afforded. The chair was ably filled by Mr. J. W. Battersby, supported by Mr. Glover, as vice-president. – When the cloth was drawn *Non Nobis Domini*[12] was sung by several eminent performers who were present. The health of the Queen, with the usual loyal toasts having been given, the chairman proceeded to give the toast of the evening, and in terms as well deserved as they were complimentary to the guest, he proposed the "health of Mr. Pelzer," which was received with enthusiasm. Mr. Pelzer returned thanks in a brief but appropriate address, and stated some interesting facts relative to the great success of his mode of teaching the million how to sing. The evening was enhanced by several beautiful glees, which were executed in the most delightful manner by the gentlemen present; but the most important feature presented on the occasion was a practical illustration of the system as taught by Mr. Pelzer, and its success. Mr. Searle, (one of Mr. Pelzer's lecturers, who is forming classes in the city,) introduced the company into a room, where there were seated twelve boys belonging to St. Peter's Orphan Society, Aungier-street, together with eight or ten young girls (private pupils of Mr. Searle). At the end

---

[10]   No copy of this newspaper has been found. Mr. J. C. Rogers was probably a singing teacher. 'Advertisements', *Freeman's Journal*, 27 June 1851. Fr Eugene O'Reilly (1768–1852) was educated in France and worked in Navan for over fifty years. He promoted the education of the poor and set up seven National Schools in his parish. *O'Reilly, Rev. Eugene (Priest & Social Reformer)* [Online]. Available from: https://www.navanhistory.ie/index.php?page=rev-eugene-o-reilly [accessed 23 August 2023].

[11]   Edw. Gilbert was proprietor of the Royal Hotel, 5, Westland-row. *Pettigrew and Oulton's Dublin Almanac* (Dublin, 1842), 739. It was in the same street as the Dublin and Kingstown Railway station (now Pearse Station) but was not listed in a contemporary guide as one of the principal hotels in Dublin. William Curry, *Picture of Dublin; or Stranger's Guide to the Metropolis* (Dublin, 1843), 329.

[12]   'Not unto us, O Lord'. A prayer of thanksgiving.

of the room was placed a black board, with the usual musical scores, notes, &c., drawn on it with chalk. Each pupil was then furnished with the book of instruction, and Mr. Searle proceeded to question them as to what the first line, first space, first note, marks, &c. were? all of which being correctly answered, he went on to the sounds. In short, after a few moments the young choir were chaunting most correctly together one of the most exquisite concerts imaginable. In fact it was electric; but when the following stanzas of the hymn daily recited by the children in the school –

> 'Almighty Lord of rich and poor,
>   by whose providing hand,
> Both life and death, and earthly store,
>   Are given throughout the land,
> Though it seemed good unto thy will,
>   To call away to thee,
> My earthly parents–thou hast still
>   In pity thought on me.' –

were sung, the effect was beyond description, and the audience (which was numerous)

[p. 5]

gave vent to their feelings by a loud burst of enthusiastic applause, which was repeated several times. One old gentleman, who appeared rather sceptical of his own senses, said, 'the children must be a long, long time, indeed, in training to sing so correctly, &c.' but, on being informed by Mr. Searle that quite three weeks had not elapsed since the class was formed, the old gentleman was instantly converted, and pledged his honour, only it was Saturday night, he would join a class; but that surely before breakfast on Monday he would be numbered amongst the pupils of Mr. Pelzer. The children were from ten to thirteen years of age. Altogether the evening was spent in a most gratifying manner, and after the health of the chair, vice-chair, Mr. Searle, and several other gentlemen had been given, the company separated – it may be truly said after enjoying, to the fullest extent, 'The feast of reason and the flow of soul.'"[13] – *The Morning Register, Oct.* 3, 1842.

PUBLIC DINNER TO MR. PELZER. – "The members of the Society of Musical Professors of Dublin entertained Mr. Ferdinand Pelzer at a public dinner, at Gilbert's Hotel, Westland-row, in token of their admiration of the system of vocal class music which he has so success-fully introduced into this country. The company comprised nearly all

---

[13] Alexander Pope, *The First Satire of the Second Book of Horace* (London, 1734), 15.

the professors who have adopted his system of instruction in Dublin, and in the other provincial towns of the province, together with many other ardent advocates, of a general musical education amongst the Irish people. The dinner was excellent, and the wines abundant, and of the choicest vintage.

Mr. Battersby acted as president, and Mr. Glover as vice-resident [*sic*].[14]

After the cloth was removed, *Non Nobis Domine* was sung by the professional gentlemen present, and the company then retired to an adjoining apartment, for the purpose of witnessing a practical exposition of the Pelzerian system of teaching. The class in attendance consisted of the children of both sexes belonging to the St. Peter's Orphan Society attached to the Carmelite Church of Whitefriar-street; and the perfect manner in which they got through the examination to which they were subjected, drew forth repeated bursts of applause from all present. They repeated the names and value of all the notes in the scale, and the musical terms in most general use, without a single mistake, and in such a manner as to show that while nothing absolutely necessary for a sound elementary course of instruction had been neglected, all mere theoretical difficulties and puzzling technicalities, of little or no practical value, had been, in the first instance wisely avoided. The G clef was alone made use of, and after showing that the pupils were thoroughly acquainted with all the notes under it, they were made to go through the entire of the intervals in the scale, both ascending and descending, which they did with the most perfect accuracy, and they afterwards sung from the music an interesting hymn, daily recited in the institution. Their performance was calculated to satisfy and please the most practised ear, and when it is considered that they have been only three weeks under instruction, their proficiency is such as must confer the highest credit on the system of Mr. Pelzer, as well as on Mr. Searle, by whom they are gratuitously taught.

After the company returned to the banquet room, the festivities of the evening were resumed; many excellent speeches were delivered, and several of the favourite glees and songs were sung.

The chairman proposed the health of their guest, Mr. Pelzer, and after dwelling on the triumphant successes which have attended Mr. Pelzer's efforts in Dublin, he concluded by expressing a hope that the country would confer on him before his departure some lasting proof of their appreciation of the immense value of his gratuitous services amongst them. The toast was received with the most unbounded applause.

Mr. Pelzer, briefly returned thanks. He said that he felt extremely honoured and delighted at the high compliment they had bestowed upon him, and his pleasure was enhanced by the reflection, that being

---

[14]   'vice-president' in original newspaper article.

all professors of the art, their approval of his system spoke in the strongest possible term of its utility. He had only to add that as natives of the country, they could be of much more service than he was in promulgating the principles of universal musical instruction amongst the people.

The healths of Mr. Lidel, Mr Searle, Mr. Glover, Vice-president, and Mr. Rogers of Navan, were then drunk.

The latter gentleman, in returning thanks, spoke in the most gratifying terms of the

[p. 6]

progress which the new system of vocal music in classes was making in the towns of Navan, Kells, and Trim, and the surrounding districts.

Several other toasts were delivered, and the company separated at a late hour, highly gratified at the result of the evening's amusement. – *The Freeman's Journal, October* 3, 1842.

———

MUSIC FOR THE PEOPLE. – "From the success that has attended the introduction of the Wilhem system in this country, we anticipated further improvements would be attempted, and probably realized, in the art of teaching singing in classes. Mr. Pelzer, a gentleman favorably known to the musical profession by his elementary works for the piano and guitar, has written a work for facilitating the acquirement of singing at sight,[15] by means of class-teaching; and, in passing through this town, from Dublin, where his method has been adopted by several first-rate professors, he gave a lesson on his system, on Monday evening, to the members of the Total Abstinence Society, assembled in the Music-hall. The method of Pelzer is remarkable for its simplicity, and for the rapidity with which elementary instruction is conveyed by it. Instead of spending the time of several lessons in mere dumb show, which the practical musician knows to be of no value, Mr. P., in a lesson of one hour, carried the class from the first rudiments of singing to performing an air from the written music with the light and shade correctly preserved." – *The Liverpool Standard, October* 14, 1842.[16]

———

[15] 'has written a little work for facilitating the acquirement of singing at sight' in original newspaper article.

[16] The newspaper article adds at the end: 'Mr. P. was assisted in giving the vocal tones by Mr. Venables, of the Music Academy, Mount-pleasant, who is about to form classes on the system, as will be seen by an advertisement in another part of this paper.' Thomas Venables taught piano, guitar, and singing; he had attended the singing classes for teachers at Exeter Hall in London. 'Advertisements', *Liverpool Mercury*, 23 July 1841, 23 September 1842. His 'Academy' was almost certainly

SINGING. – "A new system for teaching singing to classes, by Mr. Pelzer, has been introduced to the public in Southampton. A course of three gratuitous lessons has been given, which seem amply to have proved the efficiency, as well as the remarkable simplicity, of the instruction afforded by Mr. Pelzer. It would have been well for many musicians of high note and character, had their early efforts been based upon a system calculated to methodize the mind to strict time as firmly as the present class-teaching. We cannot, of course, expect that the difficulties of any art or science can be mastered in a moment; but we certainly approve of those modern methods that take the learner at once into the temple of knowledge, and bid him look about, rather than those tardy movements of the earlier masters that kept him so long waiting at the gate. A little knowledge has been called a dangerous thing; but it is a danger that the most learned must, some time or other, have encountered. Music for the people can have no debasing influence; and it is the duty of every organ of the press to encourage any effort to diffuse peaceable enjoyment in the public mind. An advertisement in another column announces that Mr. Pelzer will continue his lectures on Tuesday and Wednesday evenings next, at the Long Rooms. It will also be seen that Mr. Truss and Mr. Cromwell are about to form classes for giving instruction in those popular branches of education." – *Hampshire Independent, October* 29, 1842.[17]

MUSIC FOR THE PEOPLE. – "A successful attempt has this week been made by Mr. Pelzer to extend the system of class-teaching lately introduced into this and neighbouring towns. Three gratuitous lessons have been given at the Polytechnic Institution. At the close of the last, Mr. Vinning, the father of the Infant Sappho, addressed the assembly, and paid a high and deserved compliment, as an experienced musician, to Mr. Pelzer and his system. A vote of thanks to Mr. Pelzer was heartily responded to." *Hampshire Advertiser, October* 29, 1842.[18]

---

at his home; it was common for teachers who worked at home to describe their premises as such.

[17] The Long Rooms were the fashionable centre of Southampton when it thrived as a spa resort in the late eighteenth century, but by the 1840s their social status was in decline and they were used for meetings by, among others, the Chartists and Anti-Corn Law League. A. Temple Patterson, *A History of Southampton 1700–1914*, 3 vols (Southampton, 1966–75), ii (1971), 4, 38. Mr. Truss was a music teacher and one of the founders of the Southampton Sacred Harmonic Society, of which he was leader. 'Southampton', *Hampshire Advertiser and Salisbury Guardian*, 4 February 1843. Mr. Cromwell was organist of the Abbey Church, Romsey. He had a music shop in Southampton and taught organ, pianoforte, guitar, and singing. 'Advertisements', *Hampshire Advertiser and Salisbury Guardian*, 5 November 1842.

[18] Southampton's Mechanics Institute was opened in 1830 and renamed the Polytechnic Institution in 1842. Classes and lectures were offered there to clerks and shop

"Mr. Pelzer has been giving three gratuitous lessons in singing, to illustrate his new method of teaching music to the people in the least expensive and most simple way. The ready adoption of the instructor's rules, and the progress made by the classes, will warrant our commendation of Mr. Pelzer and his plan. His desire appears to be to encourage and diffuse a general knowledge of music. He does not attempt to depreciate the systems of others; he only requires an investigation of his own: and the inhabitants of Portsmouth and Chichester will soon have that opportunity afforded them by public exhibitions similar to those so successfully made here." – *Hampshire Telegraph, October* 31, 1842.

SINGING.—"Mr. Pelzer has this week given two more public practical lessons in his system of teaching music; and their effect upon persons previously uninstructed placed

[p. 7]

beyond a doubt the possibility of giving a knowledge of notation and time in four lessons. It was surprising to find a large body of people, called together by public invitation, uniting in one swelling sound of melody, not only directed by the ear, but also by the eye engaged upon the pages of music supplied to them. It might be fairly called an exhibition of sight-singing. The room, each night, was attended by five or six hundred respectable persons. We expect soon to stand second to none as a musical nation. Classes are now being formed by Mr. Truss and Mr. Cromwell." – *The Hampshire Independent, November* 5, 1842.[19]

MUSIC FOR THE PEOPLE. – "Mr. Pelzer, the propounder of a universal system of instruction in music and sight-singing (assisted by Mr. S. T. Cromwell), displayed its simplicity and effectiveness, at the Town-hall, Romsey, on Thursday evening. There was a large company present; and the exercises introduced on the occasion were all very creditably gone through, a considerable portion of the assembly having already been instructed in the method of Wilhem. This circumstance would of course prevent the perfect development of the progress to be made in a short space by the practice of Mr Pelzer's plan; yet it is evident that, from the absence of all extraneous and non-essential peculiarities, and the introduction of such particulars only as are really important to be enforced in rudimental study,

---

assistants. Patterson, *History*, 132. The singer Louisa Vinning (1835–1904) began her performing career in 1840 as 'The Infant Sappho'. She had been taught by her father. Kurt Gänzl, *Victorian Vocalists* (Abingdon, 2018), 716–27.

[19] The last sentence in the newspaper reads: 'Classes are now being formed by Mr. Truss and Mr. Cromwell, whose advertisements will be found in our columns. The charges it will be seen are very moderate.' Their charges for four lessons in the morning were two shillings, in the evening one shilling. Mr. Cromwell would also offer four classes for sixpence if there was demand.

a rapid march in musical knowledge may be attained by it, by learners of the most limited capacities. The lecture or lesson was extremely well received." – *The Salisbury and Winchester Journal, November* 5, 1842.

"Mr. Pelzer, the celebrated German professor of music, gave several lectures and lessons to good audiences in Chichester. This method of enabling every person to improve his vocal powers appears to be very simple, but very effective; and classes are being formed to continue Mr. Pelzer's system." – *Hampshire Advertiser, Nov.* 5, 1842.

"Mr. Pelzer has this week given two gratuitous lessons on his universal system of teaching singing and music, – a system entirely divested of the mysteries in which two useful accomplishments have hitherto been enveloped. The system is very easy and simple; and those parts introduced by Mr. Pelzer were gone through very ably before an audience of nearly one thousand. The system promises to become universal." – *Hampshire Telegraph, November* 7, 1842.[20]

"On Wednesday evening, Mr. Pelzer gave a lesson on his national system of class-instruction in music and singing, at the Athenæum, Portsea, to a very numerous and respectable company. The lesson elicited much applause for its simplicity, efficiency, and the rapid progress made in the art of singing during the evening. At the close of the lesson, a gentleman amateur, who is well known for his efficiency in sight-singing, addressed the company, and proposed a vote of thanks to Mr. Pelzer for introducing to the people his system, which was the best he had seen. This was seconded and responded to by the company." – *The Hampshire Chronicle, November* 14, 1842.[21]

"MUSIC FOR THE PEOPLE – in the cheapest and most practical form, has been afforded by Mr. Pelzer, an eminent professor, in a course of lessons at the two principal rooms in Portsea, this week; and the rapid progress made by the audience, including a large portion previously uninstructed, sufficiently evinced the superiority of Mr. Pelzer's system. Our talented townsman, Mr. Cole, has already announced his intention to form classes; and we have no doubt the system will be extensively adopted by him and by other professors. Should the people be brought to engage in a peaceful and pleasurable employment of their time, the voice of discontent would not so easily be awakened by the noisy demagogues who infest the lanes and alleys of this great and powerful kingdom. The government have recently directed their attention to a general system

---

[20]   This has been found in: 'Southampton', *Hampshire Telegraph*, 31 October 1842.

[21]   The newspaper article adds at the end: 'The admission was three pence, for which each person received 16 pages of music.' The Athenaeum housed a Mechanics' Institute and had been improved and extended by public subscription in 1841. Alan King, *The Portsmouth Encyclopaedia* (Portsmouth, 2011), 20.

of musical education; and Mr. Pelzer's claims to originality and well considered arrangements will not, we hope, be neglected by those in authority." – *Hampshire Standard, Portsmouth, Nov* 14, 1842.[22]

"Mr. Pelzer has succeeded this week in exciting the attention of the public, by giving a series of lessons in singing; showing with what facility a large number of persons can be made to understand and practise the first elements of musical instruction. The children of the Beneficial Society's school in Portsea were the most prominent in showing the excellence of Mr. Pelzer's plan; and the precision of time and tone with which the

[p. 8]

exercises were performed drew forth from the audience the warmest admiration; and a hearty vote of thanks was accorded to Mr. Pelzer at the close of the lessons.[23] *We hope this infusion of musical taste will be encouraged by clergymen of all denominations, to ensure a creditable, as it would be an attractive, execution of the congregational psalmody* – a part of the service tending, too often, to disturb rather than improve those who assemble together to sing praises unto the lord. We are happy to find that Mr. Cole is about to form classes on the above system in these towns; and are assured, from his well-known capabilities, that it could not be in better hands." – *Hampshire Telegraph, Portsmouth, Nov.* 14, 1842.[24]

"Portsmouth and Portsea have always maintained a character as being highly musical; and that distinction is being largely increased by the introduction of class-singing by Mr Pelzer, whose system, in these towns, is fast superseding the more abstruse method of Hullah; more pupils having attended the new classes the first lesson than could be obtained by three talented and diligent professors for many months previous, with John Hullah's name, and the Council of National Education, to back them. The progress made by the Children of the Beneficial Society's school is an unquestionable test of the excellence of Mr. Pelzer's plan, and of his earnest endeavour to propagate a knowledge of music. The instruction has been afforded gratuitously: and may the seed be fruitful! The ordinary education of reading and writing are merely mechanical acquirements, and only present the means of moral improvement: hence

[22] Mr and Mrs Cole taught piano forte and singing and in 1847 opened a music shop. 'Advertisements', *Hampshire Telegraph*, 3 April 1847.

[23] The Portsea Beneficial School was a free school for boys built in 1784; girls were also admitted from 1837. The building is today used by Groundlings Theatre. 'Groundlings Theatre, A Historic Building', www.groundlings.co.uk/about. [accessed 9 January 2024].

[24] The italics are not in the original newspaper article.

have arisen so many disappointments to those who were really willing to benefit the people. The tools have been placed in the hands of the lower classes; but they have never been taught to work; so that what was meant for good has only been left to wound itself. Musical education, however, speaks to the heart and the understanding; it renders the mind cheerful, and fits it for the operation of benevolent feelings. No one can be cheerful and wicked. "A laughing eye ne're made a weeping heart."[25] The voice of gladness is the voice of goodness; and long may it resound through the halls and homes of our native land! It is positively wicked to withhold the means of harmless gratification from the working people. God knows they have little to cheer them on their way: their rays of sunshine are few and far between: and, if anything can be said or done to encourage a well-directed occupation of their time, the sin of omission will be great. Mr. Pelzer's labours here closed on Friday last, with a lecture and practical lesson at the Philosophical Institution. Other arrangements to carry out Mr. Pelzer's mode of instruction, under his direction, will be made; and the class-lessons continued at a moderate price." *Hampshire Independent, Nov.* 19, 1842.

PORTSEA AND PORTSMOUTH. – "The class-singing on Pelzer's method of teaching is prosperously proceeding here. A meeting has been held every night up to Friday, when a practical lesson was given to the members of the Philosophical Society, and the continuance of the system was left to the resident professors, who have already circulated notices of their intention to form classes. The clergymen are taking deep interest in this diffusion of musical taste. Divine authority, as well as human reason, will prompt them to exertion. There are few of them who do not know the difficulty of getting the musical part of the service done even decently, and in some churches it is omitted. This will soon cease to be. A knowledge of notation and time will soon become as general as reading and writing, with this advantage, too, that other elementary instructions are dangerous weapons when not peacefully applied, while music speaks to the heart as well as the understanding, and softens one while it improves the other." – *Hampshire Advertiser, November* 19, 1842.[26]

"On Friday evening last week, Mr. S. T. Cromwell gave a gratuitous lesson in Ryde, on Mr. Pelzer's universal system of class-instruction in music and singing, to a very numerous company, many of whom were the working classes, who were more especially invited to attend on this occasion. The lesson showed simplicity and efficiency, also the rapid progress made in the art of singing during the evening. Much credit is

25 It is not known where this quotation is from.
26 Portsmouth and Portsea Literary and Philosophical Society, formed in 1818, was a middle-class institution. See King, *Encyclopaedia*, 20.

due to Mr. Cromwell for the trouble he is taking here in teaching the inhabitants a knowledge of this delighrful [*sic*] art, and particularly the working classes, who can participate in it, the charges being so very small. Should this be carried out, it will, no doubt, produce a happy effect upon society at large." – *Hampshire Advertiser,* Nov. 19, 1842.

CHORAL AND CONGREGATIONAL SINGING.

————

MR. PELZER,

Has been induced to extend his visit to DEVONSHIRE, in order to renew his Classes for Congregational Singing. The interest taken in this subject by the Clergy of all denominations, and the Resident Gentry, has shown him that in this County, so renowned for a love of Music, there is a wide and increasing field for his labours, which have been received with a degree of cordiality by all parties, exceedingly grateful to his feelings.

All Bodies who wish to improve their Congregational Singing, will receive prompt attention on addressing Mr. PELZER, Exeter. The larger the Class, the less the individual expence [*sic*], and the greater the individual pleasure and improvement.

Mr. PELZER, as a proof of the growing popularity of this subject, begs respectfully to draw attention to the following

NOTICES OF THE PRESS.

————

FROM THE HAMPSHIRE ADVERTISER, SOUTHAMPTON, MARCH 25, 1843.

MUSIC FOR THE PEOPLE. – "On Tuesday Mr. Pelzer had a Choral Class Meeting, at the Castle, Farnham, under the immediate patronage of the Lord Bishop of the Diocese; Mr. Pelzer's pupils had received only sixteen lessons. The Lord Bishop kindly granted the use of the spacious Grand Hall, which was crowded, and many were obliged to remain in the lobby. There were about 1,200 present, amongst whom were the Lord Bishop, Lord Calthorpe, Rev. Canon James, Rev. R. Sankey, and nearly the whole of the Clergy and Gentry of the surrounding neighbourhood. The whole of the pieces were in three and four parts, and were executed in a style alike creditable to the teacher and pupils. The whole was most rapturously applauded, and the piece "Lord of All," (Haydn) was personally encored by the Bishop. Miss Pelzer performed admirably on the guitar and concertina, and was much applauded in each; as was also Miss Jane Pelzer, a child of nine

---

[1]   This probably dates from 1844.

years of age, who performed several brilliant pieces on the piano forte. After the National Anthem was concluded, the Lord Bishop ascended the platform and addressed Mr. Pelzer in nearly the following words: – 'Mr. Pelzer, I feel that I should not be discharging my duty were I to allow this opportunity to pass without openly conveying to you the thanks which I feel due to you for your praiseworthy exertions – for the unceasing energy you have displayed in bringing your pupils to the perfection we have witnessed this day; and I feel assured that I am doing right in conveying to you the thanks of your classes and this numerous assemblage – (cheers) – for your unceasing efforts in the cause of parochial psalmody – in endeavouring to unite in sacred harmony the voices of those who meet to praise their God. And may your efforts be crowned with success; and may you be the humble instrument of bringing many congregations to unite in harmony in singing praises to the Almighty' – (applause). At the conclusion of the Bishop's address Mr. Pelzer was so overcome as to be hardly able to acknowledge the compliment. The Rev. Mr. Sankey addressed the meeting, and proposed a vote of thanks to the Lord Bishop for his kindness in granting the use of the room, and for the urbanity of manners ever displayed by his Lordship, which was carried with acclamation."[2]

FROM THE HAMPSHIRE ADVERTISER
AND SALISBURY GUARDIAN,
MAY 6, 1843.

"On Monday, Mr. Pelzer held a grand choral class meeting of his singers at the National School rooms, Alton. From 700 to 800 persons of the highest respectability were present. Pupils attended from Odiham, Farnham, and Basingstoke, to join the Alton classes, and sung numerous sacred pieces with great effect. Miss Pelzer and Miss Jane Pelzer delighted the audience by their solos and duetts on the piano forte and concertina, and were loudly applauded.

[p. 2]

At the end of the performance the Rev. E. James, Canon of Winchester Cathedral, and Vicar of Alton, rose and spoke as follows:–

'Ladies and Gentlemen – I trust you will pardon me if I occupy a few minutes of your time in addressing a few words to Mr. Pelzer and this numerous company' – (applause). The Rev. Gentleman then said – 'Mr. Pelzer, I am commissioned (and I feel it a pleasing duty on this occasion)

---

[2]   Two of Pelzer's daughters took part. Miss Pelzer would have been Catharina, who performed on and taught the concertina as well as the guitar in the early part of her career. Jane would have been aged about twelve in 1843.

to convey to you, publicly, the thanks of the pupils of your classes, for your strict attention, affability of manners, and your unceasing energy in endeavouring to promote the cause you have espoused, and in bringing your classes to such perfection, in so short a period, as we have this day witnessed. Not only have you given gratuitous lessons to the children of this school, and unceasing labour to your classes, but you have also given gratuitous lessons to the poor at the Union House, and I trust your labours in promoting parochial harmony has effected much moral good in this and other parishes where you have taught.[3]

'Ladies and gentlemen – Not only here has Mr. Pelzer given lessons gratis to the children of this school, but I am happy to say he has attended the Union House, and given instruction there also, thereby endeavouring to unite in harmony the voices of its inmates to praise their God.

Ladies and Gentlemen – Mr. Pelzer has been at a great expense since his visits to Alton, and has not been adequately remunerated. It is, therefore, proposed that a collection be made at the door.'

[Which amount was considerable. The plates were held by the Rev. J. Bannister, and – Barlow, Esq., of Holybourne.] Mr. Pelzer made a suitable reply, acknowledging the compliment. We may here notice the present of a large solid silver snuff box and case, made by Mr. Pelzer's pupils at Farnham, bearing the following inscription on the inside the lid: – 'Presented to Mr. Pelzer, by his pupils at Farnham, to mark their sense of his kindness and assiduity as their instructor in class singing, and to be a remembrance of March 21st, 1843.'"

———

FROM WOOLMER'S EXETER AND PLYMOUTH GAZETTE, APRIL 13, 1844.

CLASS SINGING AT POWDERHAM CASTLE. – We are glad to have it in our power to give our readers some account of the class singing, which, by the kind permission of the Earl of Devon, took place in the spacious dining-room of Powderham Castle, on Easter Tuesday. This class was a re-union of Mr. Pelzer's several classes from Kenton, Starcross, Exmouth, and Exeter, and amounted to between 250 and 300 voices. These were made up of children from the parochial schools, of ladies and gentlemen, and of tradesmen. The soprano and alto parts were divided between the ladies and the children, the girls and some of the ladies sustaining the soprano, while the rest of the ladies and the boys sang the alto. The tenor and bass were taken by a proportionate number of men's voices. The concert, which was purely vocal, was divided into two parts, secular

---

[3] The Union House was the Alton Parish Workhouse. Peter Higginbotham, 'Alton, Hampshire', *The Workhouse: The Story of an Institution*, https://www.workhouses. org.uk/Alton [accessed 7 January 2024].

and sacred. The former consisted of "Harmony," a chorus in three parts; "The Happy Choirs," in three parts; "The Mariner's Hymn," arranged as a chorus in four parts; and "Lo! the Roseate Clouds unfolding," chorus in four parts. These several pieces were performed in a very creditable manner, and to the great delight and gratification of the numerous auditory assembled. The second part consisted of "Lord of all," (Haydn); "The Nineteenth Psalm," (Haydn); "Praise the Lord for evermore;" "The Eighth Psalm;" and "The National Anthem." Sacred harmony being so peculiarly adapted to the union of voices, it is unnecessary to state that the execution of so judicious a selection was all that could be desired, and reflected very great credit on Mr. Pelzer, under whose tuition the numerous vocal orchestra had been instructed. The whole of the pieces were sung with admirable precision of note and time, so that the harmony, not always of the simplest kind, was maintained throughout. It is surprising that in the few lessons Mr. Pelzer has given his pupils, so much feeling should be imparted to their singing, and the pianos and fortes be observed with so much effect. What quota of voices each place furnished, is in itself an indifferent matter; but it is due to the people of Exmouth to state that they mustered the strongest party, and we understand the class there amounts to 200 persons. Another meeting is expected to take place at Exmouth 'ere long. Between the parts, the catch, "Poor John is dead," was executed; and received an encore. Among the guests who honoured the performance with their presence, were the Right Hon. the Earl of Fortescue, Sir John Duckworth, Bart., J. B. Swete, Esq., of Oxton, and A. Stowey, Esq., and a great number of the neighbouring gentry and clergy. It is no compliment to the Earl of Devon to say, that in uniting within the walls of his ancient castle, high and low, rich and poor, old and young, the nobility and gentry, the tradesmen and the parochial school children, he is encouraging, especially in times of unhealthy exclusiveness, even a better harmony than that of music. At the conclusion of the performance, the hall resounded with hearty cheers for Lord Courtenay (who had hastened home from the Sessions to preside over the meeting,) which the Noble Lord, with great urbanity, and just appreciation of merit, transferred to the "conductor," by demanding "three cheers for Mr. Pelzer."

———

FROM THE WESTERN TIMES, EXETER,
JUNE 1, 1844.
EXMOUTH.—On Tuesday last, a choral class meeting was held at the Globe Hotel, in this delightful watering place, of the pupils under the instruction of Mr. Pelzer. The Exmouth class, including

many of the children of the national school,[4] were joined by members from the Starcross and Kenton classes, and the pieces selected for the occasion were

[p. 3]

THE FIRST PART.	THE SECOND PART.
Harmony.	Old Hundredth Psalm.
The Happy Choirs – *Round.*	We will rejoice – *Anthem.* *– Croft.*
The Mariner's Hymn.	Lord of all. – *Haydn.*
Lo! the Roseate Clouds unfolding. – *Winter.*	Nineteenth Psalm. – *Haydn.*
Lutzow's Wild Hunt. – *Weber.*	Lord of all Power and Might – *Anthem.*
Old Father Time – *Catch.*	Non Nobis Domine.
The Russian National Hymn.	Eighth Psalm.

God save the Queen.

The pupils numbered upwards of 150, and the meeting was very well attended, there being nearly 200 visitors, composed of the principal families of the town and neighbourhood, who expressed themselves much pleased with the performance, and the manner in which the different parts were sung. It is needless to say that without the great perseverance and talent displayed by Mr. Pelzer, and his kindness to his pupils, they could not have attained such perfection in their parts, and so interesting and gratifying a scene could not have been witnessed, and it must have been pleasing to Mr. Pelzer, and have in a great degree rewarded him for his exertions, to have heard the proficiency displayed by his pupils, and the applause with which that proficiency was received. The whole passed off admirably, and the pupils only regret that their lessons from Mr. Pelzer, which have produced them such an agreeable recreation, have now ceased; but it is hoped that the inhabitants will form a choral society, and (with the aid of Mr. Stark, the organist, to whom great praise is due for the assistance he has given to Mr. Pelzer and his pupils, and whose acquaintance with music renders him equal to the task,) thus continue and improve the knowledge they have obtained under the class system.[5]

---

4   In 1811 the Church of England National Society for Promoting the Education of the Poor founded schools. Although they were subsidised parents had to pay a few pence. The government contributed small grants to them from 1833. F. M. L. Thompson, *The Rise of Respectable Society* (London, 1988), 143–44.

5   The names of the composers Winter, Weber, Croft, and Haydn were not given in the newspaper article. It is not clear who Winter was. In 1850 Mr. Stark is listed as a piano tuner in Exmouth. The Globe Inn (probably the hotel) was noted for its

---

FROM THE MORNING REGISTER, DUBLIN,
OCTOBER 3, 1842.

[As in the first leaflet, pages 4–5]

FROM THE WESTERN TIMES, EXETER,
NOVEMBER 11, 1843.
CONGREGATIONAL SINGING. – We had the pleasure of attending
Mr. Pelzer's able and interesting lecture on Tuesday evening, at the
Subscription Rooms. He does not come before the public as a miracle
worker, undertaking to level all degrees of capacity to the equal
attainment of

[p. 4]

a given subject in a given number of lessons. But he takes his stand
simply as a *teacher,* and a teacher he evidently is, by nature – apt to
instruct, and imparting the enthusiasm which he feels in the pursuit of
his delightful art. It was impossible to witness the pleasure which his
audience received without feeling impressed with the importance of
cultivating music as one of the hand-maidens of civilization, and we
have no doubt that his classes will be well attended in this city. We
shall not enter into a detail of Mr. Pelzer's method, beyond saying, that
with a black board and a piece of chalk he teaches the signs of musical
notation; with his violin he teaches the *sounds* corresponding with the
signs, and after a few attempts, the novice finds himself voluntarily
following, till in a very short time he is, in spite of himself, a willing
disciple. We would advise that those who take their idea of a singing
lesson from John Parry's song on the subject, and a very pleasant song it
is – or from the stale and standard jokes on the "Hullah-balloo" system,
to attend one of these lectures, (which we hope will be again and again
repeated,) and witness the real delight which they impart. One of the
leading features of the age is the desire to govern people through their
feelings and affections, which statesmen are beginning to discover to
be the cheapest and most effective mode. Singing will come greatly in
aid of this new method, and it requires no great stretch of imagination
to anticipate the time when sensual gratification will give place to more
refined and lasting pleasures, and complaints of demoralization and vice

large and elegant assembly room which was used for balls and concerts. White,
Directory, 232, 235.

will not be so frequently heard in our rural districts as they are now. For how small a sum might not the inhabitants of a village be brought together in pleasant and agreeable association. If the gentry wish to empty the beer shops, they must provide higher pleasures and greater comforts for the people, and of these, singing is one.[6]

―――――――

FROM THE FREEMAN'S JOURNAL, DUBLIN, SEPTEMBER 1, 1842.

[As in the first leaflet, page 1]

―――――――

FROM THE DROGHEDA ARGUS, SEPTEMBER 24, 1842.

[The second half of the extract in the first leaflet, pages 2–3, from 'A simple and successful' to the end]

―――――――

6   The italics are in the newspaper article. The 'Hullah-balloo' system would be the Wilhem system as advocated by John Hullah. The song 'ABC, Duett, the Celebrated Singing Lesson' by John Parry (1776–1851) was sung in 1840 by his son, the comic vocalist John Orlando Parry (1810–79). Gänzl, *Vocalists*, 452.

CHORAL AND CONGREGATIONAL
SINGING.

———

The importance of Congregational Singing as an aid to devotion has long been admitted; and the defects of the present system have been fully recognised in the numerous attempts made to remedy them. The English are naturally a musical people, but their habits of recreation do not lead to that development of the talent which we find in some of the continental nations. Hence unobservant strangers are frequently misled into ascribing indifference, where want of opportunity alone prevails. Having now had an extensive intercourse with the inhabitants of large towns and small villages, I have no hesitation in stating that Providence has endowed the British people with a large share of the musical faculty, and that they only want proper means by association and preliminary teaching, to develop it into maturity. We must use means for ends. Impressed with this belief, I have laboured for the last three years in endeavouring to infuse a popular love of singing. I have lectured in Dublin, Liverpool, Southampton, Portsmouth, Farnham (under the auspices of the Bishop of Winchester), Basingstoke, Alton, Andover, Exeter, Plymouth, Truro, Liskeard, Bodmin, &c., &c.

In all these places my system has been well received; and I have had the gratification to find that there was in the popular mind an innate love of harmony which convinces me that music ought to be one of the fundamental principles of popular education. *That*, however, is not now my business. I wish now, before leaving the West of England, to state that I am still open to engagement (by the Clergy and others) for the instruction of classes of school children and adults; and undertake, in Twenty popular Lessons, wherein the principles of music are taught with all possible simplicity, to teach any class part singing, so as to enable them to sing the services of the Church in a style which will tend to exalt the tone and devoutness of that important branch of Worship.
September, 1845.   F. PELZER.

———

The following are a few of the Testimonials from the Clergy and the Public Press, with which Mr. Pelzer has been honoured:–

---

¹   This dates from September 1845.

From the PLYMOUTH TIMES, Nov. 2, 1844.
To the Editor of the "Plymouth Times."

Sir, – Every friend of true religion will admit, that in Plymouth, as well as in almost every other place, there is great need of improvement in congregational singing; and that where this part of public worship is well carried out, its effect is not only pleasing to the ear, but eminently calculated to raise the tone of religious feeling in the heart.

I would not therefore but hail in our town the arrival of a person who is willing to instruct, gratuitously, the children of our National, Sunday, and other schools in this important art, and of whose proceedings you were pleased last week to make very satisfactory notice.

May I be permitted, through your columns, to call the attention of the inhabitants of this great town to the subject, for the purpose of informing them that the progress which the children have made during the present week has been considerable; as also to suggest, that a valuable opportunity is now afforded for themselves and their families, at a very small rate, to obtain this knowledge; and thereby render their attendance upon public worship both more pleasing as well as more profitable.

[p. 2]

A class for ladies and gentlemen is now forming, to be held at the Church-house in Frankfort-street, commencing on Monday next: in this class not fewer than twelve clergymen in the town and ne ighbourhood [*sic*] have enrolled their own names or those of members of their families; affording the best assurance in their power of the value of the plan, and of their confidence in Mr. Pelzer as the teacher.

Any further information may be obtained by application either at 14, Frankfort-street, or to,

Sir, your obedient Servant,   JOHN HATCHARD.
St. Andrew's Vicarage, Oct. 30th, 1844.[2]

———

From the PLYMOUTH HERALD, Nov. 2, 1844.
To the Editor of the "Plymouth Herald."

Sir, – A few days since, Mr. Pelzer, an eminent master of singing, called upon me, with an introduction from a highly esteemed clergyman of this county, stating that his method of instruction has been very successful in his neighbourhood. In consequence of this I was led to make inquiry, and finding that his efforts were chiefly directed to congregational singing, and that the plan was very simple, it seemed desirable to bring his principles to the test. With this view, Mr. Pelzer has given

---

[2]   John Hatchard is mentioned as vicar of St Andrew's Church, Plymouth in White's directory. White, *Directory*, 656.

several lessons to about 200 children connected with the Grey School, the Hele, and Lanyon Charity, the Household of Faith, the National and some of our Sunday Schools, in the Parochial Vestry of St. Andrews; the result of which has far surpassed the expectations of the various friends who have had the opportunity of hearing.

It will readily be believed, that none of these children had any previous knowledge of music, and yet after a few lessons were enabled, in the most pleasing and satisfactory way, to sing, from notes, various pieces of Church Psalmody, such as the Old Hundredth, Rousseau's Dream, the Gloria Patri, and other simple chaunts and tunes.[3]

My object in thus addressing you is to direct the attention of my parishioners and fellow-townspeople to this important matter, in the hope that great numbers amongst them may be induced to join the classes about to be formed, and to be held at the Church-house, commencing on Monday next. Their attendance will be most desirable, both on account of the advantage which even those who have been well instructed in music and singing will obtain, as also that it will enable Mr. Pelzer to give the whole of his course of instruction to these children gratuitously, conferring upon them a boon of great value, and rendering thereby their attendance upon public worship more satisfactory both to themselves and their fellow-worshippers.

I would only add in conclusion, that twelve clergymen in the town and neighbourhood have signified their co-operation in feeling with me, by either themselves or the members of their families having placed their names on the list of classes.

I am, Sir, your obedient Servant,   JOHN HATCHARD.
St. Andrew's Vicarage, Oct. 30, 1844.[4]

––––––

From FELIX FARLEY'S BRISTOL JOURNAL, JULY, 1845.
CHORAL AND CONGREGATIONAL SINGING. – When Hullah and Mainzer's systems of teaching music were first broached in this city, and elsewhere, they were received with an enthusiasm that seemed to indicate a rapid advance of the "joyous science." Since then, Mainzer has greatly declined in public opinion, and Hullah scarcely maintains his ground. He, too, is likely to be cast in the shade by Mr. Pelzer, whose system appears to us a vast improvement upon both. It must not be expected, however, that any plan can make good musicians without long practice. The elements of music may be taught, and well taught, by a judicious method, and much time and

––––––

3   'Rousseau's Dream' was a popular air at that time. It is not clear if the melody was originally by Jean Jaques Rousseau (1712–78). George Grove, 'Rousseau's Dream', in *Dictionary*, ed. Grove, iii (1883), 182.
4   Hele's and Lanyon's Charity School, the Grey School, and the Household of Faith were all charity schools described in White's directory. White, *Directory*, 659–60.

trouble will be saved by the process; but to enable a singer to hit a note at any interval, must be the result of practice far beyond a series of simple lessons at the outset. Mr. Pelzer's method of laying a good foundation has hitherto been successful, and we hope he will find his visit to Bristol profitable to himself, as well as useful to those who may avail themselves of his instructions. He has made a beginning with the Barton School children, and invites the attendance of those who take an interest in the matter, at the School Room, on Monday next. We have read numerous testimonials with which he has been furnished, highly applauding his mode of tuition; and as a specimen of the opinion entertained of him in the West of England, we copy the subjoined paragraph from the *Cornwall Gazette*, of June 20th. In quoting it we cannot but express a wish that the conduct of the clergyman and lord of the manor were more generally imitated:–

From the "Cornwall Royal Gazette," June 20, 1845.

CHORAL AND CONGREGATIONAL SNGING. – Mr. Pelzer concluded his engagements in Cornwall on Thursday, June 12, at Pelynt. [Pelynt is a small village near Looe, in Cornwall. Its population is agricultural;] and after about 30 lessons they sung the following pieces. Those marked * were sung in four parts in the church by about 50 members of the class:–

PART I. – SACRED.

*Chant. O come let us sing ....*Purcell.*
*Psalm 88th. (Pelynt)
*Psalm 19th ....*Haydn.*
*Psalm 149th. (Hanover) ....*Handel.*
*Psalm 8th. (German)
Non nobis Domine.

PART II. – SECULAR.

Harmony. Chorus.
Lutzow's Wild Hunt. Chorus...*Weber.*
Serenade. Richard Cœur de Lion.
Lo! the Roseate Clouds. Glee..*Winter.*
German Harvest Song.
Tramp Boys Tramp. Vocal Military March.
Rounds – Old father Time, Great Tom is cast.
God Save the Queen.

The professor had been eminently successful in the eastern division of the county, having been aided in the most energetic, efficient and public spirited manner, by the Rev. James B. Kitson, of Pelynt, whose class, on this occasion, had a farewell choral meeting, which was attended by a large number of the clergy and gentry of the neighbourhood. Among the pieces sung were Haydn's 19th Psalm; a chant by Purcell; Lutzow's Wild Hunt (Weber); "Lo! the roseate clouds!" glee by Winter; and, amongst many other pieces, the difficult composition of *Non nobis Domine*. The whole were sung with a degree of precision and feeling, which shewed that the hearts of the choristers were in their task; and the company were struck with admiration at the proficiency which mere labouring people and children had been able to make during so short a period. *Non nobis Domine* was sung three times; several other pieces were also repeated. It is right to state that the Pelynt class had advantages which some of the other village classes did not possess, in the zeal of the Rev. Mr. Kitson, and the talent of his schoolmaster, Mr. Churchill, who entered into the work with the greatest earnestness. The hospitable clergyman opened his house to all comers, and upwards of 100 visitors partook of a lunch provided there. In noticing this village festival, we have much pleasure in repeating what everybody says in the district, that Pelynt is highly privileged in possessing a clergyman who devotes his whole time, and very much of his substance, to promote the temporal prosperity and permanent well being of his parish. The village schools are of a superior character; the cottages of the poor, everywhere, give signs that the condition of the inmates is cared for, and a spirit of cheerful activity reigns throughout the place. The church is well filled on Sundays, the school teems with well-clad and tidy children, and the village is a pattern of neatness and order. Much of this has been produced by Mr. Kitson's pecuniary efforts, much more by his incessant exertion and untiring zeal; and although it is right to state that he has been ably sustained by the landed proprietor, James Wentworth Buller, Esq., of Downes, yet much of the work is necessarily due to the example of the rev. gentleman, who is always on the spot devoted to the practical discharge of his important duties. We hope that the example at Pelynt will not be thrown away upon our friends in the West.[5]

———

From the CORNWALL ROYAL GAZETTE, TRURO, MAY 30, 1845.
We never devote a leading article to the announcements or proposals of individuals except upon public grounds; and upon public grounds we ask a favourable attention to Mr. Pelzer's lessons advertised in another part of this paper. Music, especially sacred music, is a powerful instrument

[5] Neither the details of Pelynt village at the beginning in square brackets nor the detailed programme of the performance were in the newspaper articles.

of refinement and morals; and congregational singing is a most pleasing and animating part of public worship. The general diffusion of a correct knowledge of its principles and practice, with a view to the improvement, – perhaps we should rather say, the attainment – of congregational singing, is felt to be an object of great value. The National Society are making great exertions to effect it through their schools, and Mr. Hullah is employed at their Training College at Chelsea, that the masters they send out may be qualified to teach it.[6] The present master of the Cornwall Central Schools in this town, having been thus qualified, has exerted himself with great ability, zeal, and success, in teaching the children under his care; and Mr Hempel, the talented organist of St. Mary's, having studied the system under Mr. Hullah, has formed and taught some classes.[7] It is in no degree to detract from their zeal and success to believe that the visit of Mr. Pelzer will give a great impulse to the object they have promoted, and impart much greater facilities in future. The system of teaching of which he is the author appears to be much more effectual than Mr. Hullah's inasmuch as the object is obtained much more quickly. We have had an opportunity of hearing his explanations, as well as of witnessing, with several other ladies and gentlemen, a lesson which he gave on Monday to the children of the Central School, and we believe him to be fully entitled to confidence. We should hesitate to express this opinion so positively if it were not confirmed in the most satisfactory manner. We had to notice last March in terms of deserved commendation a choral Meeting at Liskeard, in which no less than 500 of his pupils took part, the neighbouring clergy having gladly availed themselves of his services: and we find by notices in the local Journals, that the Earl of Devon on one recent occasion, and the Bishop of Winchester on another, were so fully satisfied with the result of his teaching in their respective neighbourhoods, and so strongly impressed with its value, that they permitted choral meetings of his classes to be held in their own princely residences of Powderham and Farnham Castles; at which they, with their noble and other friends, attended. We have therefore full guarantees that Mr. Pelzer's professions are well founded, and that his visit to this part of the Country affords an opportunity not to be neglected of securing for the multitude an accomplishment so highly promotive of pleasure, refinement, and devotion.

––––––––

[6] The Training College in Chelsea was Whitelands, a teacher training college for women. It was founded in 1841 by the Church of England's National Society and in the twentieth century moved to Putney. It is now part of Roehampton University. 'The History of Whitelands College', https://www.roehampton.ac.uk/colleges/whitelands-college/history [accessed 6 January 2024]. The reference in the newspaper to the 'masters' from the college was probably a mistake.

[7] The Cornwall Central School, Truro, was established in 1812 to teach children and to train teachers. 'Truro Uncovered: Education', https://www.trurouncovered.co.uk/education_6509.aspx [accessed 9 January 2024].

From the WESTERN TIMES, EXETER, AUGUST 30, 1844.

CHORAL AND CONGREGATIONAL SINGING. – We are glad to learn by public announcements that Mr. Pelzer is about to give an extensive course of (twenty) lessons, to commence on Monday, Sept. 16. We hope that this effort to diffuse into the popular mind a love of singing will be responded to by those who enjoy the privilege of setting an example. As a teacher we never met with one more single minded, enthusiastic, and successful, than Mr. Pelzer. He has thrown himself heart and hand into this matter; but his enthusiasm is not greater than his fitness; his endowments are as manifest as his purpose is sincere. It is sad indeed if so much zeal and talent should be disregarded in a country where a love of music is not less a characteristic than a desire to advance the social and moral condition of the poor. All who read the signs of the times perceive that we are in the midst of great changes. The masses ill-educated, or uneducated, it may be almost said, partake nevertheless of the intellectual character of the age – for even, the unlettered learn by association – and those who do not possess the means of progressing of themselves are carried on by the onward movements of the general mass. Crimes even may be taken as a test

[p. 4]

of the advancement of a people. Brutal and ferocious attacks on the person give place to dexterous manœuvres and adroit manipulations. It not only requires skill to win the world's gear but skill to keep it also. – We are, however, digressing from our point. We believe it to be of the utmost importance to afford rational and agreeable means of relaxation to the masses, and we know of nothing more calculated to do so than a cultivation of a general love of singing.[8]

————

From the Rev. W. MILLS, D. D., Head master of the Exeter Free
Grammar School.

Dear Mr. Pelzer, – As you are about to close the series of twenty lessons which you have been giving in my School, you must permit me to express the great gratification, with which I have witnessed and indeed partaken in every lesson. I believe that there is not one of the eighty boys whom you have taught, who will not look back upon these lessons with pleasure: not one, who has not gained something by your attendance, while a large proportion have made a progress in the science of music and in the practice of singing which has equally pleased and surprised me and the friends who have witnessed their performances. Your method of teaching is so simple, effective, and engaging, that, in

---

[8]   'Choral and Congregational Singing', *Western Times*, 24 August 1844.

my opinion it requires only to be known, to be generally approved and adopted. I have never heard of any method, by which so much may be learned in so short a time: and by which the rules of music are so easily remembered and so perfectly understood.

To yourself I cannot speak of yourself: but to others who may refer to me I shall have real pleasure in stating the very high opinion which I entertain of your abilities as a teacher and your character as a man.

I remain, dear Mr. Pelzer, with much esteem, yours faithfully,

Exeter Free Grammar School, Dec. 16, 1843.   WILLIAM MILLS.[9]

———

Vicarage, Crediton, 30th May, 1844.

My dear Sir, – The bearer of this, Mr. Pelzer, is a gentleman who has been introducing a system of Choral and Congregational Singing, with great success in Exeter and the neighbourhood. He has formed a class here, and as we have been all much pleased and gratified at what we have seen and heard, I have no hesitation in bringing him under your notice, should he visit Dartmouth. The progress made by some of the children of our National School is quite extraordinary, and must be witnessed to be believed.

His terms are by no means expensive, and accommodated to different classes of persons.

My object has been to improve our Congregational Psalmody, and I have great hope that we shall succeed.

I have to thank you for your letter on the subject, on which I wrote to you, and regret that it could not be serviceable to you.

Yours, my dear Sir, very sincerely,

Rev. J. Tracey.   SAML. ROWE.[10]

———

Rockbeare Vicarage, 3rd Dec. 1844.

Dear Sir, – Your letter, though dated the 30th of November, did not reach me till this morning, otherwise you may be sure it would have received a much earlier acknowledgment. You will be glad to hear that the young persons who have been profiting by your instructions acquitted themselves greatly, nay, entirely to the satisfaction of myself and the congregation on Sunday last, especially in the afternoon; so that now, if we continue, as it will be our interest and our duty to do, to drill and train them regularly for some time, I have not the least doubt but that we shall succeed in our views, wishes, and hopes, to the fullest extent. I rejoice in all this; for I now indulge the hope of soon seeing a system of psalmody established in my congregation, in which

9   The Rev. William Mills was head of Exeter Free Grammar School. White, *Directory*, 146.

10   The Rev. J Tracey was vicar of Townsted Church, Dartmouth. The Rev. Samuel Rowe was vicar of Holy Cross Church, Crediton. White, *Directory*, 271, 242.

the members of it can truly unite in singing to "the praise and glory of God," instead of the former wretched display, which was nothing better than a caricature of singing, or of sacred music in its worst and most offensive shape. I hope you are proceeding well at Plymouth and the neighbourhood.

I am, dear sir, faithfully yours,

To Mr. Pelzer. H. NICHOLLS.[II]

––––––

From FELIX FARLEY'S BRISTOL JOURNAL, AUGUST 2, 1845.

CHORAL AND CONGREGATIONAL SINGING. – On Monday last, at the School-room in the Barton, Mr. Pelzer gave a public examination of the children whom he had had under his tuition for about a week. The readiness with which they answered questions on the theory of music, and the accuracy with which they sang several chaunts and a round, fully proved the superiority of Mr. Pelzer's system over those of Hullah and Mainzer, as a mode of imparting the elements of music. We shall be happy to find that he is enabled to form classes, as a means of remuneration for his gratuitous lectures.

––––––

TERMS:

For Six Evening and Six Morning Lessons, £10, exclusive of incidental expenses.

––––––

[II]   The Rev. Hy Nicholls was vicar of Rockbeare and Peyhenbury. White, *Directory*, 242.

THE GUITARIST'S COMPANION

THE GUITARIST'S
COMPANION.

In Twelve Numbers.

A COLLECTION OF POPULAR SONGS, OF DIFFERENT NATIONS, SUITED TO THE GUITAR; WITH INSTRUCTIVE EXERCISES, LITERARY OBSERVATIONS, &c.

[Image of a Girl with a Guitar]

EDITED BY FERDINAND PELZER.
THE GUITAR ARRANGEMENTS, AND WORDS OF THE VOCAL PIECES, ARE COPYRIGHT.

No. 1.

PRICE OF EACH NUMBER THREE SHILLINGS.

LONDON:
PUBLISHED FOR THE EDITOR, AT No. 7. ALBANY STREET, REGENT'S PARK; AND TO BE HAD OF ALL THE PRINCIPAL MUSIC SELLERS.

[First unnumbered page]

F. PELZER, PROFESSOR OF MUSIC, begs to inform his Pupils and Musical Students generally, that he continues to give LESSONS on the GUITAR, and also in PART and SIGHT SINGING and HARMONY, to Single Pupils or in Classes from ten to forty.

The *Art*, Instrumental or Vocal, ought never to be taught without the *Science* of Music:[1] as an Art it contributes only to the refinement of the moral feelings, but as a Science it affords an *intellectual* enjoyment. and tends in an eminent degree to develope [*sic*] and strengthen the reasoning powers, if taught in a proper manner.

---

[1] The science of music would have meant the theory of music.

The Art and the Science, therefore ought never be separated. As the knowledge of Grammar is necessary to enable us to understand and appreciate Literary Compositions, so is the knowledge of Harmony requisite for the understanding and enjoyment of Classical Music.

As all scholars are not (and cannot be) poets, so parents, without intending their children to become composers, may rationally endeavour to make them intelligent musicians, so that they may not only know and do a thing, but also understand what they know and do.

Most young beginners receive instruction from Governesses who have not themselves been taught to combine the Science with the Art. MR. PELZER undertakes to enable intelligent Ladies to instruct in the elementary principles of his system (which applies equally to Pianoforte, Harp, Guitar, or any instrument) in twelve lessons.

Address—

7, Albany Street, Regent's Park.

[Second unnumbered page]

INTRODUCTION.

———

THE *Guitar* is the Instrument of Romance; for the expression of Sentiment, Love, Chivalry, and deep poetic feeling, it is decidedly superior to any other; from the remotest ages, down, through the mediæval time of the Troubadours, to the present day, it has been associated with all the traditions of History. Every where, through the annals of the Past, we find that, with the March of the humanities, the *Guitar* is brought forth to aid and heighten the charm and attraction of romantic truth and fiction.

The Lyre of *Apollo*, its earliest representation, placed in the hand of the God of Music, in the Mythological period, was known anterior to that era by mortals, in a still more rude and simple form, by strings, or gut stretched across the Shell of the Tortoise.

To develop its universal progression as the World advanced in civilization, to evidence its adoptions by different nations, to exhibit the fondness for it invariably displayed by the Greeks, Arabians, Italians, Germans, Spaniards, and others,—to demonstrate that Mankind has ever cherished the Guitar with a fondness and affection not to be mistaken or disputed, will form an article for a future Number.[2]

The powers of the *Guitar* are much more extensive, far more varied, and its execution infinitely more perfect, than the English Amateur has hitherto given it credit for.

---

[2]   This article never materialised.

The Guitar is an Instrument

1st, of Harmony;

2d, of Melody; and

3d, of Execution.

The most natural and therefore the easiest of these properties is undoubtly [*sic*] that of Harmony. In this respect, as regards its ableness in developing the most intricate combinations, and in its facilities for Modulation through all the keys, it excels all other instruments, the Piano-forte alone excepted. We do not assert that the *Guitar,* rivals, in the wide ocean of Harmony, the Piano-forte; but we confidently affirm that within the three octaves and a half, to which the compass of the *Guitar* may be strictly said to be limited, its powers are equally varied, perfect, and inexhaustible as those of the Piano-forte itself.[3]

[p. 4]

But our little Instrument has one great advantage over the cumbersome and unwieldy, though admirable Piano-forte; viz:—that of its extreme portability. How easily is it conveyed from one place to another,—and what a small addition does it make to the Musician's travelling equipage! Even from the lap of Beauty in her carriage, may its softly-swelling tones be drawn forth, to dissipate the *ennui* of travel. No advantage of this nature attends the Piano-forte. Here it is true, we find a combination of excellencies; but where we find it, there it must remain until we return to it: no carriage companion,—no musician's solace in his pilgrimage—no portability. It is for this especial convenience that our greatest musicians were always fond of this Instrument: *Bach, Mozart, Haydn,*—even the mighty *Beethoven* himself played the Guitar; because it was an instrument of easy conveyance and capable of expressing every variety of Harmony and modulation;—*Paganini,* that extraordinary genius, the greatest of all Violinists, was also a Guitar-player: He said "I love the *Guitar* for its *Harmony;*—it is my constant companion in my travels."[4] Such an observation conveys more than the meaning of striking a few simple chords to accompany an easy lyric, such as is shown in our first three or four Songs, herein contained. It is as an instrument of *Harmony*, then, that the chief value of the Guitar exists; and no student of singing ought to be without one. We are quite sure (whatever the depressions under which its degree of favour may occasionally labour,) that the *Guitar* can never be swept out of the musical World, while singing continues to be cultivated. For those who have a *musical* ear and a *tuneful* voice may, (if, in the first instance properly taught), be in a very short time able to accompany themselves

---

3   These two paragraphs are largely from *The Giulianiad* page 3.

4   The paragraph to this point is from *The Giulianiad* page 4.

on the *Guitar*. To attain this acquirement it is not necessary, as with other instruments, to drudge along for years, ere an acceptable degree of skill be found that shall afford delight and pleasure to both the listener and performer.

The object of *The Guitarist's Companion* is to put into the hands of the Amateur such music as is strictly appropriate to the *Guitar,*—Songs and other pieces so assimilated with its character that they could not be performed with more becoming effect on any other instrument whatever; and also that the work, when completed in Twelve Numbers, should form an acceptable *Travelling Library* to the Guitarist and Singer.

If we do not succeed in this, it will not be the fault of our endeavours; and we shall be glad to receive any assistance or remarks, critical or otherwise, that may be considered suitable to the purposes announced as those we have in view.

7, ALBANY STREET, REGENT'S PARK,

LONDON.

May, 1857.

[p. 5]

The Guitar as an Accompaniment to the Voice.

———

What the Piano-forte is to an entire Orchestra, the Guitar is to a Quartett of Instruments;—what the former possesses in strength, the latter has in sweetness; the force of the one is counterbalanced by the variety of the other.

If that instrument which can be the representative of the greatest number of sounds is to be considered the best, the Piano-forte has then the decided advantage over every other;—but, for the reasons we shall now state to our readers, there are many points in which the preference may be fairly given to an instrument of less compass, which, possessing within itself peculiar powers and advantages, retains many of the good qualities of the fine instrument we have mentioned. This is precisely the case with the Guitar.[5]

As an accompaniment to the Voice, in contradistinction to the Piano-forte, the Guitar may fairly lay claim to many desirable qualifications. The Piano-forte, however out of tune, and however discordant, from variations of temperature or from any other cause, cannot, on the instant, be re-adjusted;—a disadvantage which is likely to prove very detrimental to the ear of a Tyro; whereas the Guitar can with facility be tuned, not only to any other instrument, but to suit the compass of any voice,

---

[5]   These two paragraphs are from *The Giulianiad* page 9.

that requires its aid, which prevents it from being overstrained, and thus the ear itself is protected from false intonation; hence the labour of the chest, lungs, and auditory nerves are spared in practice in every way.[6]

The Piano-forte, from its comprehensive powers, is certainly well calculated for exhibiting in the Drawing-room the full and instrumental accompaniments of modern Composers and Operatic performances; but for the plaintive ballad, the heroic verse of romance, or, for any simple melody, pourtraying some of the finest feelings of poesy— unquestionably, the fittest *media* are to be found in the all-subduing tones of the Guitar; and, it is doubtless best calculated for the *Voice*:—It supports, assists, and amalgamates with it in a pre-eminent manner, for, (be it remembered,) while it blends with, it does not drown the Voice. As an accompaniment peculiarly adapted for Singing, and the best assistance to a small weak voice, its most simple chords respond with marvellous effect.[7]

The Guitar is capable of calling up with facility, pictures which the imagination so pleasingly creates;—it is the true embodyment of that most emphatic and romantic designation, MINSTREL. "*The light Guitar*" can, as it were, evoke at will, Knights, Druids, Cavaliers, Crusaders, Troubadours, Hidalgos and Spanish Paisanos, with their Ballads, Romances, Canzonetts and Roundelays of the mediæval times; when, following "*in due array*," Baronial Halls, stately Castles, Arcadian bowers, and pastoral shepherds, come conjured up to *the mind's eye, "in its fine frenzy rolling,"* and revelling in poetic fire.[8]

From its lightness and portability, the Guitar may be made a constant companion in Town

[p. 6]

or Country, in Private or in Public, in the *Boudoui* [*sic*] or the Drawing-room, on Land or on Water, (a la Gondola,) in long or short journeys, by Rail or by Road, on River or on Lake, in Glade or in Forest, in Sunshine or in Shade, on Hill or Dale,—rivetting the attention of Pan and Æolus, who murmur their approbation in soft balmy zephyrs and purling streams;—metaphorically, the Guitar is the veritable *chere amie* to soften to us the cares and sorrows of this sublunary sphere,

---

6 This is largely taken from *The Giulianiad* page 10.
7 Much of this is taken from *The Giulianiad* page 10, to which is added the notion that the guitar can assist a weak singer.
8 William Shakespeare, *A Midsummer Night's Dream*, v. 1. 14. 'The poet's eye, in a fine frenzy rolling.' '*The light Guitar*' would be a reference to the song *The Light Guitar* by the English composer John Barnett (1801–90) first published with piano accompaniment in the mid 1820s. It was also published with the accompaniment arranged for guitar by Charles Sola in the same period.

to calm the spirits, to soothe the mind, to delight the family circle, or while away a solitary hour.[9]

The chords and harmonies, so captivating and peculiar to the Guitar, are so various and so effective that when it is in the hand of an accomplished performer, we can with no other instrument so well blend the poetry, the romance, of the subject, or drown in oblivion the cares of this *"earth's weary pilgrimage,"* living for a time, as it were, in a world of our own imagination, as when the voice dwells and lingers in *"fondest sympathy,"* with the response which the elastic touch of its chords awaken;—so harmoniously, so twin-like are the song and instrument attuned to each other, that our own divine Bard must have had these alone in view when he sung so tributarily to the *"chief Musician"* of his day:—

"If Music and sweet Poetry agree,—
"As needs they must, the Sister and the Brother,
"Then must the love be great 'twixt thee and me,
"For thou lov'st one, and I the other." *
Shakespeare's Sonnet to *Dowland* the Lutanist.[10]

———

ON TUNING THE GUITAR IN THE KEY OF E. MAJOR.

———

The Accompaniment to the Songs, in the present No. 1. are all intended for beginners, with the exception of No. 6.

To show why the Solo pieces are not for beginners we Copy here the Introduction from F. Pelzer's Instruction Book for the Guitar, tuned in the Key of E. Major.

"The object of tuning the Guitar in the Key of E. Major, is to produce certain effects in imitation of other instruments, which either cannot be produced at all, or not so effectively in other Keys. When this is not the object of the player, the Guitar OUGHT NEVER to be tuned in that Key; as the power of modulating through the Keys is thereby suspended, and the perfection of the instrument destroyed. Nevertheless, the effects which may be produced by tuning the Guitar in the Key of E. Major, are not altogether to be neglected, or to be thought inconsistent with good playing, any more than some of the effects produced by Paganini on the Violin can be condemned; tho', strictly speaking, they do not belong to Violin playing, properly so called.

---

[9] In Greek mythology Pan played the flute; Æolus was keeper of the winds. A zephyr was a breeze.

[10] This quotation and the preceding paragraph are largely taken from *The Giulianiad* page 5. The 'chief musician' was the lutenist John Dowland (1563–1626).

The Pupil therefore ought not to be taught to play the Guitar tuned in the Key of E. Major, until he is thoroughly acquainted with the instrument, tuned in the proper way.[11]

[p. 7]

THE MISSES PELZER,[12]

Give lessons on the Piano-forte, Guitar, and Concertina at their residence,

7, ALBANY STREET,
Regent's Park.

———

MR. J. MAINZER,[13]

GIVES LESSONS IN SINGING, THE GUITAR, AND PIANOFORTE,

30, RUTLAND STREET,

HAMPSTEAD ROAD.

[p. 8]

The Guitarist's Companion.

———

CONTENTS

OF

No. 2.

———

---

[11] Ferdinand Pelzer, *Instructions for the Guitar tuned in E major* (London, [1854]), 4. The capitalisation of the words 'ought never' was added in the *Guitarist's Companion*. Pelzer's approach to this tuning is in contrast to that of his daughter Catharina, who also published a method book for the guitar with this tuning at about the same time. In it she stated that the tuning was ideal for beginners who were starting to learn the instrument late in life, or who had little time to practise, because they could learn in a shorter space of time than with the usual tuning.

[12] Pelzer's unmarried daughters still living in the parental home at this time would have included some or all of Annie, who married in 1859, Giulia, who married in 1867, and Cunigunda, who married in 1876.

[13] Jacob Mainzer (Joseph Mainzer's younger brother).

2. Remarks:—On Tuning the Guitar in different Keys,

3. Instructions:—How to transpose Guitar Songs into different Keys to suit the different ranges of the Voice:

$$\text{Either} \left\{ \begin{array}{c} \text{Soprano,} \\ \text{Tenor,} \end{array} \right\} \begin{array}{c} \text{Mezza Soprano,} \\ \text{Barritone,} \end{array} \left\{ \text{or} \right\} \begin{array}{c} \text{Alto,} \\ \text{Bass.} \end{array}$$

———

Music.
Songs, with Guitar Accompaniments.

No. 1. "The Contented Mind," ....German.
    2. "Oh, *Granada!*" .... Moorish.
    3. "Oh, lov'd *Helvetia!*" ....Swiss.
    4. "The Troubadour. ....French.
    5. "Ah, ye sweet Song-Birds!" ....Italian.
    6. "What is the charm, *O'Carmela?*" .... Spanish.

Exercises.
Table for Transposing.
Theme with Variations.

To be published on the   1857.
    Price

184

APPENDIX I

'MARCH' AND 'WALTZ' FROM 'SEVEN POPULAR AIRS'.

The Giulianiad *1:1 (1833), Music 1–4, at 1.*

This, and the following two appendices, illustrate the variety of music offered in *The Giulianiad*. Many of the subsequent issues gave a similar range of material in the music sections. These 'Airs' are for elementary players.

Figure 14. 'March' and 'Waltz' from 'Seven Popular Airs', *The Giulianiad* 1:1 (1833), Music 1–4, at 1.

APPENDIX II

'SOLO BY GIULIANI (FROM HIS 3RD CONCERTO)'

The Giulianiad *1:1 (1833), Music 5.*

This extract is from the first section of the guitar part in the first movement of Mauro Giuliani's third Guitar Concerto, Opus 70; it is for an advanced player. Pelzer's eldest daughter, Catharina (Madame Sidney Pratten), was known to play this movement. In one performance on 29 June 1874 in the Beethoven Rooms, Harley Street, London, she was accompanied by Madame Lucci-Sievers, a niece of the composer. ('Concerts Various', *Musical World* 52:27 (1874), 445–47, at 446).

Figure 15. 'Solo by Giuliani (from his 3rd Concerto)', *The Giulianiad* 1:1 (1833), Music 5.

APPENDIX III

'FAIR EVENING STAR', SONG, WORDS BY E. J. J., MUSIC BY MISS ELIZ. MOUNSEY (FIRST PAGE).

The Giulianiad *1:1 (1833), Music 9–12, at 9.*

For amateurs the guitar would have been most used to accompany songs. Songs with guitar accompaniment feature in every issue of *The Giulianiad*.

Figure 16. 'Fair Evening Star', Song, Words by E. J. J., Music by Miss Eliz. Mounsey (first page), *The Giulianiad* 1:1 (1833), Music 9–12, at 9.

BIBLIOGRAPHY

PRIMARY SOURCES

Newspapers
The Age
Caledonian Mercury
Cornwall Royal Gazette
Daily Telegraph
Drogheda Argus
Drogheda Conservative Journal
Drogheda Journal
The Evening Packet
The Examiner
Exeter and Plymouth Gazette
The Express (Dublin)
Felix Farley's Bristol Journal
Freeman's Journal
Hampshire Advertiser and Salisbury Guardian
Hampshire Independent
Hampshire Telegraph and Sussex Chronicle
Hampshire and West Sussex Standard
Leeds Intelligencer
Leinster Express
Liverpool Mercury
Liverpool Standard
London Phalanx
Manchester Times
Morning Advertiser
Morning Chronicle
Morning Herald
Morning Post
Morning Register
Plymouth Herald
Plymouth Times
Salisbury and Winchester Journal
Saunders's News-Letter
Sheffield Independent

The Spectator
The Standard
The Sun
Sunday Times
The Times
True Sun
Western Times
Woolmer's Exeter and Plymouth Gazette
The World

Sources in Archives

Kew, National Archives, Records of the Copyright Office, Stationers' Company, COPY 3/1
London, City of Westminster Archives, Rate book for Poland Street in the Parish of Saint James, 1843, D182
London, London Metropolitan Archives, Middlesex Central Coroner's District Depositions, Ferdinand Pelzer, 14 July 1864, COR/B/016
Trier, Stadtarchiv Trier, Heiratseintrages Nr 49/1823 vom 22 April 1823

Other Primary Sources

Aguado, Dionisio, *Nuevo método para guitarra* (Madrid, 1843)
Anguera's Collection of Popular Ballads Composed and Arranged for the Guitar (Boston, c.1849)
Anon., 'Advertisements', *Figaro in London* 3:112 (1834), 16
——, 'Brief Chronicle of the Last Month', *Musical Times and Singing Class Circular* 2:35 (1 April 1847), 87
——, 'The Collard Jubilee Festival', *Musical World* 16:294 (1841), 312–14
——, 'The Commencement', *Musical World* 10:34 (1838), 61–63
——, 'Concerts Various', *Musical World* 52:27 (1874), 445–47
——, 'Death of Signor de Begnis', *Musical World* 24:34 (1849), 529
——, 'Diary of a Dilettante', *The Harmonicon* 10:58 (1832), 232–35
——, 'Diary of a Dilettante', *The Harmonicon* 11:62 (1833), 36–39
——, 'Drama', *Literary Gazette* 840 (1833), 123–25
——, 'Education of the Blind', *North American Review* 37:80 (1833), 20–58
——, 'The English Opera House', *Literary Gazette* 913 (1834), 501
——, 'Evening Dress', *Lady's Magazine* 4 (1823), after 486
——, 'Foreign Musical Report, Vienna', *The Harmonicon* 10:60 (1832), 284–86
——, 'Foreign Musical Report', *The Harmonicon* 11:61 (1833), 18–19
——, 'Foreign Musical Report, Constantinople', *The Harmonicon* 11:62 (1833), 41
——, 'Gossip on Musical Matters', *Court Magazine and Belle Assemblée* 2:5 (1833), 258
——, 'Instructions to my Daughter', *The Harmonicon* 8 (1830), 35

——, 'The Monster Mortar of Antwerp', *The Mechanics' Magazine, Register, Journal, and Gazette* 18:500 (1833), 374–78

——, 'Music', *The Athenæum* 278 (1833), 124

——, 'Music', *Literary Gazette* 836 (1833), 59–60

——, 'Music', *Literary Gazette* 858 (1833), 413

——, 'Of the Female Character', *Phrenology Journal and Miscellany* 2 (1824–25), 275–88

——, 'Public concerts', *The Philharmonicon* 2 (1833), 1–3

——, 'Three Rondos for Two Guitars', *The Harmonicon* 7:14 (1829), 48

——, 'Varieties', *Literary Gazette* 849 (1833), 268

——, 'Vocal Concerts', *The Athenæum* 274 (1833), 60

Azelmisia, 'The Fancy Ball', *Monthly Magazine* 26:151 (1838), 63–64

Banister, Henry, *George Alexander Macfarren* (London, 1891)

Bortolazzi, Bartolomeo, *Compleat Instructions, for the Spanish Guitar. Made Perfectly Simple and Easy* (London, [1807])

Burney, Charles, *A General History of Music*, 4 vols (London, 1776–89); 2nd edn (London, 1789)

Byron, George Gordon, *Don Juan*, 2 vols (London, 1849)

——, *The works of Lord Byron, A new, revised and enlarged edition, with illustrations*, ed. Ernest Hartley Coleridge and R. E. Prothero (New York, 1898)

Catalogue of the Universal Circulating Library, Novello, Ewer & Co. (London, [1860])

Catalogue Raisonné et historique des Antiquité Découvertes en Égypte par Joseph Passalaqua de Trieste (Paris, 1826)

Cervantes, Miguel de, *El ingenioso hidalgo don Quixote de la Mancha* (Madrid, 1604–05, 1616)

Cowper, William, 'Johnsoniana', *The County Magazine* 1:18 (1787)

Curry, William, *Picture of Dublin; or Stranger's Guide to the Metropolis* (Dublin, 1843)

Czerny, Carl, *Piano Concerto, Op. 28* (Vienna, [1822])

Darwin, Erasmus, *Zoonomia; or the Laws of Organic Life*, 2 vols (London, 1794–96)

Dickens, Charles, *Sketches by Boz* (London, 1836)

——, *David Copperfield* (London, 1850–51)

Duvernay, Flamini, *The Spanish Retreat* (London, 1829)

Edwards, Frederick George, 'Elizabeth Mounsey', *Musical Times* 46:753 (1905), 718–21

Eulenstein, Charles, *Introduction and Variations for the Spanish Guitar on Weber's Last Waltz, op 12* (London, [1832])

——, *Introduction and Variations for the Guitar on Beethoven's Celebrated Waltz* (London, [1832])

Fétis, François Joseph, 'De l'action physique de la musique', *Revue Musicale* 4 (1829), 97–110

——, 'Nouvelles de Paris, Théatre Royal Italian, Première Représentation de e Capuleti ed i Montecchi', *Revue Musicale* 50 (1833), 397–99

Gardiner, William, *The Music of Nature* (London, 1832)

——, *Music and Friends; or Pleasant Recollections of a Dilettante*, 3 vols (London, 1838, 1853)

Geary, Eleanor, *Musical Education* (London, 1841)

Giuliani, Mauro, *Giuliani's Three Rondos for two Guitars*, rev. G. H. Derwort (London, n.d.)

——, *Six Rondeaux Progressives pour Guitarre*, iii *Complete Works in Facsimiles of the Original Editions*, ed. Brian Jeffery (Vienna, [1811]; facs edn, with introduction by Brian Jeffery, London, 1984)

——, and Johann Hummel, *Grand Pot-Pourri National, Opus 93* (Vienna, [1818])

——, *Third Grand Concerto for the Guitar, with a separate accompaniment for the Piano Forte, op. 70* (London, [1833])

[Hickson, W. E.], 'Art VII,——. Part Singing', *Westminster Review* 38:1 (1842), 153–67

Home, Everard, *Lectures on Comparative Anatomy*, 6 vols (London, 1814–28)

Horace, *Q. Horatii Flacci, Carmina Expurgata: in Usum Scholarum*, ed. Vicesimus Knox and others (London, 1784)

Horetzky, Felix, *Instructive Exercises for the Guitar, Op. 15* (London, [1827])

——, *Preludes, Cadences, and Modulations in every key for the Guitar, Op. 21* (London, [1833])

Hullah, John, *Wilhem's Method of Teaching Singing, adapted to English use* (London, 1842)

Kreutzer, Joseph, *God Save the King arranged with Variations for the Spanish Guitar* (London, n.d.)

Landon, Letitia Elizabeth, *The Improvisatrice; and other Poems* (London, 1824)

Lesage, Alain-René, *L'Histoire de Gil Blas de Santillane* (Paris, 1715–35)

Macedonius, 'The Poet's Offering', in *Collections from the Greek Anthology*, ed. Robert Bland (London, 1813)

Mainzer, Joseph, *Singing for the Million* (London, 1841)

Menage, Gilles, *Menagiana ou les bons mots et remarques critiques, historiques, morales & d'erudition*, new edn, 3 vols (Paris, 1729)

Mersenne, F. Marin, *Harmonie universelle, contenant la théorie et la pratique de la musique, seconde partie* (Paris, 1637)

Miles, Mrs L., 'The Guitar', *Monthly Magazine* 24:142 (1837), 357

Moscheles, Ignaz, and Mauro Giuliani, *Grand Duo Concertant* (Vienna, [1814])

Neuland, Wilhelm, *Andantino and Rondo for Two Guitars* (London, c.1832)

——, *Fantasie pour la Guitare* (London, c.1832)

——, *Introduction and Variations on a Favorite Waltz by Himmer for the Spanish Guitar with an accompaniment for second Guitar, or* the piano forte, composed for the Celebrated Giulio Regondi, op. *16* (London, 1833)

Nüske, J. A., *Fantasia on a Celebrated Irish air* (London, [1831])

Pelzer, Ferdinand, *Introduction and Palacca from Caraffa* for two guitars (London, n.d.)

——, *Instructions for the Spanish Guitar* (London, [1830]); 2nd edn (London, c.1833)

——, *One Hundred and Fifty Exercises for Acquiring a Facility of Performance on the Spanish Guitar* (London, 1840)

——, *Music for the People on Universal Principles, Practically arranged by Ferdinand Pelzer, and Theoretically Explained by H. Doherty, esq.* (London, 1842); 2nd edn (London, 1858)

——, *A Practical Guide to Modern Pianoforte Playing* (London, 1842)

——, *Instructions for the Guitar tuned in E major* (London, [1854]

Pettigrew and Oulton's Dublin Almanac (Dublin, 1842)

Pigot and Co's Directory of Somersetshire (London, 1842)

Pollio, Marcus Vitruvius, *The Architecture of Marcus Vitruvius Pollio*, trans. Joseph Gwilt (London, 1826)

Pope, Alexander, *The First Satire of the Second Book of Horace* (London, 1734)

——, *Horace his Ode to Venus Lib IV. Ode I* (London, 1737)

——, *Memoirs of the Extraordinary Life, Works, and Discoveries of Martinus Scriblerus* (Dublin, 1741)

'Prospectus', 'Society for the Encouragement of Vocal Music among all Classes' (1838)

Rousseau, Jean-Jacques, *Dictionnaire de musique* (Paris, 1768)

Sagrini, L., and G. Osborne, *Variazione concertante sopra un tema di Rossini, per chitarra e piano forte* (London, n.d.)

Slade, Adolphus, *Records of Travels in Turkey, Greece etc. and a Cruise of the Black Sea with the Capitan Pasha in the years 1829, 1830 and 1831*, 2 vols (London, 1833)

Smellie, William, *The Philosophy of Natural History*, 2 vols (Edinburgh, 1799)

Sonnini, C. S., *Voyage dans la haute et basse Égypte*, 3 vols (Paris, [1799])

Sor, Fernando, *Fantaisie* (Paris, 1814)

——, *Six Divertimentos for the Spanish Guitar* (London, c.1815)

——, *Six Divertimentos for the Guitar* (London, c.1815–19)

——, *Six Divertimentos for the Guitar* (London, 1819)

——, *The Favorite Air, "Oh Cara armonia", from Mozart's Opera Il Flauto Magico, Arranged with an Introduction and Variations for the Guitar* (London, 1821).

——, *Method for the Spanish Guitar*, trans. A. Merrick (London, [1832])

Sosson, Alexander, *The Spanish Retreat* (London, [1830])

Sperati, Bonaventura, *New and Complete Instructions for the Spanish Guitar* (London, [1802])

Stanhope (Lord Chesterfield), Philip Dormer, 'Appendix to Lord Chesterfield's Works', in *Miscellaneous Works of the late Philip Dormer Stanhope, Earl of Chesterfield*, 4 vols (London, 1779)

Suetonius, 'The Life of Horace, believed to be an abbreviation of a Life by Suetonius', in Horace, *The Complete Odes and Epodes*, trans. David West (Oxford, 1997), xxiv–xxvi

[Thompson, T. P.], *Instructions to my Daughter for playing on the Enharmonic Guitar* (London, 1829)

——, 'Enharmonic of the Ancients', *Westminster Review* 16 (1832), 429–79

——, 'The Music of Nature', *Westminster Review* 17 (1832), 345–68

——, 'Musical Periodicals: Harmonicon-Giulianiad', *Westminster Review* 18 (1833), 471–74

Thom's Irish Almanac and Official Directory (Dublin, 1850)

Walker, Donald, *Exercises for Ladies*, 2nd edn (London, 1837)

White, William, *History, Gazetteer, and Directory of Devonshire* (Sheffield, 1850)

SECONDARY SOURCES

Angermüller, Rudolph, 'Neukomm, Sigismund Ritter von', *GMO*, 20 January 2001, https://doi.org/10.1093/gmo/9781561592630.article.19774

Anon., 'Biography, Paganini', *Literary Gazette* 653 (1829), 491–92

——, 'The Commercial History of a Penny Magazine, No. iii, Compositors work and Stereotyping', *Penny Magazine*, Monthly Supplement, 31 October 1833

——, 'The Education of Women', *Nature* 10:255 (1874), 395–96

——, 'I remember once', *Literary Garland* 1:5 (1839), 232

——, 'Varieties', *Literary Gazette* 833 (1833), 13

Appleby, Wilfrid, 'The Story of a Guitar, Chapter 1-Autobiographical', *Guitar News* 64 (1962), 6–11

Ashton, Rosemary, 'Society for the Diffusion of Useful Knowledge', *ODNB*, 24 May 2008, https://doi.org/10.1093/ref>odnb/59807

Bennett, Joseph, 'Some Recollections', *Musical Times and Singing Class Circular* 39:665 (1898), 451–53

Bernstein, Jane, 'Mounsey, Ann', *GMO*, 20 January 2001, https://doi.org/10.1093/gmo/9781561592630.article.19243

Bond, Michael, '-*IAD:* A Progeny of the Dunciad', *Publications of the Modern Language Association* 44:4 (1929), 1099–1105

Bone, Philip, *The Guitar and Mandolin* (London, 1914); 2nd, enlarged, edn (London, 1954)

Briso de Montiano, Luis, 'Dionisio Aguado', in *The Great Vogue for the Guitar in Western Europe 1800–1840*, ed. Christopher Page, Paul Sparks, and James Westbrook

'British Library Collection Items: The *Dead March* from Handel's oratorio *Saul*', https://www.bl.uk/collection-items/handel-dead-march [accessed 5 August 2023]

Britton, Andrew, 'The Guitar in the Romantic Period: Its Musical and Social Development, with Special Reference to Bristol and Bath' (unpublished doctoral dissertation, University of London, 2010)

Brown, James, *Biographical Dictionary of Musicians* (London, 1886)

Brown, James, and Stephen Stratton, *British Musical Biography* (Birmingham, 1897)

Button, Stewart, *The Guitar in England 1800–1924* (New York, 1989)

Button, Stuart, 'Ferdinand Pelzer: An Introduction to a Neglected Achievement', *British Journal of Music Education* 6:3 (1989), 241–50

Cannon, John, 'Stanhope, Philip Dormer, fourth earl of Chesterfield', *ODNB*, 4 October 2012, https://doi.org/10.1093/ref:odnb/26255

Carr, Bruce, 'Theatre Music: 1800–1834', in *Music in Britain: The Romantic Age 1800–1914*, ed. Nicholas Temperley (London, 1981), 288–306

Carter, Philip, and S. J. Skedd, 'Knox, Vicesimuus', *ODNB*, 3 January 2008, https://doi.org/10.1093/ref:odnb/15792

Cattelan, Vittorio, 'The Italian Opera Culture in Constantinople During the Nineteenth Century', *Annali di Ca'Foscari* 54 (2018), 621–56, <http://dx.doi10.30687/AnnOr/2385-3042/2018/01/028>

Chouquet, Gustave, 'Carnaval de Venise', in *A Dictionary of Music and Musicians*, ed. George Grove, 4 vols (London, 1879–89), i (1879), 316

Clarke, Sarah, 'An Instrument in Comparative Oblivion? Women and the Guitar in Victorian London' (unpublished doctoral dissertation, The Open University, 2020)

Coldwell, Robert, 'Introduction', in 'Felix Horetzky Quatre Variations Op 22', *Soundboard* 37:4 (2011), 60–61

Confalone, Nicoletta, 'Emilia Giuliani (1813–1850)', in *The Great Vogue for the Guitar in Western Europe 1800–1840*, ed. Christopher Page, Paul Sparks, and James Westbrook, 237–50

Cook, B. F., *The Townley Marbles* (London, 1985)

Crichton, Ronald, 'Braham, John', *GMO*, 20 January 2001, revised 15 May 2009, https://doi.org/10.1093/gmo/9781561592630.article.03812

Davis, Jim, and Victor Emeljanow, *Reflecting the Audience: London Theatre Going 1840–1880* (Hatfield, 2001)

Drummond, Pippa, 'The Royal Society of Musicians in the Eighteenth Century', *Music and Letters* 59:3 (1978), 268–89

Duncan, Robert, 'Literary Gazette', in *British Literary Magazines: The Romantic Age 1789–1836*, ed. Alvin Sullivan (Westport, 1983), 242–46

Eatock, Colin, *Mendelssohn and Victorian England* (Farnham, 2009)

Edgar, Anne, *Sir Edwyn Dawes – Merchant through the Suez* (Private printing, 2014)

Ehrlich, Cyril, *The Piano, a History* (London, 1976)

Elkin, Robert, *The Old Concert Rooms of London* (London, 1955)

Ensminger, John, 'From hunters to hell hounds: the dogs of Columbus and transformations of the human-canine relationship in the early Spanish Caribbean', *Colonial Latin America Review* 31:3 (2022), 354–80

Forbes, Elizabeth, 'Begnis, Giuseppe de', *GMO*, 20 January 2001, https://doi.org/10.1093/gmo/9781561592630.article.02526

——, 'Donzelli, Domenico', *GMO*, 20 January 2001, https://doi.org/10.1093/gmo/9781561592630.article.08011

——, 'Grisi, Giulia', *GMO*, 20 January 2001, https://doi.org/10.1093/gmo/9781561592630.article.11800

Fuller, Sophie, *The Pandora Guide to Women Composers* (London, 1994)

Gänzl, Kurt, *Victorian Vocalists* (Abingdon, 2018)

Goertzen, Valerie, 'By Way of Introduction: Preluding by 18th- and Early 19th-Century Pianists', *Journal of Musicology* 14 (1996), 299–337

Golby, David, *Instrumental Teaching in Nineteenth-Century Britain* (Aldershot, 2004)

Golding, Rosemary, 'Music teaching in the late-nineteenth century', in *The Music Profession in Britain, 1780–1920*, ed. Rosemary Golding (Abingdon, 2018), 128–48

——, 'Music and Mass Education: Cultivation or Control?', in *Music and Victorian Liberalism: Composing the Liberal Subject*, ed. Sarah Collins (Cambridge, 2019), 60–80

'Groundlings Theatre, A Historic Building', www.groundlings.co.uk/about [accessed 9 January 2024]

Grove, George, 'Rousseau's Dream', in *A Dictionary of Music and Musicians*, ed. George Grove, 4 vols (London, 1879–89), iii (1883), 182

Grunfeld, Frederic, *The Art and Times of the Guitar* (New York, 1969)

Guest, Ivor, 'Vestris family', *GMO*, 22 November 2023, https://doi.org/10.1093/gmo/9781561592630.article.46107

Haase, Susanne, *Der Bonner Komponist Wilhelm Neuland (1806–1889) Studien zu Leben und Werk* (Berlin, 1995)

Hall-Witt, Jennifer, 'Representing the Audience in the Age of Reform: Critics and the Elite at the Italian Opera in London', in *Music and British Culture 1785–1914*, ed. Christina Bashford and Leanne Langley (Oxford, 2006)

Heck, Thomas, 'Horetzky e la Giulianiad', *Il Fronimo* 3:12 (1975), 23–26

——, *Mauro Giuliani: A Life for the Guitar*, GFA Refereed Monographs, 2 (Palos Verdes Peninsula, 2013), [e-book]

Higginbotham, Peter, 'Alton, Hampshire', *The Workhouse: The Story of an Institution*, https://www.workhouses.org.uk/Alton [accessed 7 January 2024]

'The History of Whitelands College', https://www.roehampton.ac.uk/colleges/whitelands-college/history [accessed 6 January 2024]

Horace [Online], Chicago: Poetry Foundation, https://www.poetryfoundation.org/poets/horace [accessed 12 October 2022]

Horner, Keith, revised by Christina Bashford, 'Mori Family', *GMO*, 20 January 2001, https://doi.org/10.1093/gmo/9781561592630.article.25090

James, Douglas, 'Luigi Rinaldo Legnani' (unpublished doctoral dissertation, University of Arizona, 1994)

Jeffery, Brian, *Fernando Sor, Composer and Guitarist*, 2nd edn (London, 1994); 3rd edn (London, 2020) [e-book]

——, 'Introduction', in Mauro Giuliani, *Concerto for Guitar and Orchestra, Opus 70*, xxx: *The Complete Works in Facsimiles of the Original Editions*, ed. Brian Jeffery (Vienna, [1822]; facs. edn, with introduction by Brian Jeffery, London, 1987)

Johnson, L. G., *General T. Perronet Thompson* (London, 1957)

Kerrigan, Colm, 'Mathew, Theobald', *ODNB*, 23 September 2004, https://doi.org/10.1093/ref:odnb/18328

Kershaw, Richard, revised by Michael Musgrave, 'Berger, Ludwig', *GMO*, 20 January 2001, https://doi.org/10.1093/gmo/9781561592630.article.02783

King, Alan, *The Portsmouth Encyclopaedia* (Portsmouth, 2011)

King, Alec Hyatt, 'The London Tavern: a Forgotten Concert Hall', *Musical Times* 127:1720 (1986), 382–85

Langley, Leanne, 'The English Musical Journal in the Early Nineteenth Century' (unpublished doctoral dissertation, University of North Carolina at Chapel Hill, 1983)

Lee, Sidney, 'Introduction', in William Shakespeare, *The Passionate Pilgrim* (London, 1599; repr. with introduction by Sidney Lee, Oxford, 1905)

Lewis, Bernard, and Robert Codwell, *In Search of Sagrini* (n.p., 2021)

Loesser, Arthur, *Men, Women and Pianos* (New York, 1954)

Lucas, Stanley, 'Philharmonic Society', in *A Dictionary of Music and Musicians*, ed. George Grove, 4 vols (London, 1879–89), ii (1880), 698–701

von Lütgendorff, Willibald Leo Freiher, *Die Geigen und Lautenmacher vom Mittelalter bis zur Gegenwart*, 2 vols (Frankfurt, 1922)

Lyons, Stuart, 'Singing Horace in Antiquity and the Early Middle Ages', *Early Music History* 40 (2021), 167–205

Maas, Martha, 'Kithara', *GMO*, 20 January 2001, https://doi.org/10.1093/gmo/9781561592630.article.15077

Mack, Maynard, *Alexander Pope: A Life* (London, 1985)

Macnutt, Richard, 'Pacini, Antonio Francesco Gaetano Saverio', *GMO*, 20 January 2001, https://doi.org/10.1093/gmo/9781561592630.article.20661

Mactaggart, Peter and Ann (eds), *Musical Instruments in the 1851 Exhibition* (Welwyn, 1986)

Maczewski, A., 'Chelard, Hippolyte André Jean Baptiste', in *A Dictionary of Music and Musicians*, ed. George Grove, 4 vols (London, 1879–89), i (1879), 341

Maguire, Simon, and Elizabeth Forbes, 'Straniera, La', *GMO*, 1 December 1992, https://doi.org/10.1093/gmo/9781561592630.article.0904815

Marlat, Bruno and Catherine, *René Lacote, Luthier à Paris* (Paris, 2022)

Marshall, Julian, 'Bellini', in *A Dictionary of Music and Musicians*, ed. George Grove, 4 vols (London, 1879–89), i (1879), 212–14

——, 'Meric, Madame de', in *A Dictionary of Music and Musicians*, ed. George Grove, 4 vols (London, 1879–89), ii (1880), 313

——, 'Meyerbeer', in *A Dictionary of Music and Musicians*, ed. George Grove, 4 vols (London, 1879–89), ii (1880), 320–26

McIntosh Snyder, Jane, 'Barbitos', *GMO*, 20 January 2001, https://doi.org/10.1093/gmo/9781561592630.article.02014

Moran, John, 'Möser, Karl', *GMO*, 20 January 2001, https://doi.org/10.1093/gmo/9781561592630.article.19192

Nalbach, Daniel, *The King's Theatre 1704–1867* (London, 1972)

O'Reilly, Rev. Eugene (Priest & Social Reformer) [Online]. Available from: https://www.navanhistory.ie/index.php?page=rev-eugene-o-reilly [accessed 23 August 2023]

Orbell, John, 'Dawes, Sir Edwyn Sandys', *ODNB*, 23 September 2004, https://doi.org/10.1093/ref:odnb/48867

Page, Christopher, 'Being a Guitarist in late Georgian Britain', *Early Music* 46:1 (2018), 3–16

——, *The Guitar in Georgian England* (New Haven, 2020)

——, 'The Great Vogue for the Guitar: An Overview', in *The Great Vogue for the Guitar in Western Europe 1800–1840*, ed. Christopher Page, Paul Sparks, and James Westbrook (Woodbridge, 2023), 29–40.

Parkinson, John, *Victorian Music Publishers* (Michigan, 1990)

Parssinen, M. T., 'Popular Science and Society: The Phrenology Movement in Early Britain', *Journal of Social History* 8:1 (1974), 1–20

Pascall, Robert, 'Stockhausen [née Schmuck], Margarethe', *GMO*, 20 January 2001, https://doi.org/10.1093/omo/9781561592630.013.90000380394

Patterson, A. Temple, *A History of Southampton 1700–1914*, 3 vols (Southampton, 1966–75)

Pontigny, Victor de, revised by Paul Sparks, 'Eulenstein, Charles', *GMO*, 20 January 2001, https://doi.org/10.1093/gmo/9781561592630.article.09071.

Rainbow, Bernarr, *The Land Without Music* (London, 1967; repr. Aberystwyth, 1991)

——, *Four Centuries of Music Teaching Manuals 1518–1932* (Woodbridge, 1992)

Rawlings, Philip, 'Fielding, Sir John', *ODNB*, 23 September 2004, https://doi.org/10.1093/ref:odnb/9402

Riboni, Marco, 'Il Concerto op. 70 di Giuliani e il Concerto op. 28 di Czerny', *Il Fronimo* 187 (2019), 24–37

Rohr, Deborah, *The Careers of British Musicians 1750–1850* (Cambridge, 2001)

Rokstro, Richard, *The Flute* (London, 1890)

Romanillos, José, and Marian Harris Winspear, *The Vihuela de Mano and the Spanish Guitar, a Dictionary of the Makers of Plucked and Bowed Musical Instruments of Spain (1200–2002)* (Guijosa, 2002)

Rowland, David, 'The Piano Since c.1825', in *The Cambridge Companion to the Piano*, ed. David Rowland (Cambridge, 1998), 40–56

——, 'Composers, Publishers, and the Market in Late Georgian Britain', in *Music Publishing and Composers (1750–1850)*, ed. Massimiliano Sala (Turnhout, 2020), 85–112

Sainsbury, John, *A Dictionary of Musicians*, 2nd edn, 2 vols (London, 1827)

Sarcophagus, https://www.britishmyseum.org/collection/object/G_1805-0703-132 [accessed 1 August 2023]

Schneider, Herbert, 'Auber, Daniel-François-Esprit', *GMO*, 20 January 2001, https://doi.org/10.1093/gmo/9781561592630.aeticle.01489

Scott, Derek, *The Singing Bourgeois* (Aldershot, 2001)

Shaw, Watkins, revised by John Phillips, 'Three Choirs Festival', *GMO*, 20 January 2001, https://doi.org/10.1093/gmo/9781561592630.aeticle.27901

Spencer, Robert, '19th-Century Guitar Music: The Type of Edition We Should Play From', *EGTA Guitar Journal* 6 (1995), 15–18

Stenstadvold, Erik, '"The Worst Drunkard in London": The Life and Career of the Guitar Virtuoso Leonard Schulz', *Soundboard* 38:4 (2012), 9–16

——, 'Introduction', in Fernando Sor, *The Collected Works for Guitar*, ed. Erik Stenstadvold, 2nd edn, 14 vols (Heidelberg, 2022)

——, 'Fernando Sor (1778–1839)', in *The Great Vogue for the Guitar in Western Europe 1800–1840*, ed. Christopher Page, Paul Sparks, and James Westbrook (Woodbridge, 2023), 203–20

——, 'Printing and Publishing Music for the Guitar', in *The Great Vogue for the Guitar in Western Europe 1800–1840*, ed. Christopher Page, Paul Sparks, and James Westbrook (Woodbridge, 2023), 57–75

Stenstadvold, Erik, Gerhard Penn, and Marco Riboni, 'Idee a confronto', *Il Fronimo* 188 (2019), 50–53

Stern, Kenneth, 'Pasta [née Negri], Giuditta', *GMO*, 20 January 2001, https://doi.org/10.1093/gmo/9781561592630.aeticle.21047

Swift, R., 'Food Riots in Mid-Victorian Exeter, 1847–67', *Southern History* 2 (1980), 101–27

Tawa, Nicholas, 'Seguin, Arthur', *GMO*, 20 January 2001, https://doi.org/10.1093/gmo/9781561592630.aeticle.25332

Temperley, Nicholas, 'Xenophilia in British Musical History', in *Nineteenth-Century British Music Studies*, ed. Bennett Zon, 3 vols (Aldershot, 1999–2003), i (1999), 3–19

'The Theatre Royal: Management', in *Survey of London: Vol 35, the Theatre Royal, Drury Lane, and the Royal Opera House, Covent Garden*, ed. F. H. W. Sheppard (London, 1970), 9–29. *British History Online*, http://www.british-history.ac.uk/survey-london/vol35/pp9-29 [accessed 9 June 2022]

Thompson, F. M. L., *The Rise of Respectable Society* (London, 1988)

Thomson, Peter, 'Kean, Edmund', *ODNB*, 8 January 2015, https://doi.org/10.1093/ref:odnb/15204

'Truro Uncovered: Education', https://www.trurouncovered.co.uk/education_6509.aspx [accessed 9 January 2024]

Tyler, James, 'The Guitar in the Sixteenth Century', in *The Guitar and its Music*, James Tyler and Paul Sparks (Oxford, 2002), 5–45

Warrack, John, 'Schröder-Devrient [née Schroder], Wilhelme', *GMO*, 20 January 2001, https://doi.org/10.1093/gmo/9781561592630.article.25090

——, 'Sontag [Sonntag], Henriette', *GMO*, 20 January 2001, https://doi.org/10.1093/gmo/9781561592630.article.26234

——, revised by Elizabeth Forbes, 'Haizinger [Haitzinger], Anton', *GMO*, 20 January 2001, https://doi.org/10.1093/gmo/9781561592630.article.1219

Weinmann, Alexander, and John Warrack, 'Diabelli, Anton', *GMO*, 20 January 2001, https://doi.org/10.1093/gmo/9781561592630.article.07710

Westbrook, James, 'General Thompson's Enharmonic Guitar', *Soundboard* 38:4 (2012), 45–52

——, *Guitar Making in Nineteenth-Century London: Louis Panormo and his Contemporaries* (Halesowen, 2023)

Weston, Pamela, 'Willman, Thomas Lindsey', *GMO*, 20 January 2001, https://doi.org/10.1093/gmo/9781561592630.article.30367

White, Jerry, *London in the 19th Century* (London, 2007)

Winnington-Ingram, R. P., 'Greece; Ancient', in *The New Grove Dictionary of Music and Musicians*, ed. Stanley Sadie, 29 vols (London, 1980), vii, 659–72

Yates, Stanley, 'Introduction', in Ernest Shand, *Guitar Music from Late Victorian England*, ed. Stanley Yates (Tennessee, 2022)

Zuth, Josef, *Handbuch der Laute und Gitarre* (Vienna, 1926)

INDEX

Page numbers followed by 'n' refer to footnotes.

Thomas, Miss   64
Thompson, T. P.   35n10, 95–6, 111, 114,
    118
  Instructions to my Daughter for
    playing on the Enharmonic
    Guitar   33, 107–11, 119
Total Abstinence Society   150
Townley marbles   96
Tracey, Rev. J.   172
Training College, Chelsea   170
Trier   1, 17, 18
Trim   150
troubadour   61, 178, 181
trumpet   35, 52, 56
trumpeters   51
Truro   165
Truss, Mr.   151, 152
Turkey   81
Turks   81
Turner, John   17

Valentine, J.   29n3
Vea, Miss T.   65
Venice   66
Venus, temple of   70
Vestris family   59
Victoria, the (the 'Old Vic')   122
Vienna   9, 16, 37, 50, 65, 66
Vinning, Louisa (Infant Sappho)   151

violin   7, 35, 40, 45, 52, 53, 66, 68, 90,
    116, 119, 182
violoncello   40, 68
Vocal concerts, London   67
Vocal Society   67n73
vogue for guitar   6–7, 16

Walker, Donald   33, 96, 112
Weber, Carl Maria von   29, 31, 86, 87,
    119, 161, 168, 169
Weippert, Nelson   93, 104, 105
Welsh (publisher)   120
Western Times   160, 162, 171
Westminster Review   34, 57, 87, 111
Wilde, Miss   115
Wilhem, G. L. Bocquillon   18, 142, 144,
    145, 150, 152
Willis's Rooms   107
Wilman, Thomas   93
Wilson, [John]   92, 104
Winchester, Bishop of   165, 170
Winter, (composer)   161, 168, 169
Wolf, ?Ludwig   104, 105
Woodham, Fanny   32, 106
Woolmer's Exeter and Plymouth Gazette
    159
Worcester Music Meeting   122
World, The   142

Yates, [Frederick Henry]   124

LONDON RECORD SOCIETY

The London Record Society was founded in December 1964 to publish transcripts, abstracts and lists of the primary sources for the history of London, and generally to stimulate interest in archives relating to London. Membership is open to any individual or institution. Prospective members should apply to the Hon. Membership Secretary, Dr Penny Tucker, Hewton Farmhouse, Bere Alston, Yelverton, Devon, PL20 7BW (email londonrecordsoc@btinternet.com).

The following volumes have already been published:

35. *London and Middlesex Exchequer Equity Pleadings, 1685–6 and 1784–5: A Calendar*, edited by Henry Horwitz and Jessica Cooke (2000)

36. *The Letters of William Freeman, London Merchant, 1678–1685*, edited by David Hancock (2002)

37. *Unpublished London Diaries: a Checklist of Unpublished Diaries by Londoners and Visitors, with a Select Bibliography of Published Diaries*, compiled by Heather Creaton (2003)

38. *The English Fur Trade in the Later Middle Ages*, Elspeth M. Veale (2003; reprinted from 1966 edition)

39. *The Bede Roll of the Fraternity of St Nicholas*, edited by N. W. and V. A. James (2 vols, 2004)

40. *The Estate and Household Accounts of William Worsley, Dean of St Paul's Cathedral, 1479–1497*, edited by Hannes Kleineke and Stephanie R. Hovland (2004)

41. *A Woman in Wartime London: the Diary of Kathleen Tipper, 1941–1945*, edited by Patricia and Robert Malcolmson (2006)

42. *Prisoners' Letters to the Bank of England 1781–1827*, edited by Deirdre Palk (2007)

43. *The Apprenticeship of a Mountaineer: Edward Whymper's London Diary, 1855–1859*, edited by Ian Smith (2008)

44. *The Pinners' and Wiresellers' Book, 1462–1511*, edited by Barbara Megson (2009)

45. *London Inhabitants Outside the Walls, 1695*, edited by Patrick Wallis (2010)

46. *The Views of the Hosts of Alien Merchants, 1440–1444*, edited by Helen Bradley (2012)

47. *The Great Wardrobe Accounts of Henry VII and Henry VIII*, edited by Maria Hayward (2012)

48. *Summary Justice in the City: A Selection of Cases Heard at the Guildhall Justice Room, 1752–1781*, edited by Greg T. Smith (2013)

49. *The Diaries of John Wilkes, 1770–1797*, edited by Robin Eagles (2014)

50. *A Free-Spirited Woman: The London Diaries of Gladys Langford, 1936–1940*, edited by Patricia and Robert Malcolmson (2014)

51. The Angels' Voice: *A Magazine for Young Men in Brixton, London, 1910–1913*, edited by Alan Argent (2016)

52. *The London Diary of Anthony Heap, 1931–1945*, edited by Robin Woolven (2017)

53. *The Dinner Book of the London Drapers' Company, 1564–1602*, edited by Sarah A. Milne (2019)

54. *Thomas Kytson's 'Boke of Remembraunce' (1529–1540)*, edited by Colin J. Brett (2020 for 2019)

55. *The London Jubilee Book, 1376–1387: An edition of Trinity College Cambridge MS O.3.11, folios 133–157*, edited by Caroline M. Barron and Laura Wright (2021)

56. *Records of the Jesus Guild in St Paul's Cathedral, c.1450–1550: An Edition of Oxford, Bodleian MS Tanner 221, and Associated Material*, edited by Elizabeth A. New (2022)

57. *London Through Russian Eyes, 1896–1914: An Anthology of Foreign Correspondence*, edited and translated by Anna Vaninskaya and translated by Maria Artamonova (2022)
58. *The Brewers' Book, Part 1, 1418–25: An Edition of the Minute Book of William Porlond, Clerk of the Brewers' Company*, edited by Caroline Anne Metcalfe (2024)

Previously published titles in the series are available from Boydell and Brewer; please contact them for further details, or see their website, www.boydellandbrewer.com